THE 38TH PARALLEL WAR

A TACTICAL HISTORY OF THE KOREAN WAR

DANIEL WRINN

CONTENTS

TUNE IN TO MY PODCAST: ALTERNATIVE MILITARY HISTORY

Check out my podcast exploring the "what ifs" of military history, where alternative scenarios and fresh perspectives dive into the pivotal moments that shaped our world.

Go to danielwrinn.com to listen.

"It was the wrong war, in the wrong place, at the wrong time, with the wrong enemy."

— GENERAL OMAR BRADLEY

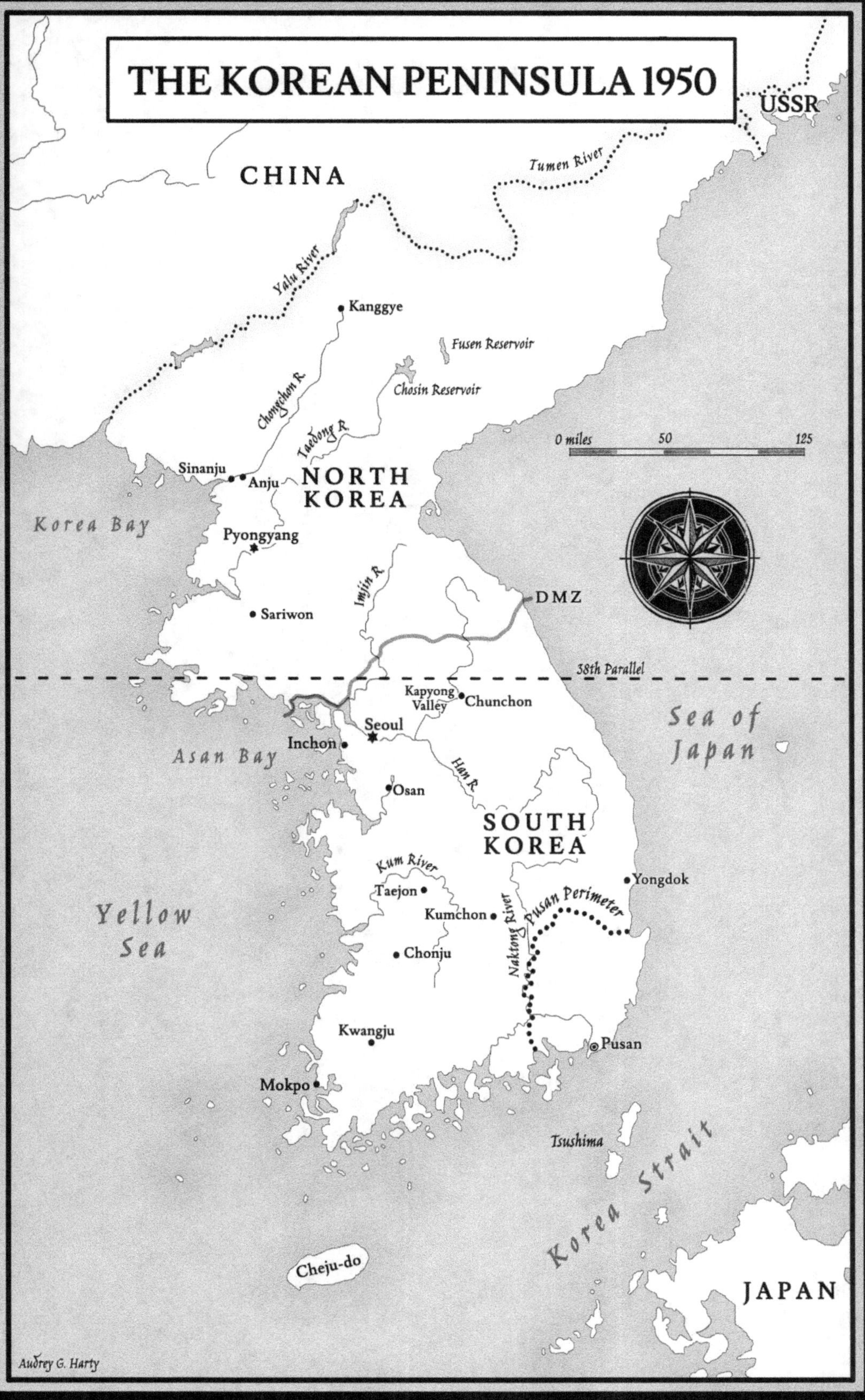

THE KOREAN PENINSULA 1950
USSR
CHINA
Tumen River
Yalu River
Kanggye
Fusen Reservoir
Chongchon R.
Chosin Reservoir
Taedong R.
Sinanju
Anju
NORTH KOREA
Korea Bay
Pyongyang
Imjin R.
DMZ
Sariwon
0 miles   50   125
38th Parallel
Kapyong Valley
Chunchon
Sea of Japan
Seoul
Inchon
Asan Bay
Han R.
Osan
SOUTH KOREA
Kum River
Yongdok
Taejon
Naktong River
Pusan Perimeter
Yellow Sea
Kumchon
Chonju
Kwangju
Pusan
Mokpo
Tsushima
Korea Strait
Cheju-do
JAPAN
Audrey G. Harty

PREFACE

The Korean War, often called the "Forgotten War," is far from forgotten by those who lived it. Though it may not command the same attention as World War II or Vietnam, the conflict on the Korean Peninsula was no less significant in shaping the world we know today. It was the first major confrontation of the Cold War, a battle fought not just with weapons but with ideas, alliances, and ideologies that would define global politics for decades. The war marked a turning point, showing the limits of diplomacy and the necessity of military force in an age where superpowers competed for influence across the globe.

This book explores the battles, strategies, and decisions that shaped the course of the war, while shedding light on the human cost of combat. From the desperate defense of the Pusan Perimeter to the daring Inchon Landing, and from the bitter cold retreat at Chosin Reservoir to the brutal hill battles of 1951, these pages take you into the trenches, onto the battlefields, and behind the lines where critical decisions were made.

At its core, this book offers a tactical exploration of the conflict—how soldiers fought across mountains, rivers, and frozen landscapes, and how commanders made the hard choices that often meant the difference between survival and disaster. But it also reveals the personal side of the war. It was a conflict fought by individuals—soldiers, Marines, airmen, sailors, and civilians—each with their own stories of courage, endurance, and sacrifice.

The Korean War was about more than just controlling territory—it was about the fight to contain the spread of communism, the struggle to defend freedom, and the determination to draw the first lines of what would become a decades-long Cold War. The 38th Parallel, once a mere line on a map, became the epicenter of this ideological struggle.

This preface is not just an introduction to a history book—it is a call to remember a war that continues to shape our modern world. The tensions on the Korean Peninsula are still felt today, and the lessons learned from this conflict remain relevant for policymakers and military leaders alike. Understanding what happened between 1950 and 1953 is crucial not only for honoring those who fought but also for appreciating the strategic complexities of modern warfare.

It is my hope that this book will serve as more than just a tactical history. It is a tribute to the men and women who endured unimaginable hardship in the fire and ice of the Korean War, and a reminder that even the wars we do not always speak of can have lasting consequences.

Whether you are a student of military history, a veteran seeking to revisit these events, or a reader curious about one of the most pivotal conflicts of the twentieth century, I invite you to step into the pages that follow and explore the battles that defined The 38th Parallel War.

Daniel Wrinn

INTRODUCTION

"The 38th Parallel wasn't just a border—it was where ideologies collided, where diplomacy failed, and where soldiers fought to draw the first lines of a new global order."

— DANIEL WRINN

The Korean War (1950–1953) emerged as a pivotal conflict in the broader ideological struggle between communism and capitalism. It represented the first major military clash of the Cold War, shaping global geopolitics for decades to come. This war was not merely a regional conflict—it was a battle between superpowers, with the Korean Peninsula becoming a proxy battleground for the competing visions of world order. On one side, the United States and its allies sought to promote democracy and free-market economies, while the Soviet Union and China aimed to expand their communist ideology across the globe.

The roots of the conflict lay in the complex legacy of Korea's liberation from Japanese colonial rule at the end of World War

II. Korea had endured thirty-five years of harsh Japanese domination, and when the empire fell in 1945, the peninsula was left in political disarray. Although Koreans hoped for independence, the post-war settlement divided the nation at the 38th Parallel, effectively creating two spheres of influence. The Soviet Union took control of the northern half, installing Kim Il-sung as the head of a communist regime. Meanwhile, the United States occupied the southern half, where Syngman Rhee emerged as the leader of a capitalist government backed by Western powers.

This division was originally intended as a temporary arrangement, with the hope that elections would eventually reunify Korea. However, as Cold War tensions escalated, the two sides grew farther apart, solidifying the separation into two ideologically opposed states. Both North and South Korea claimed to be the legitimate government of the entire peninsula, and their mutual hostility simmered, fueled by their superpower patrons. The establishment of these rival regimes in 1948 marked the beginning of what would become one of the most volatile flashpoints of the twentieth century.

By 1950, the Cold War had already produced several crises, but Korea would mark the first time that the ideological conflict erupted into full-scale war. The Korean War was not just a local dispute—it became a global struggle, drawing in forces from multiple nations under the banner of the United Nations on one side and Chinese and Soviet support on the other. The conflict reflected the broader geopolitical reality of the Cold War: battles fought not only with weapons but with ideologies, propaganda, and diplomacy.

The Korean War also demonstrated the limits of international cooperation in the post-World War II order. Despite the formation of the United Nations, the competing interests of the major powers often paralyzed effective diplomacy, leaving smaller nations caught in the crossfire of global ambitions. Korea was a tragic example of this dynamic—a country torn apart by foreign influence, where ideological rigidity prevented peaceful solutions and only deepened the suffering of its people.

As the war began on June 25, 1950, with the North Korean invasion of the South, it became clear that this conflict would not be easily contained. The United States saw the invasion as a direct challenge to its policy of containment, fearing that the fall of South Korea would set off a domino effect of Communist takeovers across Asia. For China and the Soviet Union, the war was a test of their ability to expand Communist influence and push back against Western encroachment.

The fighting that followed was brutal, marked by rapid advances, retreats, and staggering casualties on both sides. Major cities changed hands multiple times, leaving devastation in their wake. The Korean War was also a technological turning point, showcasing modern warfare tactics such as large-scale amphibious landings, jet aircraft dogfights, and the use of strategic bombers. However, it was also a deeply personal conflict —brothers fought against brothers, families were torn apart, and millions of civilians suffered as the frontlines shifted unpredictably.

Ultimately, the war ended in a bitter stalemate in 1953, with the signing of an armistice that re-established the 38th Parallel as the dividing line between North and South Korea. However, no formal peace treaty was ever signed, leaving the peninsula technically at war to this day. The conflict's legacy remains unresolved, with North and South Korea still divided, and the Korean War standing as a stark reminder of how ideological rivalries can fracture nations and devastate lives.

GLOBAL AGENDAS AT WAR IN KOREA

Several nations and leaders, each pursuing distinct political, ideological, and strategic objectives, played pivotal roles in the Korean War. For North Korea, the conflict represented an opportunity to reunify the peninsula under Communist rule, believing swift action would exploit South Korea's perceived weakness.

South Korea, on the other hand, saw the war as a fight for survival and legitimacy, relying on U.S. military support to resist invasion. Meanwhile, the United States viewed the conflict through the lens of Cold War containment, determined to prevent the spread of communism throughout Asia.

The Soviet Union and China also became deeply involved, each seeing the war as a chance to challenge American influence in the region while promoting their respective visions for global communism. What began as a civil struggle quickly escalated, drawing in foreign powers that transformed the conflict into a defining battleground of the Cold War.

NORTH KOREA (DPRK)

North Korea, under Kim Il-sung, aimed to reunify the Korean Peninsula under Communist rule. Kim believed that the southern government led by Syngman Rhee lacked widespread popular support, seeing it as an opportunity to swiftly topple the South before the United States and its allies could intervene. Drawing on the support of the Soviet Union and China, Kim was confident that a lightning invasion would lead to a quick victory, consolidating Communist control over the entire peninsula.

Kim Il-sung's decision to invade the South was not made unilaterally; he sought the approval of Soviet leader Joseph Stalin and Chinese leader Mao Zedong. Both supported the effort, though Stalin initially hesitated, fearing a direct confrontation with the United States. Once assured of China's potential involvement, Stalin granted his approval. With the Soviet Union's military backing in the form of weapons, strategic planning, and training, Kim launched the invasion on June 25, 1950, triggering the Korean War.

North Korea's leadership underestimated the resolve of the

United Sates and the United Nations, misjudging both the speed of international mobilization and the willingness of Western powers to fight. Kim's forces quickly captured Seoul, but they faced fierce resistance as the U.N. coalition regrouped, shifting the war from a swift invasion into a prolonged conflict.

SOUTH KOREA (ROK)

South Korea, under the authoritarian leadership of Syngman Rhee, sought to consolidate control over the southern half of the peninsula while resisting Communist infiltration from the North. Rhee's regime was backed by the United States, though it faced challenges from internal opposition and economic instability. Rhee viewed the North Korean government as illegitimate and shared the ambition of reunifying the peninsula—though under capitalist and nationalist principles.

When the invasion began, South Korean forces (Republic of Korea Army or ROK) were initially overwhelmed, poorly equipped, and underprepared for war. Rhee appealed to the U.S. and the international community for immediate assistance, playing a crucial role in framing the conflict as a struggle between democracy and communism. His leadership, however, was not without controversy, as his authoritarian tendencies and suppression of political dissent created domestic unrest.

UNITED STATES AND UNITED NATIONS

For the United States, the Korean War was a critical test of its policy of containment—the effort to stop the spread of communism. President Truman feared that allowing North Korea to conquer the South would set a dangerous precedent, potentially leading to a domino effect of Communist takeovers across Asia. In response, the United States rapidly mobilized military forces under the banner of the United Nations, securing support from allied nations.

Truman's decision to intervene reflected a broader strategic imperative to demonstrate the U.S.'s commitment to opposing the expansion of communism anywhere in the world. General Douglas MacArthur, the commander of U.N. forces, played a key role in organizing the defense of South Korea and launching the counteroffensive that recaptured Seoul. However, tensions between Truman and MacArthur would later arise, particularly over MacArthur's desire to expand the war into China, leading to his eventual dismissal in April 1951.

The U.S. and U.N. involvement transformed the conflict into a multinational effort, with countries like the United Kingdom, Canada, Australia, Turkey, and the Philippines contributing troops. The war became a proving ground for post-World War II alliances, demonstrating both the strengths and limitations of collective security through the U.N.

SOVIET UNION

The Soviet Union's involvement in the Korean War was driven by Stalin's desire to expand Communist influence without provoking a direct confrontation with the United States. Although initially hesitant, Stalin ultimately supported North Korea's invasion, providing Kim Il-sung with military advisers, weapons, and strategic guidance. However, Soviet support was covert; Stalin avoided deploying Soviet troops directly, concerned about the risk of escalating the conflict into a full-scale war between superpowers.

Stalin saw the Korean War as an opportunity to challenge U.S. influence in Asia and test the limits of American resolve. By backing North Korea, Stalin hoped to destabilize the U.S.-led order in the Pacific without crossing into open conflict.

CHINA

China's involvement in the Korean War was initially cautious but became decisive as the conflict progressed. Mao Zedong feared that the U.S. presence on China's border posed a direct threat to Chinese security, especially following the American-led invasion at Inchon and the rapid advance of U.N. forces toward the Yalu River. In late 1950, China intervened, sending hundreds of thousands of "volunteer" soldiers to fight alongside North Korean forces.

For Mao, the Korean War was both an ideological struggle and a matter of national security. China's intervention not only reinforced the global Communist movement but also solidified Mao's position as a leader within the Communist bloc. Chinese troops, though initially underestimated by U.N. forces, proved to be a formidable fighting force, forcing the war into a stalemate.

Each of these key players entered the Korean War with distinct ambitions and strategies, but their actions intertwined to produce a conflict far more complex and enduring than any had initially anticipated. Their motivations—whether ideological, strategic, or driven by security concerns—ensured that the Korean War would become a defining event in the Cold War, with consequences that continue to shape the political landscape of East Asia today.

A SYMBOLIC AND STRATEGIC DIVISION

The 38th Parallel was not merely a line on a map; it embodied the deep ideological schism that defined the Cold War. Hastily drawn in 1945 as World War II came to an end, the parallel divided Korea into two political spheres of influence: a communist North under the guidance of the Soviet Union and a capitalist South backed by the United States. Initially intended as a temporary measure to facilitate Korea's transition to independence, the division soon hardened into a permanent and volatile split due to growing diplomatic tensions between the two superpowers. As both sides entrenched themselves in opposing ideologies, North and South Korea emerged as bitter rivals, each claiming to be the sole legitimate government of the entire peninsula. This mutual rejection of the other's authority made conflict all but inevitable.

The significance of the 38th Parallel went beyond geography; it became a flashpoint for Cold War confrontation, symbolizing the global struggle between communism and capitalism. While the division was artificial, the political realities it created were very real. Families were torn apart, economies developed in isolation, and both Koreas were shaped by the ambitions of their powerful allies. The ideological battlelines running through the Korean Peninsula were a microcosm of the larger Cold War conflict, where local disputes were quickly magnified into global crises.

On June 25, 1950, North Korean troops, under the command of Kim Il-sung, crossed the 38th Parallel in a full-scale invasion of the South. This bold offensive was driven by the belief that the South's government, led by Syngman Rhee, was fragile and that a quick military victory would spark a popular uprising in the South, unifying Korea under Communist rule. The North's strategy assumed that the United States and other Western powers would be slow to react, if they intervened at all. However, rapid mobilization of U.N. forces under U.S. leadership quickly came to the aid of the ROK.

As a result, the 38th Parallel became the focal point for brutal battles and shifting frontlines throughout the war. Cities along the border, such as Kaesong and Seoul, changed hands multiple times, suffering immense destruction in the process. Though the war ended with an armistice in 1953, the 38th Parallel—or a line slightly north of it— remained the de facto boundary between the two Koreas. Frozen in time as a militarized border, it's now known as the Demilitarized Zone (DMZ). To this day, the Demilitarized Zone stands as one of the most heavily fortified borders in the world, a stark reminder of the unresolved tensions from a war that technically never ended.

This division not only shaped the fate of Korea but also set the tone for future Cold War conflicts, where proxy wars would be fought in regions far from the capitals of the superpowers driving them. The Korean War proved that the ideological conflict between communism and capitalism would not be confined to Europe but could erupt anywhere in the world, such as Vietnam, Africa, and Central America, with devastating consequences for the nations caught in the middle. The 38th Parallel, both as a physical boundary and a symbol of ideological intransigence, became a powerful reminder of the costs of division and the human toll of geopolitical rivalry.

PURPOSE AND FOCUS OF THIS BOOK

This book is a tactical, in-depth analysis of the Korean War, going beyond the battles to examine the strategies, decisions, and personal experiences that defined the conflict. It highlights pivotal engagements such as the defense of the Pusan Perimeter, the bold Inchon Landing, and the grueling retreat from the Chosin Reservoir, offering insight into how terrain, logistics, and command decisions shaped the war's outcome.

A central focus is the human element—exploring the courage, resilience, and struggle for survival amid the harsh realities of war fought in extreme conditions. The narrative sheds light on the enduring legacy of the Korean War, not only in shaping modern military doctrine but also in perpetuating the geopolitical divide between North and South Korea that persists today.

With an emphasis on objectivity, the book avoids ideological bias, focusing instead on the tactical realities faced by soldiers and commanders from both sides. It is crafted for readers interested in military history, strategy, and the complexities of Cold War conflicts. By analyzing the Korean War through a tactical lens, it provides new insights into a conflict often overshadowed by World War II and the Vietnam War but crucial to understanding the development of modern geopolitics and military operations.

EARLY SETBACKS AND THE DEFENSE OF SOUTH KOREA

"We'll hold until we're told to pull out. If we can't hold, we'll die trying."

— CAPTAIN WILLIAM B. MCMAINS, U.S. ARMY, DURING THE BATTLE OF TAEJON

When North Korean forces launched a surprise invasion of South Korea on June 25, 1950, the Republic of Korea (ROK) and its allies were thrown into disarray. The attack, meticulously planned by the North under Kim Il-sung's leadership, sought to take advantage of South Korea's unpreparedness and swiftly reunify the peninsula under Communist rule. North Korean forces, equipped with Soviet-made tanks, artillery, and aircraft, advanced rapidly, overwhelming the lightly armed South Korean troops and throwing the entire region into crisis.

In the initial days, U.S. and South Korean forces found themselves scrambling to respond. Many of the U.S. soldiers stationed in Japan, who were hastily deployed to Korea, had not seen combat since World War II and lacked the equipment and supplies needed for a high-intensity conflict. The first American units to arrive were understrength and ill-equipped to confront the disciplined and battle-hardened Korean People's Army (KPA), whose tactics and Soviet equipment gave them a clear advantage. The KPA advanced quickly, capturing key southern cities such as Kaesong and Seoul within days, further eroding morale and complicating defensive efforts.

A series of fierce battles in July 1950 tested the mettle of U.S. and ROK forces. One of the first major confrontations occurred at Osan, where Task Force Smith—a small U.S. force sent to slow the North Korean advance—was decisively defeated. This encounter exposed critical weaknesses, including insufficient anti-tank weaponry and poor communication between units. Despite the setback at Osan, the battle bought valuable time, alerting U.S. commanders to the seriousness of the situation and enabling them to coordinate reinforcements.

As the KPA pushed farther south, U.S. and South Korean forces fell back repeatedly, abandoning several strategic positions under pressure. However, these retreats were not without purpose—each delay allowed the defenders to regroup and establish a more coherent front. By late July, the retreating forces made their final stand at the Pusan Perimeter, a defensive line anchored around the port city of Pusan (now Busan) in the southeastern corner of the peninsula. Encircled and outnumbered, the defenders prepared for a desperate fight, knowing that holding the perimeter was essential to preventing the complete collapse of South Korea.

The defense of South Korea in these early weeks was marked by confusion, frustration, and hard lessons learned in the field. The U.S. Military command quickly realized that the Korean War would not be a brief conflict resolved with limited intervention. The defeat at Osan and the collapse of several key defensive positions underscored the need for better coordination, more effective equipment, and the mobilization of additional forces. The early setbacks provided an opportunity to assess the enemy's capabilities and adjust strategies accordingly. The troops, though battered, gained crucial experience that would prove essential in the brutal battles to come.

Ultimately, the early phase of the war revealed the seriousness of the North Korean threat and demonstrated the importance of resilience in the face of adversity. While North Korea had the advantage of surprise, superior equipment, and initial momentum, the determination of U.S. and ROK forces to hold the Pusan Perimeter marked the beginning of a shift in the war's trajectory. These early battles were not just a test of tactics and logistics but also of willpower and endurance, setting the stage for a prolonged conflict that would reshape the political landscape of the peninsula.

BATTLE OF OSAN

The Battle of Osan on July 5, 1950, marked the first direct U.S. engagement of the Korean War and exposed the harsh realities of the conflict. It shattered the assumption that American forces could achieve a swift victory with minimal resistance, setting the tone for the intense and grueling battles that would follow. This encounter signaled the beginning of the United States' deeper military involvement in Korea and forced U.S. leaders to confront the need for improved preparation, better coordination, and modern equipment to face the well-supplied and determined North Korean forces.

The strategic importance of the battle lay not in its outcome —Task Force Smith was decisively defeated—but in its objective: slowing the rapid advance of the Korean People's Army (KPA) long enough for reinforcements to arrive. Every hour gained was critical in the early days of the war, as North Korean forces sought to conquer South Korea before the United States and its allies could effectively respond. The soldiers deployed to Osan were not expected to win; instead, their mission was to buy time by engaging the enemy and forcing them to regroup, even at great personal cost.

The U.S. soldiers who fought at Osan were far from ready for the conflict they found themselves in. Many had been stationed in Japan as part of the post-WWII occupation force, with little combat experience and minimal training for a large-scale war. Their deployment to Korea was rushed, and they were sent into battle with outdated equipment and insufficient supplies—factors that would quickly become painfully apparent as they faced the KPA's Soviet-supplied tanks and seasoned infantry.

TASK FORCE SMITH

Task Force Smith was a hastily assembled unit from the 24th Infantry Division, comprising around 540 soldiers under the command of Lieutenant Colonel Charles Smith. The unit was formed as part of the U.S. Army's initial response to the North Korean invasion, rushed from its post-WWII occupation duties in Japan to the unfamiliar terrain of South Korea. Despite their mission to delay the North Korean advance, the soldiers were ill-prepared for the realities of combat against a formidable enemy.

The composition of Task Force Smith reflected the challenges of a peacetime military suddenly thrown into a full-scale conflict. Many of the troops had little to no recent combat experience, with most of their service limited to garrison and occupation roles in postwar Japan. Their training focused more on main-taining order than engaging in modern warfare, leaving them unfamiliar with the tactics and strategies required to confront a battle-hardened force like the Korean People's Army (KPA). The sudden shift from occupation duty to combat revealed a critical vulnerability—these troops were not prepared for the brutal reality of a mechanized conflict.

Adding to their challenges, Task Force Smith was equipped with outdated weaponry, including WWII-era M1 rifles, light mortars, and bazookas, all inadequate for confronting the Soviet-made T-34 tanks deployed by the KPA. Their anti-tank capabilities were insufficient, with recoilless rifles and bazookas proving ineffective against the heavy armor of the advancing tanks. This lack of proper equipment and firepower would have devastating consequences when they finally faced the enemy at Osan.

The soldiers of Task Force Smith were further hampered by limited logistical support. Rushed into action without proper reconnaissance or preparation, they lacked critical supplies, including ammunition and anti-tank mines. Communication between the American troops and their South Korean allies was also inconsistent, further complicating efforts to coordinate defenses. Despite these challenges, Task Force Smith was given the mission of holding the line at Osan, tasked with buying time for reinforcements to arrive and delaying the KPA's rapid push south.

In many ways, the formation and deployment of Task Force Smith symbolized the U.S. Military's unpreparedness for the Korean War. It reflected the broader assumption that North Korean forces could be easily deterred and that U.S. intervention would be enough to halt the invasion. However, the rushed mobilization and reliance on under-equipped, inexperienced troops foreshadowed the difficulties the United States would face in the months to come. Task Force Smith entered the battlefield with a sense of duty and determination, but the challenges they encountered would highlight the urgent need for a more robust military response in Korea. Their stand at Osan was not just a tactical moment but a prelude to a broader lesson: the war would require far more than symbolic gestures—it demanded full-scale commitment and preparation.

NORTH KOREAN ADVANCE

The Korean People's Army entered the Korean War with a clear strategy and overwhelming momentum, quickly crossing the 38th Parallel and driving deep into South Korea. Their primary objective was to achieve rapid reunification by overwhelming the South's defenses before the United States or other foreign powers could intervene effectively. The KPA's offensive was carefully planned, with Kim Il-sung and his generals relying on speed, surprise, and overwhelming force to capitalize on South Korea's lack of preparedness.

The North Korean forces were bolstered by Soviet military aid, which included T-34 tanks, trucks, artillery, and small arms—far superior to the equipment available to South Korean and hastily deployed U.S. forces. The KPA had been trained extensively by Soviet advisers, adopting modern tactics that emphasized mechanized warfare and close coordination between infantry and armor. The T-34 tanks, a proven weapon during World War II, formed the backbone of the KPA's offensive and would prove devastating against poorly equipped ROK units and Task Force Smith.

The momentum of the KPA advance was unrelenting. Within days of crossing the 38th Parallel, North Korean forces captured key towns and cities, including Kaesong and the South Korean capital of Seoul, creating panic and disrupting defensive efforts. The speed and coordination of the invasion gave the North a psychological edge, eroding morale among South Korean defenders and complicating U.S. efforts to organize an effective response.

Kim Il-sung and his military leadership were confident that the war would be brief and decisive. They believed that South Korea, under Syngman Rhee's unpopular government, lacked both the military strength and public support to mount a serious defense. The North Koreans also assumed that the United States, still recovering from the costs of World War II, would be reluctant to engage in another foreign war, particularly in Asia. This confidence, combined with the KPA's early successes, drove their aggressive push southward.

The initial phase of the North Korean advance reflected the tactical advantages of preparation, surprise, and superior equipment. However, the rapid pace of their offensive created logistical challenges, stretching supply lines and leaving key units vulnerable to counterattacks. Although the KPA succeeded in overwhelming South Korean forces in the opening weeks, their reliance on a swift victory underestimated the determination of U.S. forces and the impact of international intervention. The KPA's early gains set the stage for a brutal and drawn-out conflict that would ultimately test their endurance and strategy.

Geography of Osan

The terrain at Osan played a significant role in shaping the events of the battle. Task Force Smith chose a hill overlooking a critical roadway that the North Korean forces would use to continue their advance southward. This elevated position gave the American troops a slight tactical advantage, allowing them to observe the enemy's approach and position their limited artillery and mortars to maximize impact. However, the surrounding landscape, with open fields and little cover, also left the Americans exposed once the battle began, making it difficult to retreat without sustaining heavy casualties.

The road cutting through Osan was a vital artery for the advancing KPA, part of their broader strategy to quickly push south and capture key cities like Suwon and Pusan. Task Force Smith's position along this route aimed to create a bottleneck, slowing the enemy's progress just enough to allow reinforcements to establish a more robust defensive line. However, the strategic importance of the location would mean little without the necessary firepower and coordination to hold it effectively.

Commanders hoped that a determined stand at Osan would

buy time for additional U.S. and South Korean forces to organize farther south, setting the stage for a more effective defense at the Pusan Perimeter. The plan relied on the element of surprise. Task Force Smith intended to ambush the advancing North Korean column, disrupt their momentum, and force them to pause and reorganize. Positioned on the hill, American mortars and artillery were intended to neutralize enemy infantry and vehicles, while bazookas were expected to take on the tanks.

However, this plan was based on a dangerous overestimation of American capabilities and a profound underestimation of the KPA's strength. The U.S. command believed that even a small force like Task Force Smith could make a significant impact by stalling the North Koreans, assuming that the KPA was poorly trained and lightly equipped. In reality, the North Korean army was not only well-prepared but also equipped with superior Soviet-made T-34 tanks and experienced infantry.

Task Force Smith's limited anti-tank weapons, including WWII-era bazookas and recoilless rifles, proved grossly inadequate for the task ahead. The underestimation of the KPA's capabilities would become painfully clear as the battle unfolded, with American forces quickly overwhelmed by the tanks and infantry of the advancing North Koreans. Despite the soldiers' bravery and determination, the plan to delay the enemy proved unrealistic, revealing the urgent need for better equipment, intelligence, and preparation as the Korean War escalated.

The Battle Begins

The Battle of Osan erupted in the early morning hours of July 5, 1950, as Task Force Smith awaited the arrival of the advancing KPA column. Positioned on the hillside overlooking the main road, the American troops initiated the ambush as the first North Korean units, consisting of infantry and trucks, came into view. The Americans opened fire with mortars, rifles, and artillery, successfully catching the enemy off-guard. Some enemy trucks were destroyed, and disoriented KPA soldiers scrambled for cover, temporarily halting the column's forward momentum.

These initial moments of the battle provided a brief glimmer of hope for Task Force Smith. The destruction of a few vehicles and the disruption of infantry movement suggested that their ambush might buy enough time for reinforcements to arrive. However, the early successes were fleeting. The North Korean troops quickly regrouped, adapting to the surprise attack with disciplined precision. As the American mortars continued to fire, the KPA shifted their strategy, preparing for a more coordinated assault involving armor and infantry.

Shortly after the ambush began, the situation took a devastating turn. A column of Soviet-supplied T-34 tanks advanced down the road, spearheading the KPA's push through Osan. Task Force Smith's soldiers, having never encountered this type of heavily armored vehicle before, scrambled to engage the tanks with the limited anti-tank weapons they had on hand. They fired bazookas and recoilless rifles at the approaching tanks, but the weapons proved ineffective. Shells bounced harmlessly off the thick armor of the T-34s, leaving the Americans stunned and defenseless against the armored behemoths.

The failure of the anti-tank weapons marked a critical moment in the battle. Without the means to stop the T-34s, the American defensive line began to collapse. As the tanks rumbled through the ambush site, KPA infantry followed closely behind, firing on the disorganized U.S. troops and seizing the high ground. Task Force Smith, already stretched thin and lacking any air or artillery support, struggled to maintain cohesion as enemy forces overran their positions.

The breakthrough of the T-34s not only shattered the American defenses but also demonstrated the stark difference in preparation between the two sides. The U.S. troops were neither equipped nor trained to confront a mechanized enemy of this caliber, and their outdated weapons proved no match for Soviet-engineered armor. The tanks rolled on, with KPA forces continuing their advance south, leaving the Americans with no choice but to retreat.

With the T-34 tanks breaking through the American lines, the KPA infantry wasted no time in exploiting the breach. Following closely behind the armor, they launched a series of coordinated assaults on the scattered positions of Task Force Smith. North Korean soldiers, armed with rifles, machine guns, and grenades, quickly closed the distance, engaging the Americans in close-quarters combat. The combination of tanks and infantry proved overwhelming. The U.S. troops, who had already suffered heavy losses, found themselves surrounded and outgunned.

As the KPA soldiers advanced, they targeted the weakened defensive positions with precision, seizing the hilltop and neutralizing pockets of resistance. The Americans fought with determination, but their numbers were too few, and their defenses were stretched too thin to withstand the coordinated attack. Communication between units broke down, and the frontlines crumbled under the relentless pressure. Without sufficient reinforcements or air support, Task Force Smith was isolated and overwhelmed, with no hope of regaining the upper hand.

Faced with the collapse of their positions and mounting casualties, the soldiers of Task Force Smith were ordered to retreat after holding the lines for three hours. The withdrawal, however, quickly devolved into chaos. With enemy infantry pressing from multiple directions and tanks cutting off escape routes, the retreat became a desperate scramble for survival. Soldiers abandoned their positions, leaving behind essential equipment, artillery, and even some of their wounded comrades. Those too injured to move were captured by the advancing North Koreans or left to fend for themselves.

The retreat under fire was marked by confusion and panic as American troops scattered across the battlefield. Some soldiers managed to escape through nearby fields and small villages, while others were cut down by enemy fire as they tried to flee. The lack of coordination during the retreat magnified the already heavy losses. In the end, more than a third of Task Force Smith's soldiers were killed, wounded, or captured, and the unit was effectively destroyed as a fighting force.

This disastrous retreat illustrated the grim reality of the early days of the Korean War: American forces were unprepared for the scale and intensity of the conflict. The defeat at Osan not only demonstrated the tactical shortcomings of Task Force Smith but also highlighted the consequences of underestimating the KPA's capabilities. The chaotic withdrawal left a lasting impression on leaders from the U.S. Military, forcing them to reassess their strategy and prepare for the long, difficult road ahead.

Though the retreat was a tactical failure, it was not without strategic value. The stand at Osan, however brief, had delayed the North Korean advance just enough to buy critical time for additional U.S. forces to establish a more defensible position farther south at the Pusan Perimeter. The soldiers of Task Force Smith, though overwhelmed and ill-equipped, had fulfilled their mission in the most harrowing way possible—at great personal cost and under the most difficult conditions imaginable.

Casualties

The Battle of Osan resulted in significant losses for Task Force Smith. Out of the approximately 540 soldiers who engaged the North Korean forces, around 150 were killed, wounded, or captured. The survivors retreated in disarray, leaving behind equipment and many of their injured comrades. The defeat shattered the unit's cohesion, marking a grim beginning to U.S. involvement in the Korean War. In contrast, North Korean forces sustained only minimal damage. The rapid success of the KPA at Osan emboldened their advance, reinforcing the belief among

North Korean leaders that they could achieve swift victory and reunify the peninsula under Communist rule before U.S. reinforcements could mount a meaningful defense.

The quick defeat of Task Force Smith highlighted the unpreparedness of American forces for the scale and intensity of the Korean conflict. The shock of the engagement forced commanders to confront several critical weaknesses: outdated equipment incapable of countering the Soviet-made T-34 tanks, a lack of coordination between units, and a severe underestimation of the capabilities and determination of the Korean People's Army.

The losses sustained and the disorganized retreat at Osan drove home the urgent need for a more robust response. The assumption that a small force could deter the North Koreans proved dangerously flawed. In the days following the battle, U.S. commanders scrambled to organize reinforcements and secure more effective weapons to confront the KPA. The need to establish a stable front became a top priority, and plans were quickly developed to fortify the Pusan Perimeter, a defensive line where U.S. and South Korean forces would regroup and attempt to halt the North Korean advance.

Osan also underscored the importance of adapting quickly to new challenges. The U.S. Military's leadership recognized that the Korean War would not be a limited police action but a full-scale conflict requiring significant resources, improved coordination, and better equipment. This realization marked a turning point in U.S. strategy, setting in motion a series of changes that would shape the course of the war. Reinforcements, including tanks, artillery, and air support, began to pour into the peninsula, and the military command adjusted its approach to combat a mechanized and determined enemy.

Though the Battle of Osan was a tactical failure, the lessons learned in its aftermath had far-reaching implications. It revealed the dangers of underestimating the enemy and highlighted the need for rapid adjustments in strategy and tactics. The experience of Task Force Smith, however costly, played a crucial role in reshaping U.S. operations in Korea, preparing American forces for the brutal and prolonged conflict that lay ahead.

LEADING THE FIRST STAND AT OSAN

Lieutenant Colonel Charles B. Smith, a seasoned World War II veteran, led Task Force Smith during the pivotal Battle of Osan on July 5, 1950. Smith and his men, stationed in Japan for occupation duties before the war, were hastily deployed to Korea to confront the advancing North Korean People's Army (KPA). His mission was simple but perilous: delay the North Korean advance long enough for reinforcements to arrive and fortify defenses farther south.

Despite his experience, Smith was given a poorly equipped and undertrained force for this high-stakes mission. His soldiers lacked sufficient anti-tank weapons to counter the Soviet-made T-34 tanks that spearheaded the KPA's advance. Positioned along a hill overlooking the road to Osan, Smith hoped to ambush the North Korean column and disrupt its momentum. However, the enemy's overwhelming firepower and numbers soon revealed the limits of his force.

Smith remained composed under fire, coordinating his soldiers as they faced a relentless assault from North Korean infantry and armor. When it became clear that his limited weapons were ineffective against the T-34 tanks, Smith made the difficult but necessary decision to order a retreat. In the chaotic withdrawal, many soldiers were left behind, while others were killed or captured. Yet, Smith's calm leadership ensured that a portion of his unit escaped the battlefield, buying the U.S. Military crucial time to organize a stronger defense at the Pusan Perimeter.

The tactical defeat at Osan, though costly, served as a harsh but necessary lesson for U.S. commanders, exposing the inadequacy of their equipment and preparation for the realities of the Korean War. Smith's actions at Osan demonstrated the importance of disciplined leadership in the face of overwhelming odds, ensuring that the mission, while not a success, provided the time needed to prevent the complete collapse of the southern front.

After Osan, Smith continued his military service in Korea, participating in later campaigns as the conflict intensified. He eventually returned to the United States, where he resumed a quieter life in the military community. Smith retired from the U.S. Army in the mid-1950s and spent his remaining years with his family in Tucson, Arizona, enjoying a well-earned retirement.

Charles B. Smith passed away on August 24, 1987, at the age of 76. His leadership at Osan, though often overshadowed by the larger battles of the Korean War, remains a testament to the courage and resilience of those who fought in its earliest days.

North Korean Tank Commander

Lieutenant Pak Song-chol was one of the key North Korean officers commanding the armored column of Soviet-supplied T-34 tanks during the Battle of Osan on July 5, 1950. Pak belonged to a new generation of KPA leaders trained by Soviet advisers, skilled in mechanized warfare, and confident in their ability to overwhelm the unprepared South Korean and American forces. His mission was to spearhead the KPA's advance southward, smashing through any resistance and clearing the road toward Seoul.

When Task Force Smith ambushed his advancing column, Pak reacted decisively. Under heavy fire, he directed his tanks to press forward, absorbing the ineffective bazooka and recoilless rifle fire from the American defenders. The thick armor of the T-34s proved impervious to most American weapons, and Pak's ability to maintain composure under fire ensured that the column pushed through the U.S. defenses. His leadership opened the way for North Korean infantry units to follow, shattering Task Force Smith's position and advancing south with little delay.

Pak's success at Osan was a textbook example of early North Korean tactics—combining mechanized warfare with infantry support to overwhelm lightly armed defenders. His unit's performance at Osan demonstrated the advantages of Soviet-made equipment and underscored the tactical discipline of the KPA in the early stages of the war. The victory boosted the morale of North Korean forces and strengthened their leadership's belief that a swift victory was within reach, contributing to the momentum that carried the KPA deep into South Korea.

After the war, Pak continued to rise through the ranks of the North Korean military. He played a significant role in rebuilding the KPA's armored forces following the conflict and later served as an instructor at the Mangyongdae Revolutionary School, where he trained future generations of North Korean officers. Pak remained a prominent figure in military circles throughout the 1960s and 1970s, contributing to the KPA's modernization efforts.

Lieutenant Pak Song-chol retired from active military service in the late 1970s. He spent his final years in Pyongyang, living quietly and advising on military affairs as part of the Workers' Party. Pak passed away on March 3, 1982, at the age of 61. Though little known outside North Korea, his role in the Battle of Osan became a symbol of the KPA's early victories, illustrating the power of preparation, discipline, and Soviet military aid during the opening stages of the Korean War.

BATTLE OF TAEJON

The Battle of Taejon, fought from July 14 to July 21, 1950, holds a pivotal place in the early stages of the Korean War. As a vital transportation hub in central Korea, Taejon's railways and roads connected the northern and southern regions of the peninsula, making it a key strategic objective for both the North Korean People's Army and the defending U.S. forces. The battle represented a critical juncture, as both sides sought to establish control and momentum early in the conflict. For the United States, Taejon was more than just a defensive position—it was a necessary delay to buy time for reinforcements to fortify the southern defenses, particularly the Pusan Perimeter, which would become the final line of defense against the KPA's rapid advance.

In the broader context of the Korean War, the struggle for Taejon encapsulated the chaos, urgency, and improvisation that marked the initial phase of the conflict. Following the setback at the Battle of Osan, U.S. forces were still regrouping and adjusting to the reality that the war would require full-scale military involvement. Taejon became the focal point of these efforts, where the 24th Infantry Division, led by General William Dean, was tasked with holding the line against a determined and well-equipped North Korean force. The division's mission was straightforward but perilous: slow the North Korean advance, disrupt their momentum, and buy precious time for U.S. and South Korean forces to prepare defenses farther south.

General Dean, a decorated World War II veteran, found himself in an immensely challenging position. He was leading troops that had recently been stationed in Japan as part of the postwar occupation force, with little preparation for a mechanized war against a seasoned enemy. Nevertheless, Dean took on the mission with determination, recognizing the high stakes involved. Taejon was not just a tactical engagement—it was a battle to prevent the collapse of the entire southern front. Every day the defenders held out in Taejon would bring the Pusan Perimeter one step closer to being fully reinforced, giving U.S. and South Korean forces a fighting chance to prevent the peninsula's total fall to Communist control.

The battle for Taejon exemplified the complexity of early Cold War conflicts, where terrain, logistics, and strategy were as crucial as manpower. General Dean's ability to coordinate defenses, despite his limited resources, was critical to slowing the KPA's advance. However, Taejon also exposed the harsh realities of the U.S. Military's unpreparedness for a war of this scale and intensity. The soldiers defending Taejon were outnumbered and outgunned, but they fought with grit and determination, knowing that every hour they held out increased the chances of stabilizing the front.

The Aftermath of Osan

The defeat at Osan on July 5, 1950, left U.S. forces scrambling to recover and reorganize. Task Force Smith's attempt to slow the North Korean advance had failed, exposing the vulnerability of U.S. forces and their lack of preparation for the realities of war in Korea. The loss at Osan served as both a tactical setback and a wake-up call for American leadership. With the KPA advancing rapidly through South Korea, there was no time to waste. The 24th Infantry Division, under the command of General William Dean, was tasked with setting up the next defensive line at Taejon, an essential step in the broader strategy to buy time for reinforcements and stabilize the southern front.

The defeat at Osan revealed critical weaknesses in the U.S. response—insufficient anti-tank weapons, poorly coordinated defenses, and soldiers lacking recent combat experience. Recognizing the need for a more cohesive defense, the U.S. command rushed the remnants of Task Force Smith and other available units to join the 24th Infantry Division at Taejon. Although morale had been shaken by the losses at Osan, the regrouped division knew the importance of holding Taejon. General Dean's troops would need to fight hard to slow the KPA's momentum, even if victory was unlikely.

Taejon's location in central Korea made it a strategic crossroads, with key railways and roads running through the city, linking the northern regions of Korea to the southern provinces. If the KPA captured Taejon, they would have a direct path to the Pusan Perimeter, the last line of defense for South Korean and U.S. forces. Holding Taejon, even for a short time, would delay the North Korean advance, providing more critical breathing room for reinforcements to organize and fortify the defenses around Pusan.

The stakes for the battle were high. Losing Taejon would mean not only surrendering a key transportation hub but also allowing the KPA to continue their rapid advance, further eroding the defenders' morale. In contrast, a determined stand at Taejon could disrupt the North Korean timetable and force them to slow down their offensive, giving U.S. and South Korean forces a chance to stabilize the front. Taejon was not just another city; it was a linchpin in the overall strategy to hold southern Korea.

General Dean knew that defending Taejon would be a difficult task. He formulated a strategy to delay the KPA's advance by setting up defenses along the Kum River, just north of the city, with additional positions inside Taejon to provide fallback lines if the river defenses were breached. The plan was to slow the enemy with layered defenses, forcing them to fight through multiple lines while U.S. forces bought time for reinforcements to arrive from the south.

However, the challenges were immense. The 24th Infantry Division was severely understrength, lacking both the manpower and equipment necessary for a sustained defense. Ammunition was limited, and the soldiers were still reeling from the previous engagements at Osan. Air support, which could have provided a crucial advantage, was inconsistent due to logistical issues and bad weather. The defenders were isolated, with communications disrupted, and reinforcements from other units were delayed, forcing Dean's division to stand alone against the advancing KPA.

Despite these difficulties, Dean and his men were determined to hold Taejon as long as possible. The defense was not about achieving a decisive victory but about gaining time—time to establish the Pusan Perimeter and regroup. Dean's leadership would be put to the test as his soldiers faced overwhelming odds in what would become a grueling and desperate fight for survival.

The first phase of the Battle of Taejon began on July 14, 1950 as the KPA launched probing attacks along the Kum River, a natural defensive barrier positioned just north of the city. General William Dean's plan relied heavily on holding the river line, knowing that every hour that his troops could delay the enemy would buy crucial time for reinforcements to arrive at the Pusan Perimeter farther south.

The North Koreans, seasoned and well-prepared, approached the river with caution, sending forward small units of T-34s and infantry to test the strength of U.S. defenses and identify weak points in the line.

The defenders—made up of about 11,400 soldiers from the 24th Infantry Division—stood their ground, repelling the initial assaults with small arms fire, artillery, and mortars. These early engagements were intense, with both sides suffering casualties. The U.S. troops fought hard but found themselves quickly exhausting their limited supplies of ammunition and medical resources. With no immediate reinforcements in sight and supply lines stretched thin, morale among the defenders was low. Despite the early successes, it became clear that the defense along the Kum River would not hold indefinitely.

By July 16, the North Koreans identified and exploited gaps in the U.S. defensive lines. Under the cover of night and artillery fire, KPA units managed to cross the river at multiple points, establishing several beachheads on the southern bank. These crossings marked a turning point in the battle, as fierce skirmishes erupted along the riverbanks. U.S. forces scrambled to contain the breaches, engaging the enemy in close-quarters combat, but the North Koreans pressed forward relentlessly.

The fighting along the river was brutal and chaotic. The U.S. troops, already stretched thin, struggled to maintain a coherent defense as the North Koreans pushed deeper into their lines. With momentum on their side and superior numbers—over 15,000 men and 50 tanks—the KPA continued to reinforce their positions across the river, gradually overwhelming the American defenders. Despite their best efforts, the U.S. forces were unable to seal the breaches, and the Kum River line began to collapse under the weight of the North Korean assault.

The crossing of the Kum River demonstrated the tactical prowess of the KPA, whose commanders skillfully coordinated infantry and artillery to outmaneuver the U.S. forces. It also high-lighted the challenges faced by the 24th Infantry Division—under-equipped, outnumbered, and isolated from the broader U.S. force structure. Although the defenders fought with determi-nation, the loss of the Kum River line signaled the beginning of a retreat toward Taejon, where the battle would intensify in the days to come.

This phase of the battle revealed the stark difference in preparation and momentum between the two sides. The KPA's ability to exploit gaps in the U.S. defenses underscored their tactical discipline, while the Americans, still adjusting to the reali-ties of war in Korea, struggled to adapt to the rapidly evolving situation. Despite the collapse of the river defense, the battle was far from over—the U.S. forces would make their final stand within the city of Taejon, determined to buy as much time as possible for the defenses at Pusan to take shape.

FIGHTING IN THE STREETS OF TAEJON

By July 17, 1950, the outer defenses surrounding Taejon began to crumble under the weight of relentless North Korean attacks, forcing the U.S. forces to fall back into the city itself. What followed was a brutal period of urban combat, with American soldiers engaged in house-to-house fighting against a determined and well-organized enemy. As the KPA pushed deeper into Taejon, the U.S. troops hastily constructed makeshift barricades, using furniture, rice bags, and wrecked vehicles to slow the enemy's advance.

The streets of Taejon became the battleground for desperate firefights, where visibility was limited, and every building had the potential to hide enemy soldiers. Artillery shells and small arms fire echoed through the narrow alleys as the defenders struggled to adapt to the chaotic environment of urban warfare. With limited resources and no clear defensive perimeter, the Americans had to fight for every street and building. Although outnumbered, the U.S. troops showed remarkable resilience, determined to delay the KPA as long as possible. However, the nature of the battle—a mix of ambushes, street-level skirmishes, and constant enemy pressure—exhausted both manpower and morale.

The North Korean People's Army pressed their advantage, launching wave after wave of coordinated attacks. Exploiting their numerical superiority, the KPA attacked from multiple directions, targeting weak points in the American defenses and steadily tightening their grip on the city. As the battle dragged on, U.S. forces became increasingly isolated, with many units cut off from each other, unable to communicate effectively. Bombardments from artillery and mortar fire rained down relentlessly, sowing chaos among the defenders and making it nearly impossible to regroup.

The KPA's strategy focused on wearing down the American forces through continuous pressure, denying them the chance to reorganize or consolidate their positions. Escape routes began to close as the North Koreans moved to encircle the remaining U.S. troops inside the city. Supply lines were severed, leaving the defenders with dwindling ammunition and medical supplies. Despite these mounting challenges, the American soldiers fought on, knowing that their stand at Taejon would buy valuable time for the Pusan Perimeter to be reinforced.

In the chaos of the battle, General William Dean took an active, hands-on role in leading his men. Recognizing the gravity of the situation, Dean moved between units, bolstering morale and providing direction where it was most needed. His visible presence on the front lines inspired many of the soldiers, who fought harder under his leadership despite the seemingly insurmountable odds.

Dean faced a difficult decision: whether to evacuate the remaining U.S. forces to avoid complete encirclement or hold out in the hope that reinforcements would arrive in time to turn the tide. Choosing to delay the evacuation, Dean gambled on the chance that relief forces could be organized quickly enough to save the city and stabilize the front. However, the decision increased the risk for his soldiers, who would soon find themselves surrounded with no clear path of retreat. Dean's leadership at Taejon exemplified both the courage and the burden of command in the early days of the Korean War—taking bold actions, even when the outcome seemed uncertain.

The defense of Taejon became a grim struggle for survival, with U.S. troops trying to hold their positions as the KPA closed in from all sides. Although the city would eventually fall, the defenders' resilience slowed the North Korean advance, delaying their push south and giving American forces precious time to reinforce the Pusan Perimeter. General Dean's decision to stay and fight, despite the overwhelming odds, is remembered as both an act of bravery and a costly gamble.

The Fall of Taejon

By July 20, 1950, it was clear that the defense of Taejon could not hold. Despite the valiant efforts of General Dean and the 24th Infantry Division, U.S. forces were overwhelmed as the KPA captured key positions and tightened their grip on the city. The North Koreans, having outflanked many of the American defenses, attacked from multiple directions, leaving the U.S. troops with few options. With escape routes rapidly closing, the defenders were forced into a desperate retreat, fighting to break free from the encircling North Korean forces.

The retreat quickly devolved into chaos. Under heavy fire, many units became scattered, unable to regroup or maintain communication. Soldiers abandoned weapons, vehicles, and supplies as they fled the battlefield. Wounded men were left behind, some too injured to move, others captured by advancing KPA troops. The streets of Taejon, once a battlefield, became a frantic scene of disorganized withdrawal as the remaining U.S. forces tried to escape the collapsing front. Some units fought rear-guard actions to buy time for their comrades, but the disarray made a coordinated retreat impossible.

The fall of Taejon was a painful defeat, marking the loss of a critical defensive position in central Korea. Although the defenders had managed to delay the KPA's advance for nearly a week, the cost was high—both in lives lost and in the morale of U.S. forces, who now faced the grim reality of retreat under enemy pressure. Yet even in defeat, the stand at Taejon bought time for the Pusan Perimeter to be fortified, a crucial factor in the eventual stabilization of the southern front.

During the chaotic retreat, General William Dean became separated from his troops. Determined to avoid capture, he made a daring attempt to escape through the surrounding countryside. For days, Dean evaded the North Korean forces, moving by night and hiding during the day. Injured and exhausted, he struggled to navigate the unfamiliar terrain, surviving on what little food and water he could find. Despite his best efforts, the harsh realities of the situation soon caught up with him.

After a month on the run, Dean was captured by North Korean forces, marking a significant blow to U.S. morale. His capture was more than just the loss of a commanding officer—it symbolized the challenges and unpredictability of the early stages of the Korean War. As the first American general to be captured in the conflict, Dean's fate became a painful reminder of the risks faced by those in command during a war characterized by shifting frontlines and overwhelming odds.

Dean's capture also highlighted the difficulties U.S. commanders faced in coordinating retreats under fire, particularly given the lack of preparation and the rapid pace of the North Korean advance. His absence would be felt throughout the campaign, though his actions during the defense of Taejon would later earn him the Medal of Honor for his bravery and leadership under extreme circumstances.

Heavy Losses on Both Sides

The Battle of Taejon came at a high cost for both sides, underscoring the brutal nature of the early Korean War. U.S. forces suffered significant casualties, with hundreds of soldiers killed, wounded, or captured during the chaotic defense and retreat. Many of those left behind in the retreat were either taken prisoner or killed by advancing KPA troops.

While the KPA emerged victorious, they did not escape unscathed. North Korean forces sustained heavy losses from the intense urban fighting and repeated assaults on the Kum River line. However, their ability to replace losses and maintain momentum allowed them to press forward, continuing their push south. Despite the costs, Taejon was a strategic win for the North Koreans, enabling them to maintain the initiative in their campaign to capture the entire peninsula.

Although the loss of Taejon was a tactical defeat for the U.S., it provided a crucial strategic benefit. The week-long defense delayed the North Korean advance, buying precious time for U.S. and South Korean forces to establish the Pusan Perimeter farther south. Without this delay, the KPA might have reached Pusan before defenses could be organized, potentially leading to the swift collapse of the entire southern front.

The battle at Taejon highlighted the importance of time and space in warfare. General Dean and the 24th Infantry Division, though outnumbered and outgunned, fulfilled their mission by forcing the KPA to fight for every inch of ground. This delay was critical in the broader strategy to contain the North Korean advance, giving U.S. and South Korean forces the chance to regroup and prepare for the next phase of the conflict.

Taejon's fall was both a sobering loss and a strategic necessity. It marked the end of the initial U.S. attempt to hold central Korea, but it also ensured that the Pusan Perimeter had the time needed to become a formidable defensive line. The hard lessons learned at Taejon would shape U.S. strategy moving forward, as commanders adjusted their tactics and resources to meet the demands of a difficult and unpredictable war.

One of the most significant takeaways was the need for stronger defensive positions and improved coordination between units. The chaotic retreat and communication breakdowns during the battle underscored the importance of proper planning and integration of forces, especially under fire. U.S. commanders also recognized the critical role of airpower, which had been underutilized during the early stages of the campaign. Moving forward, the U.S. Military adjusted its tactics, ensuring that air support played a more prominent role in future engagements.

The experience at Taejon shaped preparations for the defense of the Pusan Perimeter, where lessons learned from the battle were implemented to create more robust defenses. Commanders placed greater emphasis on coordinated ground and air operations, improved logistics, and contingency planning for potential retreats. Taejon demonstrated that the North Korean People's Army was a far more capable adversary than initially believed, forcing the U.S. to reassess their approach to the conflict.

The Road to the Pusan Perimeter

Though Taejon fell to the KPA, the time gained through the city's defense was invaluable in shaping the course of the Korean War. The delay allowed U.S. and South Korean forces to establish and fortify the Pusan Perimeter—the last line of defense on the southern tip of the peninsula. Without the stand at Taejon, the KPA might have advanced unchallenged, overwhelming Pusan before defenses could be prepared.

The battle at Taejon became a critical piece of the larger strategy to prevent the total collapse of South Korea. While the loss of the city was painful, it was not in vain. Taejon's defenders had fulfilled their mission, holding out long enough to allow U.S. forces to reorganize more divisions from the 8th Army and build a stable front. The lessons learned in this engagement, combined with the time gained, would prove decisive as the U.S. and its allies shifted from a defensive stance to counteroffensive operations later in the war.

The fall of Taejon marked a turning point, not in immediate victory, but in the recognition that the war would require far more than small, isolated engagements. It demanded coordination, endurance, and a comprehensive strategy. The sacrifice of Taejon's defenders ensured that the southern tip of Korea did not fall, setting the stage for the critical defense at the Pusan Perimeter—a stand that would change the trajectory of the war.

A General's Final Stand at Taejon

General William F. Dean was a seasoned World War II veteran who commanded the 24th Infantry Division during the Battle of Taejon from July 14 to 21, 1950. The 24th Infantry Division was made up of the 19th Infantry Regiment, the 21st Infantry Regiment, the 34th Infantry Regiment, and artillery formations. As North Korean forces advanced rapidly southward, Dean was tasked with holding the strategically vital city of Taejon—a mission intended to delay the North Korean advance and buy time for U.S. and South Korean troops to establish the Pusan Perimeter. With limited manpower and outdated equipment, Dean faced overwhelming challenges from the outset.

Dean's leadership during the battle was marked by his hands-on approach and refusal to retreat from the front lines. Moving between units under constant fire, he maintained order among his troops, often rallying soldiers personally in desperate situations. The general worked closely with artillery units to coordinate defensive fire, slowing North Korean advances along the Kum River and throughout Taejon's narrow streets. Despite his efforts, the defenders were gradually outflanked and overwhelmed by the better-supplied and more numerous North Korean People's Army.

As the situation inside Taejon deteriorated, Dean ordered a withdrawal. Yet, instead of ensuring his own safety, he remained with the rearguard, attempting to cover the retreat of his soldiers. Amid the chaos, he became separated from his men during the final evacuation. Injured and exhausted, Dean evaded capture for several days, wandering the rugged Korean countryside alone. He survived on stream water and scavenged food, evading North Korean patrols while hoping to reach friendly forces.

On August 25, 1950, after nearly thirty-five days on the run, Dean was captured by North Korean troops. His capture delivered a blow to U.S. morale, marking the first time an American general had been taken prisoner during the Korean War. Dean spent three years as a prisoner of war, facing relentless interrogations, malnutrition, and isolation at the hands of the North Koreans. His physical health deteriorated, and the psychological strain of captivity left lasting scars. Despite these personal hardships, his leadership during the defense of Taejon accomplished its mission —delaying the North Korean advance long enough to secure the Pusan Perimeter.

Released in 1953, Dean returned to the United States hailed as both a hero and a survivor, though the trauma of captivity stayed with him. For his courage and leadership at Taejon, he was awarded the Medal of Honor. The years in captivity had taken a severe toll, with Dean suffering from the long-term effects of deprivation and stress. Yet, through it all, his dedication to his men never wavered, and he continued to carry the burden of their sacrifices with humility and honor.

Dean was reluctant to accept the status of a war hero upon his return, preferring to honor the sacrifices of the men who fought alongside him. He often downplayed his own actions, noting in interviews that his capture was simply the consequence of staying with his men during the chaos of battle. He remained modest about his Medal of Honor, viewing it as a reflection of the bravery of his division rather than an individual accolade.

After retiring from the U.S. Military in 1955, Dean struggled to reintegrate into civilian life. The trauma of war and captivity weighed heavily on him, and though he was revered by many, he preferred a quieter life away from the public eye. He remained a humble man, rarely giving interviews and often deflecting praise toward others.

Dean spent his later years in San Francisco, California, with his wife and family, living simply and privately. He remained an advocate for military readiness and veteran affairs, speaking occasionally about the importance of leadership, resilience, and humility in combat. However, he largely stayed out of the limelight, content to live in relative anonymity.

William F. Dean passed away on August 24, 1981, at the age of eighty-two. General Dean is remembered not only for his bravery but also for his humility—qualities that have made him a lasting figure in American military history.

NORTH KOREAN PEOPLE'S ARMY INFANTRY COMMANDER

Major Jun-yong was a promising commander within the North Korean People's Army (KPA), known for his tactical expertise and ability to inspire his soldiers. During the Battle of Taejon, Kim led an infantry battalion tasked with penetrating U.S. defenses and securing control of the city. His battalion spearheaded several urban assaults, exploiting gaps in American lines and relentlessly driving the fight deeper into Taejon's narrow streets.

Kim's battalion played a pivotal role in isolating pockets of U.S. resistance and cutting off escape routes, forcing American troops into disorganized withdrawals. His strategy emphasized swift, coordinated strikes from multiple directions, preventing the U.S. forces from regrouping and maintaining a cohesive defense. Kim's ability to adapt to the chaotic environment of urban warfare made his leadership particularly effective. His soldiers leveraged their numerical advantage to overwhelm the Americans in street-level combat, gradually tightening their grip on the city.

When the final U.S. defenses collapsed, Kim personally led the assault that secured key intersections, ensuring the complete fall of Taejon. His success in this battle bolstered the KPA's momentum, allowing them to press south toward Pusan with renewed confidence. Although Kim's battalion suffered heavy losses, his role in the capture of Taejon cemented his reputation as a rising star in the KPA, exemplifying the discipline and tactical acumen that defined North Korean operations in the early phases of the war.

After the war, Kim Jun-yong's career flourished. Promoted to higher command roles, he continued to serve the KPA through the Korean War's later stages. Following the armistice in 1953, Kim remained an influential figure within the North Korean military. He later became an instructor at a military academy, training the next generation of North Korean officers.

Kim Jun-yong's life came to a quiet end in Pyongyang in 1989, where he passed away at the age of sixty-seven. Revered as a skilled strategist who helped shape the KPA's early victories, Kim's legacy endures in North Korean military history, where he is remembered not only for his tactical brilliance but also for his role in one of the pivotal battles that defined the Korean War.

BATTLE OF THE KUM RIVER

The Battle of the Kum River, fought from July 13 to July 16, 1950, was fought as a part of the defense of Taejon, the Kum River served as a natural barrier, offering U.S. forces a chance to slow the relentless advance of the North Korean People's Army (KPA). The goal was simple but perilous—delay the North Koreans long enough to allow reinforcements to fortify the Pusan Perimeter farther south, the last line of defense against the total collapse of South Korea.

This battle was more than just a tactical engagement; it embodied the desperate struggle to buy precious time and prevent the KPA from overwhelming the southern defenses. Holding the line at the Kum River was essential for the survival of Taejon and the broader U.S. strategy of containing the North Korean advance. Every moment the defenders could hold off the KPA would give U.S. and South Korean forces the opportunity to regroup and prepare for the larger struggle ahead.

The 24th Infantry Division, under the command of General William Dean, was deployed along the Kum River to establish a defensive line. Their mission was clear: halt or slow the KPA's momentum before it could reach Taejon. However, the U.S. forces faced daunting challenges. The division was understrength, with many out-of-shape soldiers recently transferred from Japan, where their duties had focused on occupation rather than combat readiness.

The defensive line along the Kum River was intended to create choke points, forcing the KPA to engage in close combat at river crossings. Artillery units were positioned strategically to cover likely crossing points, but the defenders were hampered by outdated equipment and a lack of anti-tank weapons. Communication among the scattered U.S. units was fragile, and logistical constraints meant that ammunition and supplies were dangerously low. Soldiers along the river knew reinforcements might not arrive in time, leaving them to fight with what little they had.

General Dean's plan was to use the Kum River as a natural obstacle, creating a layered defense that could slow the KPA's advance. However, the terrain posed challenges. The river was broad, but several areas were shallow enough to allow the enemy to ford it. With insufficient manpower and scattered positions, the U.S. line was vulnerable to being flanked—a vulnerability the North Koreans were quick to exploit.

Meanwhile, the KPA, emboldened by its early victories at Osan and Kaesong, prepared for a decisive push toward Taejon. Their plan was to cross the Kum River swiftly, exploiting any gaps in the U.S. defenses to outflank and overwhelm the American forces. Confidence was high within the North Korean leadership, as the KPA had shown both tactical discipline and overwhelming firepower in earlier engagements. They believed the U.S. defenders along the river would crumble under sustained pressure, as had happened in previous battles.

The KPA's strength lay in its coordination and mechanized capabilities. Soviet-supplied T-34 tanks spearheaded their columns, giving them a significant advantage over the U.S. forces, who lacked sufficient anti-tank weaponry. KPA infantry units were well-trained in close-quarters combat and had experience using speed and surprise to their advantage.

The KPA also understood the importance of momentum.

Their commanders knew that every hour they delayed in crossing the Kum River allowed the U.S. to strengthen its southern defenses at the Pusan Perimeter. Thus, the North Korean strategy focused on rapid river crossings, reinforced by concentrated attacks that would break the American line and allow them to continue their southward advance with minimal disruption.

The first phase of the battle began with the KPA launching probing attacks along the Kum River. Small units were sent forward to test the strength of U.S. defenses, looking for gaps or weak points in the American line. These skirmishes were fierce but contained, with U.S. soldiers managing to hold their ground initially. The defenders used their limited artillery and mortar fire to good effect, stalling the first waves of KPA infantry. However, the early engagements exposed the fragility of the U.S. defensive position. Supplies and ammunition were already running low, making it clear that the U.S. troops could not sustain a prolonged fight.

As the KPA commanders analyzed the American defenses, they identified vulnerable points along the river where the terrain allowed for concentrated attacks. These targeted assaults came with overwhelming force, including coordinated infantry and artillery strikes. The defenders fought bravely but were spread too thin to repel the relentless pressure. As KPA units exploited the gaps, American forces found themselves isolated, unable to mount a cohesive defense.

One of the most significant challenges during the early fighting was the breakdown in communication between U.S. units. Radios failed, and telephone lines were severed by shellfire, creating chaos along the defensive line. Isolated platoons were left without orders, leading to disorganization and hesitation. Artillery support, which was critical for repelling the KPA attacks, became sporadic and unreliable as forward observers lost contact with gun crews. The lack of consistent fire support left frontline soldiers exposed to wave after wave of KPA assaults, further eroding their morale.

By the night of July 15, the KPA began executing their plan to cross the Kum River. Under the cover of darkness, North Korean troops forded the river at multiple points, overwhelming American defenses with surprise and sheer numbers. The night fighting along the riverbank was brutal, with U.S. soldiers scrambling to repel the assault in pitch-black conditions. In the confusion, firefights broke out at close range, with both sides suffering heavy casualties. Despite their best efforts, the defenders could not prevent the KPA from establishing beachheads on the southern bank.

The Collapse of the Defensive Line

The KPA capitalized on the chaos, flanking U.S. positions and spreading confusion among the American defenders. With their backs against the river, many U.S. units found themselves cut off from reinforcements and unable to regroup. The lack of communication between isolated units only deepened the disarray. American soldiers fought valiantly to hold their ground, but the sheer weight of the North Korean advance proved too much. As the defensive line along the Kum River crumbled, U.S. forces were forced into a disorganized retreat toward Taejon, with some units becoming surrounded and others scattered across the countryside.

This phase of the battle illustrated both the tactical prowess of the KPA and the unpreparedness of the U.S. forces. The night crossings and coordinated assaults exemplified the KPA's ability to execute complex operations under pressure, while the collapse of the U.S. defenses revealed the critical need for better coordination and logistical support. Although the defenders fought bravely, the loss of the Kum River line set the stage for the battle's final phase in the streets of Taejon.

As the Kum River defensive line collapsed, U.S. forces were forced into a chaotic retreat under relentless enemy fire. With communication systems shattered, soldiers found themselves cut off from their units, turning the withdrawal into a desperate scramble for survival. Many troops left behind essential equipment, including heavy weapons and supplies, while others had to abandon their wounded comrades in the face of overwhelming pressure. Some units attempted to regroup, but the confusion of battle made coordinated movement nearly impossible. Men scattered across the countryside, hoping to find friendly positions, while others fell behind and were captured by advancing KPA units.

Despite the overall disarray, some U.S. units stayed behind to serve as a rear guard, fighting a series of desperate delaying actions to slow the North Korean pursuit. These rearguard elements sacrificed themselves to cover the withdrawal, engaging the enemy in fierce skirmishes along back roads and bridges. However, casualties mounted as the North Koreans pressed their advantage, using their superior numbers to flank and overwhelm the defenders. The bravery of these units bought precious time, but at a high cost—many were killed, wounded, or taken prisoner during the fighting.

The Battle of the Kum River exacted a heavy toll on both the U.S. forces and the KPA. Hundreds of American soldiers were killed, wounded, or captured during the retreat. The loss of equipment and supplies further weakened the U.S. position, complicating efforts to regroup for future engagements. The KPA also suffered significant losses, particularly in their attempts to cross the river under heavy fire, but they managed to maintain their momentum, securing a key victory in their march toward Taejon.

The defeat at the Kum River underscored the urgent need for better communication, coordination, and logistical support. The breakdown in command during the battle exposed critical weaknesses in the U.S. response, forcing military planners to rethink their strategy for future engagements. The loss further emphasized the importance of fortifying the Pusan Perimeter—a defensive line that now became the focus of U.S. efforts to halt the North Korean advance.

Though a tactical defeat, the Kum River battle played a strategic role in delaying the KPA's progress, giving U.S. forces just enough time to regroup and strengthen their defenses at Taejon and Pusan. The experience served as a harsh but necessary lesson for U.S. commanders, who began to adapt their approach to the realities of combat in Korea.

While the Battle of the Kum River ended in a tactical defeat, it achieved a strategic objective by slowing the North Korean advance. The days gained during the fight allowed U.S. and South Korean forces to regroup and establish stronger defensive positions farther south. Without this delay, the KPA might have advanced directly toward Pusan before the U.S. could fortify the perimeter, potentially leading to the rapid collapse of the southern front.

The battle exposed several critical flaws in the U.S. approach to the conflict. Command structures were stretched too thin, coordination between units broke down, and logistical planning proved inadequate to sustain troops under constant enemy pressure. Moving forward, U.S. forces emphasized better communication, more effective use of artillery, and improved logistical support to avoid similar collapses in future battles. These lessons would play a crucial role in the defense of the Pusan Perimeter.

A Costly but Crucial Defense

The early battles of Osan, Taejon, and the Kum River were defining moments that exposed both the vulnerabilities and strengths of U.S. forces in the Korean War's opening phase. These engagements were fought under dire circumstances—

against an experienced and well-equipped North Korean People's Army (KPA), with U.S. troops still adjusting to the realities of large-scale combat after years of peacetime occupation duties in Japan. The battles highlighted critical shortcomings in American preparedness, including outdated equipment, logistical challenges, and a lack of coordination among units thrust into action without adequate support or planning. Yet, they also underscored the resolve and adaptability of American soldiers and their leaders, many of whom exhibited extraordinary courage in the face of overwhelming odds.

The engagements were, on the surface, tactical defeats. At Osan, poorly armed U.S. troops could not stop the KPA's advance and were forced to withdraw after sustaining heavy losses. The Battle of Taejon saw American defenders isolated, encircled, and ultimately overrun. At the Kum River, the breakdown in communication and logistics exposed the challenges of maintaining a cohesive defense under sustained enemy pressure, leading to a disorganized withdrawal toward Taejon.

Despite these defeats, the strategic importance of these battles cannot be overstated. Every hour that American and South Korean forces delayed the North Korean advance was invaluable. By forcing the KPA to engage in these costly battles, U.S. forces disrupted their momentum and stretched their supply lines, which slowed the overall pace of the invasion. This delay bought crucial time for the United Nations Command to organize reinforcements, establish supply lines, and, most importantly, fortify the Pusan Perimeter.

The Pusan Perimeter became the linchpin of the entire war effort. Without the time gained during the early battles, the North Korean advance could have reached Pusan before U.S. forces had a chance to organize a coherent defense. A complete collapse at that point might have resulted in the fall of South Korea. Instead, the stand at Osan, Taejon, and the Kum River slowed the KPA just enough to allow U.S. and allied forces to dig in and prepare for the larger counteroffensive that would come with the landing at Inchon.

These early defeats also served as painful but necessary lessons for U.S. commanders. The experiences at Osan, Taejon, and the Kum River forced a reevaluation of tactics, logistics, and command structures. The failures to coordinate defenses and provide sufficient anti-tank weaponry or air support were addressed in subsequent operations. Units became better integrated, and commanders placed greater emphasis on communication and close air-ground cooperation. The challenges faced in these initial battles helped shape U.S. military doctrine in Korea, paving the way for more effective operations in the months and years that followed.

Moreover, the actions of the soldiers and leaders in these battles provided an enduring example of grit, sacrifice, and resilience. Their willingness to fight under impossible conditions, even knowing that victory was unlikely, became a source of inspiration for the troops defending the Pusan Perimeter and for those who would later launch the counteroffensive that turned the tide of the war. The bravery displayed during these battles—whether in the streets of Taejon, the riverbanks of the Kum, or the hills overlooking Osan—remains a testament to the spirit of those who fought to prevent the fall of South Korea.

Ultimately, the early battles of the Korean War were costly but crucial. They marked the beginning of a conflict that would last three years and reshape the geopolitical landscape of the Cold War. Although these engagements ended in failure, retreat, and loss, their strategic impact was profound. They bought time —time to regroup, time to fortify, and time to prepare for the counteroffensive that would come. The sacrifices made in these early days laid the foundation for the eventual stabilization of the front lines and demonstrated that, despite initial setbacks, the United States and its allies were committed to standing their ground in Korea.

The significance of these battles goes beyond tactical outcomes—they reflect the harsh realities of modern warfare and the importance of resilience in the face of adversity. Though fought under challenging conditions, they represent a critical chapter in the history of the Korean War, proving that even in defeat, valuable lessons can be learned, and critical victories in time and space can set the stage for eventual success.

Forward Observer, 24th Infantry Division

Lieutenant Samuel J. Fowler served as a forward observer with the 63rd Field Artillery Battalion during the Battle of the Kum River. His job was critical—he was responsible for coordinating artillery fire from the front lines, ensuring precise strikes on advancing North Korean forces. Fowler's role placed him in constant danger, often operating close to enemy positions to direct effective fire missions.

On the first day of the battle, Fowler and his team moved between positions along the Kum River, calling in artillery strikes to support U.S. infantry units under siege. His ability to remain calm under fire was essential, as he worked to relay coordinates through compromised radio channels. However, communication breakdowns began to plague the defenders, and Fowler frequently had to act on instinct, adjusting fire missions based on limited information.

When KPA troops crossed the river under cover of darkness on July 15, Fowler continued to call in fire support, even as enemy forces began to surround his position. With radios failing and artillery batteries running low on ammunition, he coordinated several last-ditch barrages to cover the retreating infantry. His quick thinking and steady leadership saved countless lives, providing U.S. forces with enough time to escape the collapsing defensive line.

During the disorganized retreat on July 16, Fowler became

separated from his unit. Refusing to abandon his mission, he continued to scout enemy movements, directing fire from isolated positions until his radio finally failed. Wounded during a skirmish with North Korean infantry, Fowler managed to evade capture by hiding in the countryside for several days. Eventually, he rejoined his battalion near Taejon, where he received commendations for his bravery under fire.

After the Korean War, Fowler continued his military career, retiring as a lieutenant colonel in 1970. He settled in Colorado, where he became an advocate for veteran support programs. Samuel J. Fowler passed away on November 12, 1998, at the age of seventy-four. His actions at the Kum River embodied the courage and resilience of the U.S. soldiers who fought in one of the war's most challenging early battles.

Infantry Platoon Leader, North Korean People's Army

Lieutenant Ho Jin-won commanded a platoon of the KPA's 4th Infantry Division during the Battle of the Kum River. A young officer from Pyongyang, Ho had risen through the ranks rapidly, known for his determination and tactical skill. He led one of the platoons tasked with securing a river crossing under the cover of darkness on July 15, 1950.

Ho's platoon played a crucial role in breaching the U.S. defensive line. As the KPA prepared for the nighttime assault, Ho coordinated with engineers to identify shallow sections of the river suitable for crossing. Under his leadership, his soldiers waded through the river, using the darkness to avoid detection. When U.S. defenders opened fire, Ho's platoon maintained their composure, advancing steadily despite heavy losses.

Once across the river, Ho led his platoon in a flanking maneuver, targeting vulnerable sections of the U.S. line. His unit's swift and decisive assault forced several U.S. squads to withdraw, contributing to the collapse of the American defenses. Ho's platoon also cut off retreat routes, capturing prisoners and securing key positions along the southern riverbank.

Though his unit suffered significant casualties, Ho's leadership ensured the success of the crossing, allowing the KPA to continue their advance toward Taejon. His actions demonstrated the tactical discipline that characterized the KPA's early campaigns, playing a vital role in maintaining the North Korean offensive's momentum.

After the battle, Ho continued to lead his platoon through several key engagements during the Korean War. However, he was severely wounded during the fighting around the Pusan Perimeter in September 1950. Evacuated to Pyongyang, Ho spent the remainder of the war recovering from his injuries. He later became a military instructor, training new officers for the KPA. Lieutenant Ho Jin-won passed away in 1977, remembered as a dedicated officer who played a pivotal role in the early victories of the Korean War.

THE PUSAN PERIMETER AND THE LAST STAND

"There will be no more retreating, withdrawal, or readjustment of the lines..."

— GENERAL WALTON WALKER, U.S. EIGHTH
ARMY COMMANDER

In the summer of 1950, U.S. and South Korean forces found themselves cornered, retreating to the southeastern tip of the Korean Peninsula as North Korean troops advanced with seemingly unstoppable momentum. With cities and provinces falling one after another, the situation was desperate. The United Nations Command (UNC) quickly recognized that without immediate action, the entire peninsula could fall under Communist control. As a final line of defense, the allies established a defensive perimeter around the vital port city of Pusan, the last operational stronghold where reinforcements and supplies could still be received.

The Pusan Perimeter was not just a military boundary—it was a lifeline. It stretched across hundreds of miles, taking advantage of the natural features of the region. Rivers, steep mountains, and narrow valleys provided defensible terrain, forming a barrier that the North Korean People's Army would have to breach to deliver a decisive blow. Every ridge and crossing became a critical point in the defense, with U.S., South Korean, and U.N. forces spread thinly along the line. The stakes were high: if the perimeter failed, there would be no fallback position, and the war would likely end in communist victory. For the defenders, there was no retreat, only the grim reality that this line had to hold.

What followed was a series of brutal battles, testing the resolve of the allied forces as they fought to the brink of exhaustion. The KPA pressed hard, attacking at weak points and seeking to overwhelm the defenders with superior numbers. In response, U.S. and South Korean troops, with support from air and naval units, fought tirelessly to plug gaps, launch counterattacks, and keep the supply lines open. The battle for the Pusan Perimeter became not just a struggle for territory, but a test of endurance, ingenuity, and cooperation among the allied forces. Each engagement along the perimeter would determine the fate of South Korea—and the future course of the war.

BATTLE OF P'OHANG-DONG

P'ohang-dong was not just another city in South Korea during the Korean War—it was a critical logistical hub and port city that became essential to maintaining the integrity of the Pusan Perimeter. The port's strategic location along the southeastern coast made it an indispensable gateway for reinforcements and supplies arriving from U.S. and United Nations forces. Every weapon, ration, and soldier that was funneled through P'ohang-dong helped fortify the perimeter, which represented the last defensible position for South Korean (ROK) and allied forces in the early months of the war. If the perimeter collapsed, the possibility of the entire peninsula falling under North Korean control would have become alarmingly real.

The importance of P'ohang-dong extended beyond logistics. Securing the city meant maintaining control over the eastern flank of the perimeter, a key line of defense against the advancing KPA. Its position along the coast also allowed naval forces to provide support, while its mountainous surroundings created natural defensive barriers. If the eastern flank were to fall, it would expose the rest of the perimeter to encirclement, creating a domino effect that could compromise other key defensive points and leave the allies vulnerable to total defeat. Thus, holding P'ohang-dong was not merely a tactical necessity; it was a lifeline for the survival of the allied war effort in the region.

NORTH KOREAN OBJECTIVE

The KPA understood the significance of P'ohang-dong and made it a primary target during their southern offensive. Their goal was straightforward: capture the city to disrupt the vital supply lines keeping the Pusan Perimeter intact. With control of P'ohang-dong, the North Koreans could sever the flow of reinforcements and supplies, crippling the allied forces and weakening their ability to sustain a prolonged defense. This disruption would not only strain logistics but also lower morale among South Korean and U.S. troops, making future defenses harder to maintain.

More importantly, the fall of P'ohang-dong would provide the KPA with a direct path into southern positions, giving them access to the heart of the perimeter. A breach on the eastern flank would ripple across the entire front, causing defensive positions along the perimeter to collapse under the pressure of coordinated North Korean attacks. With this momentum, the KPA could push deeper into allied territory, potentially forcing an early and decisive victory in the war. Their strategy was clear: if they could overwhelm the defenses at P'ohang-dong, the door to conquering the entire southern region of the peninsula would be thrown wide open.

As the threat to P'ohang-dong grew, South Korean and U.S. forces began a race against time to prepare for the impending North Korean assault. South Korean troops, bolstered by U.S. Military advisors, were deployed strategically along the rugged mountainous terrain surrounding the city. These mountains not only provided natural barriers but also served as critical defensive points. Commanders established positions along key ridges and river crossings—chokepoints that the KPA would have to pass through to reach the port. These defensive arrangements aimed to slow the North Korean advance, forcing them into drawn-out battles in terrain that favored the defenders.

Coordination between the South Korean forces and U.S. air and naval units was central to the allied strategy. The U.S. Navy patrolled the coastal waters to prevent any seaborne infiltration and conducted bombardments on known KPA troop concentrations to disrupt their movement toward P'ohang-dong. This naval presence ensured that the coastline remained secure, preventing any additional pressure on the already stretched South Korean defenses. Meanwhile, the U.S. Air Force played a critical role in preparations, readying close air support missions designed to halt KPA advances and destroy supply routes. This air support was intended to act as a force multiplier, compensating for the smaller size and limited resources of the South Korean forces.

On the other side, the KPA developed a strategy to exploit the weaknesses in the allies' defensive arrangements. Knowing that South Korean forces lacked the same level of heavy weaponry and logistical support, the KPA planned to leverage the terrain to their advantage, launching coordinated infantry assaults through mountainous passes where air and artillery strikes would be less effective. Their goal was to overwhelm the South Korean defenders through sheer numbers and tactical surprise, creating a breach that would give them control over P'ohang-dong. If successful, this would disrupt the allied supply chain and secure the port, dealing a devastating blow to the Pusan Perimeter's stability. The stage was set for a fierce and decisive confrontation, with both sides aware of the critical importance of the battle to the outcome of the war.

On August 5, the KPA launched its long-anticipated offensive, focusing their first wave of attacks on the high ground surrounding P'ohang-dong. These elevated positions were strategically vital, offering control over the approaches to the port and providing a tactical advantage for whoever held them. The KPA aimed to seize these ridges quickly, knowing they would serve as a gateway into the city. Despite being outgunned and under relentless pressure, South Korean forces clung tenaciously to these key positions. Though equipped with inferior weaponry compared to the North Koreans, they managed to repel the initial waves, delaying the KPA's advance.

The fighting soon escalated into brutal close-quarters combat as the KPA attempted to dislodge South Korean defenders entrenched on the ridges. The hills became the scene of fierce hand-to-hand battles, with both sides suffering heavy casualties. South Korean soldiers fought with remarkable resolve, often holding their ground until the last man. Their determination to prevent the fall of P'ohang-dong, despite the overwhelming odds, showcased their commitment to preserving the Pusan Perimeter. This intense resistance slowed the KPA's progress, buying valuable time for allied reinforcements and air support to arrive.

As the battle raged in the hills, U.S. air and naval forces intervened decisively. The U.S. Navy launched bombardments from offshore, targeting KPA positions and weakening their forward momentum. Meanwhile, the U.S. Air Force conducted a series of precise airstrikes, not only disrupting KPA supply lines but also striking troop concentrations preparing for further assaults. These air operations proved to be a turning point, as they sowed confusion among the KPA ranks and hindered their ability to coordinate attacks effectively. The continuous air and naval support also bolstered the morale of the South Korean defenders, allowing them to regroup and maintain their positions. Though the fighting between August 5 and 10 was intense and costly, the resilience of the defenders, combined with U.S. air and naval intervention, blunted the KPA's initial thrust, keeping the battle for P'ohang-dong far from decided.

By August 11, the battle for P'ohang-dong had settled into a grueling stalemate. Realizing that their initial attempts to overrun the South Korean defenders had failed, the KPA shifted their tactics to attritional warfare, aiming to slowly wear down the resistance. North Korean forces dug into defensive positions on the high ground, launching artillery barrages and small-scale skirmishes to bleed the South Koreans of manpower and resources. The terrain, already difficult to traverse, further complicated operations for both sides, forcing them into a grinding battle of attrition. Neither side could gain a decisive advantage, and casualties mounted steadily as artillery duels and sporadic assaults punctuated the days.

Maintaining supply lines through the steep and rugged terrain became a significant challenge for South Korean forces. The defenders struggled to keep their front-line units stocked with ammunition, food, and medical supplies. With many of the supply routes vulnerable to enemy fire or blocked by shifting lines, units on the front often operated with limited resources. Fatigue also began to take a toll, as the soldiers fought day and night under constant pressure from the KPA. Despite these hardships, the South Korean troops remained committed to holding their positions, understanding that the fall of P'ohang-dong would open the door to the collapse of the entire Pusan Perimeter.

Amid these dire conditions, U.S. and South Korean efforts to sustain the defense became critical. The port of P'ohang-dong, though under threat, remained operational, allowing U.S. forces to deliver supplies and reinforcements directly to the embattled defenders. These reinforcements helped alleviate some of the exhaustion among South Korean units and provided much-needed ammunition and medical support. As the battle progressed, coordination between air, naval, and ground forces improved, further strengthening the defense. U.S. airstrikes targeted enemy artillery and disrupted KPA logistics, while naval bombardments kept pressure on North Korean positions along the coast. These coordinated efforts not only boosted the morale of the South Korean troops but also gave them the means to continue holding their ground despite the heavy attrition.

The period between August 11 and 15 was marked by a brutal deadlock, with neither side willing to concede ground. While the KPA sought to grind down the defenders through relentless pressure, the South Korean forces, supported by U.S. reinforcements and firepower, held firm. Though the battle had not yet reached its climax, the ability of the defenders to withstand the KPA's attritional tactics during this period would prove critical in the coming days.

FINAL NORTH KOREAN PUSH

Sensing that their window of opportunity was closing, the KPA launched a final series of desperate offensives between August 16 and 18. Their goal was to break through the South Korean defenses and seize control of P'ohang-dong before additional reinforcements could arrive. These concentrated attacks focused on key mountain passes and river crossings, where the South Korean defenses were most vulnerable. The KPA hoped that a breakthrough in these areas would create chaos within the allied lines, allowing them to penetrate deep into the defensive perimeter and capture the critical port city.

The fighting during these final days was intense and unrelenting. North Korean forces, exhausted but determined, threw everything they had into the battle, engaging in brutal combat along the steep, narrow mountain paths. South Korean defenders fought tenaciously, knowing that a breach at this stage could lead to the collapse of the entire eastern flank. Both sides suffered heavy losses, with some battles devolving into hand-to-hand fighting amid the difficult terrain. The KPA's desperation was evident as they pressed forward in waves, determined to overwhelm the exhausted South Korean units and push them back toward the city.

Despite the intensity of the KPA's assault, South Korean forces mounted fierce counterattacks to reclaim any ground lost during the North Korean offensives. These counterattacks were carefully timed, striking back just as the KPA's momentum began to falter. In several instances, South Korean troops drove the North Koreans from key positions, using the mountainous terrain to their advantage. With reinforcements now arriving more steadily through the port, the defenders were better prepared to meet the KPA head-on.

U.S. air support proved decisive in turning the tide of the battle. Fighter planes and bombers conducted close air support missions, targeting enemy troop concentrations and disrupting their ability to coordinate attacks. These strikes, combined with naval bombardments from offshore, decimated KPA units and shattered their morale. The sustained air support allowed South Korean forces to regroup quickly and launch additional counterattacks, preventing the KPA from achieving a breakthrough.

By August 18, it became clear that the North Korean push had failed. The KPA, exhausted and depleted, could no longer sustain their offensive. South Korean defenders, with U.S. support, had weathered the storm, solidifying their control over P'ohang-dong and securing the eastern flank of the Pusan Perimeter. This final push marked the end of the KPA's hopes to capture the port city, setting the stage for the eventual stabilization of the allied defenses and a shift in momentum in favor of the United Nations forces.

Victory and Aftermath

By August 19, it became clear that the KPA could no longer sustain their offensive. After suffering heavy losses during their final push, North Korean forces began a hasty withdrawal from the battle, abandoning their hopes of capturing P'ohang-dong. Exhausted, depleted, and unable to overcome the combined South Korean and U.S. resistance, the KPA had no choice but to pull back to avoid complete encirclement and destruction. Their retreat marked the end of the immediate threat to the port city and solidified the defense of the eastern flank of the Pusan Perimeter. With P'ohang-dong firmly in U.N. control, the port remained operational, ensuring that reinforcements and supplies could continue flowing into the region to support the broader war effort.

The victory, however, came at a high cost. Both sides suffered significant casualties during the brutal fighting. Many South Korean units were reduced to a fraction of their original strength, with some companies nearly wiped out during the intense close-quarters battles in the hills. The defenders' perseverance, though heroic, left them physically and emotionally drained. Meanwhile, the KPA sustained catastrophic losses, with large numbers of troops killed, wounded, or captured during the fighting. A South Korean report showed 3,800 KPA soldiers killed and 181 captured, though the number of KPA killed is likely double that. The defeat at P'ohang-dong severely weakened their ability to press deeper into the Pusan Perimeter, marking a turning point in the conflict and preventing them from gaining the upper hand in the southern campaign.

A decisive factor in the battle was the role of U.S. air and naval power. Airstrikes by the U.S. Air Force repeatedly disrupted

KPA supply lines and shattered troop concentrations, preventing the North Koreans from coordinating their assaults effectively. At the same time, naval bombardments from offshore ensured that the coastline remained secure and provided vital fire support for ground troops engaged in the fiercest fighting. The seamless coordination between ground, air, and naval units became a critical component of the allied victory. This battle highlighted the importance of integrated operations, demonstrating how close cooperation between different branches of the military could turn the tide of engagements, even when outnumbered or under pressure.

The victory at P'ohang-dong was more than just a tactical success; it provided a blueprint for future operations throughout the Korean War. The ability to synchronize air, sea, and ground forces became a hallmark of U.N. and U.S. strategy, influencing the way subsequent battles were fought. With the eastern flank of the Pusan Perimeter secure, the allies could now shift their focus to stabilizing other sectors, eventually mounting counteroffensives that would drive the KPA back. The hard-fought defense of P'ohang-dong ensured that the war's momentum would shift in favor of the south, setting the stage for the campaigns that would follow.

The victory at P'ohang-dong had profound strategic implications for the broader defense of the Pusan Perimeter. By securing the eastern flank, the ROK and U.S. forces stabilized a critical sector that had been under constant threat. The successful defense ensured that the KPA would not gain access to the port city, which was essential for the continued flow of reinforcements and supplies into the southern region. With P'ohang-dong intact, the southern defenses grew stronger, providing a solid foundation for the allies to hold the line and plan future counteroffensives. The ability to maintain supply routes through the port was instrumental in keeping the Pusan Perimeter operational during one of the most critical phases of the war.

The battle also provided valuable lessons that would influence allied strategy throughout the remainder of the conflict. The importance of seamless air-ground coordination became evident, as close air support from U.S. aircraft played a decisive role in blunting the North Korean offensives. Naval firepower was equally crucial, with offshore bombardments helping to neutralize KPA positions and secure the coastline. The integration of these elements highlighted the need for synchronized operations across different military branches, a strategy that would shape the allies' approach in future battles. Additionally, the difficulties faced in maintaining supply lines through the mountainous terrain around P'ohang-dong underscored the importance of better logistical planning when fighting in such environments. These hard-earned lessons improved the allies' ability to manage future operations in similarly challenging conditions.

For the KPA, the defeat at P'ohang-dong forced a significant shift in strategy. With their eastern offensive stalled and their forces badly depleted, the North Koreans were compelled to redirect their focus to other sectors of the Pusan Perimeter. The loss of momentum from the failed assault at P'ohang-dong was a blow to the KPA's strategic ambitions, as they had hoped to use the port city as a springboard for deeper incursions into allied territory. Instead, they were left scrambling to find new opportunities elsewhere along the perimeter. The failed offensive not only weakened their overall position but also provided the allied forces with a critical psychological and tactical victory, setting the stage for a shift in the momentum of the war.

Fighting for Survival

During the Battle of P'ohang-dong, Yi Kyung-jae was among the seventy-one South Korean student soldiers defending Pohang Girls' Middle School on August 11, 1950. With minimal training and limited weapons, these student soldiers were thrust into the role of frontline defenders against an elite North Korean force—the 766th Independent Infantry Regiment. Yi and his fellow students were tasked with holding the school, a critical position that could give the North Koreans a foothold in the town.

Despite overwhelming odds, the student soldiers fought fiercely, stalling the North Korean advance for eleven hours, giving the ROK 3rd Division time to move the rear command at Pohang Girls' Middle School southward. Their decisive actions made it possible for the 3rd Division and citizens of Pohang to retreat safely.

Yi's unit endured relentless attacks from infantry and armored vehicles, but their resolve bought crucial time for allied reinforcements to arrive. Tragically, only thirteen of the original seventy-one students survived the battle, with most of the company killed in combat or executed after being captured.

Yi survived the war and later became an educator, dedicating his life to ensuring that future generations remembered the bravery and sacrifice of his fallen classmates. He passed away in 2006 in Daegu, South Korea, where a memorial now stands honoring the student-soldiers' valor.

A Determined Offensive

Senior Colonel O Jin Woo led the elite 766th Independent Infantry Regiment during the assault on P'ohang-dong. His mission was to capture the strategically important Pohang Girls' Middle School, which would serve as a base of operations for further advances into the Pusan Perimeter. Despite logistical challenges and a lack of reinforcements, O's unit pressed forward, believing that seizing control of the school would tilt the battle in their favor.

O's regiment launched multiple coordinated attacks, but the resistance from the seventy-one student soldiers proved more formidable than expected. His soldiers fought through waves of artillery fire and fierce close-quarters combat but were unable to break through before U.N. reinforcements arrived. As the tide of battle shifted, O was forced to retreat with his remaining troops. Following the war, he quickly rose through the military and political hierarchy, and was a vice-chairman of North Korea's National Defense Commission from 1972 until his death. He passed away in 1995 at seventy-seven and is remembered for his close association with Kim Il Sung and his leadership during some of the most intense battles of the Korean War.

FIRST BATTLE OF NAKTONG BULGE

The Naktong River played a critical role in the defense of the Pusan Perimeter, serving as a natural barrier on the western front of the allied defenses. As one of South Korea's longest rivers, the Naktong created a formidable obstacle for advancing North Korean forces. Its wide, fast-flowing waters and the rugged terrain surrounding its banks made large-scale crossings difficult and dangerous. For the United Nations Command (UNC), which was scrambling to prevent a collapse of the perimeter, the Naktong River became a crucial line of defense. Holding this line meant not only blocking the North Koreans from penetrating further into southern territory but also ensuring that reinforcements, supplies, and troops could continue to flow through the vital port of Pusan to sustain the war effort.

From the perspective of the allied forces, the Naktong River provided a temporary buffer that bought them time to organize, dig in, and prepare for further assaults. With U.S., South Korean, and other U.N. forces spread thin along the perimeter, natural barriers like the Naktong gave the defenders a much-needed advantage. If properly defended, the river could halt or slow the North Korean advance, preventing them from creating openings in the western sector of the perimeter. The high ground along the river's southern bank offered favorable positions for artillery units, allowing them to bombard enemy troops as they attempted to cross. As such, the Naktong became not just a physical boundary but a symbol of hope for the defenders, who knew that holding this river was essential to preventing the war from slipping into total disaster.

However, the North Korean People's Army recognized the importance of the Naktong River as well and made it a primary target in their campaign to break the Pusan Perimeter. Their objective was to breach the allied defenses by establishing a bridgehead across the river, creating a "bulge" that could pierce the U.N. lines. Such a breakthrough would allow the KPA to push deeper into southern territory, opening a path to Pusan, the critical logistical hub that sustained the entire allied defense. Capturing Pusan would not only cut off reinforcements and supplies to U.N. forces but also likely force the collapse of the perimeter itself, leading to the complete defeat of the allied effort in Korea.

For the KPA, the Naktong River represented both an opportunity and a challenge. If they could establish a foothold on the southern side, they would gain a strategic advantage that could shift the balance of the war in their favor. A successful crossing would also deal a psychological blow to the allied forces, further straining their already stretched defenses. But the North Koreans understood that crossing the Naktong would be no easy task. The river's terrain, combined with U.S. air and artillery superiority, meant that any attempt to breach the perimeter would require careful planning and sustained effort. The battle that followed would prove to be one of the most intense and critical engagements of the Korean War, with both sides fully aware that the outcome could determine the fate of the entire conflict.

Initial North Korean Assaults

The First Battle of Naktong Bulge began with a series of surprise night crossings by the KPA. Under the cover of darkness, KPA units exploited the river's winding currents and used stealth to move across the Naktong River, catching the U.N. forces off guard. With careful planning, the KPA sent small groups of soldiers across in makeshift boats, rafts, or by swimming, targeting vulnerable points along the riverbank. The North Koreans relied on the element of surprise, hoping to avoid detection by U.S. and ROK defenders stationed along the perimeter.

These initial efforts proved successful. Before U.N. forces could react, the KPA managed to establish small bridgeheads on the southern side of the river. These footholds, while precarious, gave the North Koreans a critical opportunity to push farther into allied territory. From these positions, KPA units began ferrying more troops and equipment across the river, aiming to reinforce the bridgeheads and prepare for a larger offensive. Their strategy was clear: establish a firm grip on the southern bank and use it as a staging ground for an assault deeper into the perimeter.

The sudden breach of the perimeter forced the U.N. forces to respond rapidly. U.S. and South Korean (ROK) commanders quickly recognized the danger posed by the bridgeheads and mobilized their troops to contain the situation. Infantry units were rushed to the areas where KPA forces had crossed, while artillery units scrambled to reposition and target the North Korean positions. With no time to waste, the U.N. forces launched immediate counterattacks, determined to prevent the KPA from consolidating their gains and expanding their foothold.

The counterattacks were fierce and well-coordinated, as U.S. and ROK troops engaged the North Koreans in brutal close-quarters combat. Artillery fire and air support were used to great effect, bombarding the bridgeheads to disrupt the KPA's efforts to bring in reinforcements. Although the KPA fought tenaciously to hold their positions, the U.N. forces' rapid and aggressive response prevented them from establishing a stable beachhead. The battle along the riverbank became a back-and-forth struggle, with both sides suffering heavy casualties in the intense fighting.

By containing the initial breach, U.N. forces bought themselves precious time to reinforce the western flank of the perimeter. However, the KPA's successful night crossings made it clear that the Naktong River would remain a volatile front, with the potential for disaster if the North Koreans could mount another major assault. The initial engagements set the tone for what would become one of the most grueling battles of the Korean War, with both sides fully committed to securing control of the river at any cost.

The terrain around the Naktong River posed severe challenges for both the North Korean and U.N. forces, shaping the nature of the battle in critical ways. The rugged landscape consisted of steep ridges, dense vegetation, and unpredictable river currents, making movement difficult and hazardous for soldiers on both sides. The river itself was wide, fast-moving in places, and prone to sudden shifts in depth, complicating crossings. For North Korean troops attempting to move across the river under fire, every crossing was a life-threatening endeavor. Meanwhile, the hilly terrain on the southern side of the river became a battleground where ambushes, counterattacks, and brutal close-quarters combat unfolded, adding to the battle's intensity.

North Korean forces leveraged the terrain to their advantage, using thick vegetation and the natural folds of the land to shield their movements from U.N. airstrikes and artillery bombardments. However, they too struggled with the environment, as transporting troops and supplies across the river under constant enemy fire was a grueling task. The steep ridges offered cover but also forced soldiers to engage in exhausting uphill assaults and ambushes, leaving units vulnerable to fatigue and disorganization. For every step gained, the KPA had to overcome both the U.N.'s resistance and the punishing geography of the region.

The same terrain that challenged the KPA also hindered the U.N. forces. The steep ridges and narrow passes complicated the deployment of tanks and other armored vehicles, limiting their mobility and effectiveness. With the terrain favoring infantry engagements, U.S. and South Korean forces had to rely heavily on foot soldiers to fight off the North Korean assault, a grueling endeavor given the harsh conditions. Supply lines also became a critical concern. Transporting ammunition, food, and medical supplies through the rugged environment was slow and hazardous, placing additional strain on already exhausted troops. Artillery units, while crucial to the defense, had difficulty maintaining consistent fire support due to the challenges of moving heavy guns through the hilly landscape.

The combination of the difficult terrain and the chaotic nature of the battle tested the endurance of soldiers on both sides. U.N. forces had to fight not only against the enemy but also against the natural elements, which slowed down reinforcements and made it challenging to coordinate operations effectively. For the North Koreans, every assault came with the risk of ambushes or counterattacks from U.N. troops who were now familiar with the terrain and determined to protect their positions at all costs. The landscape turned the fight into a series of brutal skirmishes, with progress measured in yards rather than miles.

In the end, the harsh environment around the Naktong River ensured that neither side could rely on straightforward tactics or overwhelming force. Both armies were forced to adapt to the terrain, using a mix of small-unit tactics, ambushes, and strategic positioning to gain even the slightest advantage. These conditions made the First Battle of Naktong Bulge one of the most physically and mentally taxing engagements of the Korean War, highlighting the importance of logistics, endurance, and terrain awareness in determining the outcome of the conflict.

U.S. artillery played a decisive role in the First Battle of Naktong Bulge, providing the firepower needed to halt the North Korean advance and disrupt their operations. One of the key advantages for U.N. forces was the ability to position artillery units on elevated terrain along the southern side of the Naktong River. From these high vantage points, U.S. gunners could rain down shells on KPA positions, targeting bridgeheads and disrupting their supply lines with precision. The steep hills and ridges overlooking the river gave the U.S. artillery a clear view of the battlefield, allowing them to adjust their fire in real-time and deliver devastating blows to the North Korean troops struggling to maintain their foothold across the river.

These artillery bombardments proved essential in containing the KPA's initial advances. As North Korean forces attempted to ferry reinforcements and supplies across the river to support their bridgeheads, U.S. shells rained down on them, wreaking havoc. Every attempt to strengthen their positions on the southern bank was met with a storm of artillery fire, forcing the KPA to scatter and seek cover. The sustained shelling not only inflicted heavy casualties but also disrupted the North Koreans' logistical operations, cutting off vital supplies of ammunition and food. Without a steady flow of reinforcements, the KPA's forward units became isolated and vulnerable to U.N. counter-attacks.

Beyond its physical impact, the artillery bombardments had a significant psychological effect on the KPA troops. The relentless shelling demoralized the North Korean soldiers, sapping their will to fight and reducing their ability to coordinate further attacks. Communication lines between units were severed as artillery shells pounded key points, leaving KPA commanders struggling to organize cohesive offensives. The chaos caused by the shelling forced the North Koreans into a defensive posture, halting their momentum and giving U.N. forces the breathing room they needed to regroup and counterattack.

The strategic use of artillery throughout the battle exemplified the importance of coordinated fire support in modern warfare. With infantry and armor limited by the difficult terrain, U.S. artillery became the linchpin of the defense, holding the line when other options were unavailable. The high ground provided U.N. forces with a tactical advantage that the KPA could not overcome, despite their repeated efforts to cross the river and establish a lasting foothold. In the end, the continuous artillery fire not only prevented the KPA from reinforcing their positions but also played a decisive role in breaking their will to fight, setting the stage for the eventual collapse of the North Korean offensive at Naktong Bulge.

Intense Fighting and Counterattacks

As the battle for the Naktong Bulge intensified, North Korean forces made determined efforts to expand their bridgeheads and establish a permanent presence on the southern side of the river. Realizing that their initial footholds were precarious, the KPA launched multiple waves of attacks, seeking to widen their positions and break deeper into U.N. territory. The fighting along the riverbanks and surrounding hills became ferocious, with both sides locked in brutal close-quarters combat. Every inch of ground was fiercely contested, as the KPA pushed to connect their bridgeheads into a larger front that would give them the momentum needed to launch offensives farther into the heart of the Pusan Perimeter.

The terrain only added to the chaos. The steep hills and dense vegetation along the river made movement difficult, turning skirmishes into grueling encounters where ambushes and sudden counterattacks were common. U.N. troops defending the ridges and river crossings were forced to fight tooth and nail, facing relentless assaults from KPA soldiers determined to widen the breach. Some battles raged for hours as the lines shifted back and forth, with neither side willing to yield. Exhausted and often cut off from reinforcements, U.N. troops relied on their training and discipline to hold their positions in the face of overwhelming pressure.

In response to the North Korean offensives, U.S. and ROK forces mounted aggressive counterattacks to reclaim lost ground and prevent the KPA from consolidating their bridgeheads. These counteroffensives were not just reactive; they were calculated efforts to push the KPA back across the river and reestablish a secure defensive line. Infantry units led the charge, moving swiftly to engage KPA soldiers in close combat. With artillery fire providing suppressive support from the high ground and U.S. air support striking enemy positions, the counterattacks gained momentum.

The coordination between infantry, artillery, and air units was a critical factor in the success of the U.N. counteroffensives. Artillery units targeted KPA positions along the riverbanks, disrupting their movements and making it difficult for them to reinforce their front lines. At the same time, U.S. aircraft conducted close air support missions, bombing enemy concentrations and supply routes, further weakening the KPA's ability to maintain their foothold. These combined efforts allowed the U.N. forces to regain the initiative, driving the North Koreans back inch by inch.

The relentless counterattacks eventually began to turn the tide of the battle. U.N. forces managed to reclaim key positions along the river and surrounding hills, denying the KPA the opportunity to expand their bridgeheads. The combination of artillery fire, airstrikes, and determined infantry assaults proved overwhelming, forcing the North Korean forces into a defensive posture. Although the KPA fought stubbornly, the coordinated firepower of the U.N. forces ensured that the attackers could not gain a lasting advantage.

By the end of this phase of the battle, the U.N. forces had not only halted the KPA's attempts to widen the bridgehead but had also pushed many of the remaining North Korean units back across the river. The fierce fighting along the Naktong River demonstrated the tenacity of both sides, but it also highlighted the effectiveness of the U.N.'s integrated battle strategy. Through close coordination between ground, air, and artillery units, the U.N. forces were able to repel the North Korean offensive and maintain control of the western flank of the Pusan Perimeter, preventing a catastrophic breach that could have altered the course of the war.

By the conclusion of the First Battle of Naktong Bulge, the North Korean People's Army was forced to abandon its offensive and withdraw across the Naktong River. After days of fierce fighting, relentless U.N. counterattacks, and devastating artillery and air bombardments, the KPA's foothold on the southern bank became untenable. Exhausted and suffering from heavy casualties, the North Koreans lacked the manpower and resources to sustain their offensive. What had begun as a promising attempt to breach the Pusan Perimeter ended in retreat, with KPA soldiers scrambling to cross the river under U.N. fire. Many units left behind weapons, equipment, and wounded comrades, reflecting the chaotic nature of the withdrawal.

The KPA's failure to break through the western flank of the Pusan Perimeter had significant consequences for their broader strategy. Their defeat at Naktong Bulge not only drained their manpower but also depleted valuable resources, weakening their ability to launch large-scale offensives in the future. With supply lines already stretched thin, the loss of so many troops and the failure to gain new ground left the North Koreans in a vulnerable position. The momentum they had gained in the early stages of the war began to falter, giving U.N. forces the breathing room they desperately needed to regroup and reinforce their defenses along the entire perimeter.

The victory at Naktong Bulge had an equally profound impact on the U.N. forces. With the KPA driven back across the river, the U.N. solidified control over the western flank of the Pusan Perimeter, ensuring that no further crossings could threaten the stability of their defenses. U.S. and South Korean forces immediately reinforced key positions along the riverbank, creating a formidable line that the KPA would find difficult to penetrate in subsequent attempts. The control of the Naktong River proved essential in maintaining the integrity of the perimeter, as it denied the North Koreans an easy route into southern territory.

Perhaps most importantly, the victory at Naktong Bulge provided a significant boost to the morale of the U.N. forces. Until this point, the war had largely been marked by a series of North Korean victories and retreats for the allied forces. The successful defense of the Naktong River marked a turning point, demonstrating that the U.N. forces *could* withstand and repel the KPA's aggressive offensives. This psychological shift was crucial for the defenders, giving them the confidence to continue holding the perimeter and preparing for future counteroffensives.

In the grander context of the Korean War, the outcome of the First Battle of Naktong Bulge reinforced the importance of the Pusan Perimeter as the last bastion of allied resistance. By preventing the KPA from breaking through the western flank, the victory bought critical time for additional reinforcements and supplies to arrive from the United States and other allied nations. The defeat of the North Koreans at the Naktong River also marked the beginning of a shift in the war's momentum, paving the way for future U.N. counterattacks that would eventually drive the KPA back north. Ultimately, the battle at Naktong Bulge not only preserved the perimeter but also strengthened the resolve of the U.N. forces to defend South Korea and turn the tide of the conflict.

A Resolute Defense at Naktong

Lieutenant Charles E. Payne commanded C Company, 34th Regimen, during the First Battle of Naktong Bulge, where his leadership was pivotal in preventing a North Korean breakthrough. His company was stationed along the Naktong River, a critical point in the U.N. defensive line. When North Korean forces launched relentless assaults to widen their bridgeheads, Payne's unit found itself isolated and under fire from all directions. With communication lines severed, Payne rallied his troops, organizing defensive positions and holding off the attackers despite overwhelming odds.

At a critical moment in the battle, one of Payne's soldiers, Private Robert Witzig, volunteered to navigate through enemy lines to call for reinforcements. Although Witzig was seriously injured by shrapnel during the attempt, his success ensured that U.S. forces could regroup and prevent the collapse of the western flank. Payne's cool-headed leadership in this high-stakes environment not only saved his unit but also helped stabilize the overall defensive line at a crucial point in the battle.

Payne's life and death after the war aren't well known, but he is remembered as a hero of the Korean War.

Leading the Assault

Captain Kim Song-ju played a critical role in the North Korean assault on the Naktong River. As a company commander in the KPA 1st Battalion, 4th Infantry Division, he was tasked with establishing and reinforcing bridgeheads on the southern bank. Kim led his men in night crossings of the river, using the cover of darkness to avoid U.S. artillery fire and gain a foothold on the enemy's side. Under his command, North Korean soldiers seized parts of Obong-ni Ridge, a strategically important feature, and attempted to push deeper into U.N.-held territory.

Despite early successes, Kim's forces faced relentless U.N. artillery and air strikes that disrupted his supply lines and eroded his unit's strength. As U.N. counterattacks intensified, Kim's troops were forced to fight tenaciously to hold their ground. However, the battle's tide eventually turned against the North Koreans. Severely wounded during the chaotic withdrawal back across the Naktong, Kim was evacuated to Pyongyang, where he spent the remainder of the war recovering from his injuries.

Following the war, Kim transitioned to a career as a military instructor, training new officers for the KPA. His experiences in the battle at Naktong shaped his teachings on the importance of tactical flexibility and the need for thorough preparation in river crossings and offensives. Kim Song-ju is remembered as a dedicated soldier who exemplified the aggressive spirit of the early North Korean campaigns.

BATTLE OF THE BOWLING ALLEY

Taegu, located in the northern sector of the Pusan Perimeter, was a key logistical and transportation hub that played a pivotal role in the defense of South Korea during the early stages of the Korean War. Its strategic location at the crossroads of several major roadways and rail lines made it essential for moving troops, supplies, and equipment to support allied forces along the perimeter. If Taegu were to fall into North Korean hands, it would jeopardize the entire defensive line, cutting off reinforcements and disrupting the flow of critical supplies necessary to sustain U.N. operations in the region.

Furthermore, Taegu's loss would have created a direct path for North Korean forces to push deeper into the southern areas of the peninsula, accelerating the collapse of the Pusan Perimeter. The U.N. Command understood that holding Taegu was not only a tactical necessity but also a symbolic one—it represented the last bastion of resistance in the north of the perimeter. With the success of the U.N. defense hinging on logistical stability, the city's defense became a priority. U.S. and South Korean commanders poured resources and manpower into ensuring that Taegu remained secure, knowing that its fall could tilt the balance of the entire war in favor of the North Koreans.

The battle that took place near Taegu became known as the "Battle of the Bowling Alley," named for the narrow, valley-like terrain where much of the fighting occurred. The valley's shape funneled troops into a confined corridor, resembling the lanes of a bowling alley, forcing advancing forces into tight, predictable formations. For the defenders, this terrain presented both an opportunity and a challenge. The confined space allowed U.S. and South Korean forces to concentrate their defenses, using artillery and tanks to create devastating kill zones along the valley walls. Any attempt by the North Korean People's Army to advance through the valley exposed their troops to heavy fire from well-positioned defenders.

However, the same narrow corridor that gave defenders an advantage also made the battle particularly intense and grueling. Nighttime assaults became the KPA's preferred strategy, as they hoped to use the darkness to mask their movements through the valley and avoid the superior air power of the U.N. forces. The confined space turned the valley into a brutal battleground, where firefights were fought at close range, and both sides experienced heavy casualties. The terrain's limitations meant that reinforcements and supplies could not always reach the front lines quickly, further compounding the intensity of the fighting.

In this narrow corridor, the defenders faced relentless waves of North Korean troops determined to break through and seize Taegu. The "Bowling Alley" became a microcosm of the larger Pusan Perimeter defense—a last stand where every inch of ground was fought over fiercely. The battle's outcome would play a critical role in determining whether the northern sector of the perimeter would hold or collapse, setting the stage for the wider U.N. counteroffensives that followed.

Nighttime Attacks to Avoid Air Strikes

The KPA knew that U.N. forces possessed overwhelming air superiority, with fighter planes and bombers capable of devastating enemy positions during daylight hours. To mitigate this disadvantage, the KPA launched most of their assaults at night. Under the cover of darkness, North Korean troops advanced through the narrow confines of the "Bowling Alley," hoping to avoid detection and bombardment by U.S. aircraft. These nighttime maneuvers were a strategic necessity for the KPA, but they also posed significant risks. With the valley's confined shape forcing soldiers into tight formations, the North Koreans became easy targets for concentrated U.N. artillery fire once their positions were detected.

The valley's natural layout funneled North Korean forces into predictable paths, giving U.N. troops a tactical advantage despite the limited visibility. Artillery units and machine-gun emplacements along the valley walls could fire down on advancing KPA troops with deadly accuracy. Even under the cover of night, the KPA struggled to mount a coordinated assault in such a restricted space, often suffering heavy casualties before reaching the U.N. lines. Nonetheless, the North Koreans pressed forward night after night, hoping to overwhelm the defenders with sheer numbers.

The ultimate goal of the KPA's relentless assaults was to capture the strategically vital city of Taegu. A breakthrough in this sector would not only hand the North Koreans control of a key logistical hub; it would destabilize the northern flank of the Pusan Perimeter. If the KPA succeeded, it would leave U.N. forces vulnerable, cutting off vital supply routes and potentially triggering the collapse of the entire defensive line. A victory at Taegu would allow the North Koreans to advance deeper into southern Korea, jeopardizing the survival of the U.N. forces and hastening the fall of the peninsula.

To achieve this, the KPA relied on repeated frontal assaults, throwing waves of infantry at the U.N. positions. These attacks came at a high cost, with the confined space of the valley turning each push into a bloodbath. North Korean commanders understood that victory would require overwhelming the defenders with sheer force, and they accepted the heavy casualties as part of their strategy. Every assault aimed to wear down U.N. forces, hoping that the defenders would eventually buckle under the pressure. Despite their numerical advantage, the KPA struggled to gain ground against the well-coordinated U.N. defenders, who used the narrow terrain and superior firepower to their advantage. The initial assaults set the tone for the brutal, drawn-out battle that would determine the fate of Taegu and the northern sector of the Pusan Perimeter.

Positioning Along the Valley Walls

The U.S. and ROK forces effectively used the natural topography of the Bowling Alley to strengthen their defensive posture. Recognizing the tactical advantage offered by the valley's steep walls, commanders fortified key positions along the elevated terrain on either side of the narrow corridor. By occupying the high ground, the defenders could direct devastating fire down onto advancing North Korean troops, forcing them into a confined path where they were vulnerable to enfilading fire from multiple angles.

This strategic positioning allowed U.N. forces to create overlapping fields of fire, ensuring that any KPA advance was met with a relentless barrage of bullets and artillery shells. Artillery units were placed on ridges and hills overlooking the valley, while tanks were stationed at chokepoints to intercept enemy troops before they could reach the defensive line. South Korean infantry units reinforced these positions, coordinating closely with U.S. forces to ensure that every section of the line was covered.

The defenders relied heavily on the combined firepower of M24 Chaffee light tanks and artillery batteries to repel the relentless KPA assaults. The tanks were strategically placed at the valley's narrowest points, creating roadblocks that channeled North Korean forces into pre-sighted kill zones. Artillery played a crucial role in disrupting KPA formations before they could fully organize their attacks. With heavy artillery positioned on the ridges, the defenders could rain down shells on enemy troops as they advanced through the valley, inflicting devastating casualties.

The constant bombardment shattered KPA morale and complicated their efforts to reinforce their front-line units. U.S. forces kept up a near-continuous barrage of fire, preventing the North Koreans from consolidating any ground they had gained. Every time the KPA launched an attack, they were met with coordinated artillery fire, tank shells, and machine-gun bursts from entrenched positions along the valley walls, grinding their momentum to a halt.

Despite the overwhelming firepower of the U.N. forces, the North Koreans were determined to break through the defenses, resulting in intense close-quarters combat as the battle progressed. In several instances, KPA troops managed to reach the U.N. lines, forcing the defenders into brutal hand-to-hand fighting. The narrow confines of the valley amplified the chaos, with soldiers engaging in knife fights, bayonet charges, and desperate grappling for control of machine-gun nests and artillery positions.

South Korean units played a pivotal role in holding the line during these critical moments, especially in sectors where the North Koreans launched concentrated attacks. Under heavy fire, ROK soldiers fought alongside their U.S. counterparts, preventing the collapse of key sections of the defense. Their tenacity was instrumental in keeping the KPA at bay and ensuring that the valley remained under U.N. control.

Together, the strategic use of terrain, the coordination between infantry and armored units, and the defenders' resilience in close combat proved decisive in turning back the North Korean assault. Each engagement in the valley further eroded the KPA's strength, buying valuable time for U.N. forces to stabilize the northern sector of the Pusan Perimeter. The combination of firepower, tactical positioning, and the defenders' resolve created an insurmountable obstacle for the North Koreans, solidifying the defense of the Bowling Alley.

As the North Korean assaults continued to lose momentum, U.S. forces launched decisive counterattacks during daylight hours, exploiting the KPA's exhaustion and disorganization. With tanks at the forefront, U.S. infantry advanced strategically, targeting weakened North Korean positions along the narrow valley. M24 Chaffee tanks spearheaded these offensives, using the confined terrain to funnel enemy forces into predictable paths where their firepower could be maximized. The tanks, supported by machine-gun fire and artillery, pushed the KPA back toward the northern edges of the Bowling Alley.

Although KPA forces had avoided U.N. air attacks by operating at night, the daylight counterattacks brought U.S. aircraft back into play. Fighter-bombers targeted enemy supply lines, artillery positions, and reinforcements behind the front lines. These airstrikes further disrupted the KPA's ability to sustain their offensive, isolating forward units and cutting off their supply of ammunition and food. The close coordination between infantry, armor, and air support allowed U.N. forces to dismantle North Korean strongpoints systematically, driving them back step by step.

Heavy KPA Casualties

The North Koreans suffered staggering losses during both their failed nighttime assaults and the U.N. counteroffensives. With each attack repelled by overwhelming artillery and tank fire, KPA units were left decimated, often with entire companies reduced to mere remnants. U.S. forces capitalized on these losses, applying continuous pressure to prevent the KPA from regrouping or reinforcing their lines. The attrition took a severe toll not only on the North Koreans' operational capabilities but also on their morale. Though exact numbers are difficult to ascertain, reports suggest that around 5,700 KPA soldiers were killed, and likely thousands injured or captured in the Battle of the Bowling Alley. Meanwhile, approximately 2,000 U.N. soldiers were killed during this battle, plus thousands more injured or missing.

The sheer scale of KPA casualties, combined with the failure to breach the U.N. defenses, began to break the resolve of the North Korean troops. Their inability to achieve a breakthrough, despite multiple high-casualty assaults, led to growing disillusionment among the ranks. Commanders struggled to maintain order and motivation as the offensive stalled. The relentless artillery bombardments and armored counterattacks left the KPA exhausted, forcing them to retreat under the cover of night to avoid further devastation.

The U.N.'s coordinated counterattacks proved to be the turning point in the Battle of the Bowling Alley. By regaining control of key positions and inflicting heavy casualties, the defenders ensured the stability of the northern sector of the Pusan Perimeter. With the KPA in retreat, U.N. forces could regroup and shift focus to other vulnerable areas of the perimeter, marking the beginning of a shift in momentum that would shape the course of the Korean War.

The North Korean People's Army was ultimately unable to penetrate the defenses of the Bowling Alley and was forced to abandon its assault. After days of brutal fighting and suffering devastating casualties, the KPA withdrew from the valley to regroup and reorganize. The narrow terrain, relentless U.N. artillery fire, and coordinated counterattacks by U.S. and South Korean forces left the North Koreans depleted and unable to sustain further offensives. Their retreat marked a significant setback for the KPA, as the failure to capture Taegu dealt a blow to their strategic ambitions in the northern sector.

The loss of momentum in this part of the front created ripple effects across the battlefield. Without control of Taegu, the KPA struggled to maintain pressure along the northern flank of the Pusan Perimeter. The resources and manpower exhausted during the battle left the North Koreans vulnerable, forcing them to divert attention to consolidating their remaining forces rather than continuing aggressive operations.

The successful defense of the Bowling Alley was pivotal in stabilizing the northern sector of the Pusan Perimeter. U.N. forces, bolstered by their victory—though it came with heavy losses of their own—were able to reestablish control over key positions and secure the area around Taegu. This victory not only provided much-needed breathing room but also strengthened morale among U.N. troops, who now had proof that they could withstand and repel the determined North Korean offensives.

With the northern sector stabilized, U.N. forces were able to regroup, resupply, and prepare for future operations. The lessons learned from this engagement—particularly the effective use of terrain, artillery coordination, and infantry-tank cooperation— were integrated into upcoming campaigns. The battle's outcome marked a turning point in the conflict, shifting the momentum slightly in favor of the U.N. forces. It provided them the opportunity to plan for counteroffensives, which would eventually culminate in the Inchon landings and push the North Korean forces back across the 38th Parallel.

The U.N.'s victory at the Bowling Alley not only ensured the continued survival of the Pusan Perimeter but also signaled the beginning of a gradual shift in the war's dynamic, with U.N. forces increasingly taking the initiative against a weakened North Korean army.

Holding the Line

Colonel John Michaelis commanded 27th Infantry Regiment, known as the "Wolfhounds," during the Battle of the Bowling Alley. His leadership was critical in holding the narrow valley north of Tabu-dong, a strategic route on the road to Taegu. Faced with relentless North Korean attacks, Michaelis organized a defensive strategy that capitalized on the high ground along the valley walls. Under his command, tanks, artillery, and infantry coordinated to block the advancing North Korean units, creating overlapping fields of fire that decimated enemy forces as they moved through the valley.

Despite the overwhelming pressure, Michaelis ensured that his troops maintained discipline and cohesion. His ability to adapt to changing battlefield conditions allowed the 27th Infantry to withstand multiple night attacks by the KPA. Michaelis's efforts not only prevented a breakthrough but also secured the northern sector of the Pusan Perimeter, keeping the vital city of Taegu under U.N. control. After the war, Michaelis continued his military career, rising to the rank of a four-star general in 1969. He passed away in 1985 at seventy-three, remembered as a skilled and determined leader during one of the Korean War's fiercest battles.

Leading the Charge

General Kim Ung was a senior officer leading the North Korean 13th Infantry Division in their assault on the Bowling Alley. His goal was to break through the U.N. defenses and capture Taegu, which would open a path to Pusan and threaten the survival of the U.N. forces. Kim coordinated relentless nighttime attacks, hoping to exploit the cover of darkness and overwhelm the U.S. and South Korean troops guarding the valley.

Although his forces initially achieved some success, they struggled to maintain momentum under heavy U.N. artillery and airstrikes. The confined terrain of the valley made it difficult for Kim's divisions to maneuver effectively, forcing them into repeated frontal assaults that resulted in devastating casualties. Despite his best efforts, the relentless resistance from the U.N. forces under Michaelis's command forced the NKPA to retreat.

After the battle, Kim Ung continued to serve in the North Korean military, but the defeat at the Bowling Alley weakened his divisions' ability to mount further offensives. He remained a high-ranking figure in the North Korean military hierarchy until his death in 1989 in Pyongyang, remembered as a determined but ultimately unsuccessful commander in the Korean War.

SECOND BATTLE OF NAKTONG BULGE

By late August 1950, the North Korean People's Army (KPA) was determined to break through the Pusan Perimeter and deliver a decisive blow to the U.N. forces defending the southeastern tip of the Korean Peninsula. With equipment, supplies, and tactical guidance provided by the Soviet Union, the KPA launched the Second Battle of Naktong Bulge as part of a larger, coordinated offensive. Soviet-supplied T-34 tanks and artillery strengthened North Korean forces, giving them the firepower needed to mount a more aggressive attack compared to earlier efforts.

The renewed assault aimed to shatter the U.N. defensive lines along the Naktong River, which had become a focal point in the fight for control of the Pusan Perimeter. The KPA deployed fresh troops alongside veterans who had previously fought in the region, hoping to overwhelm the U.N. defenses with relentless attacks. North Korean commanders knew that time was of the essence—each passing day allowed U.N. reinforcements and supplies to bolster the perimeter. For North Korea, success at Naktong would mean the collapse of the southern defenses and the potential end of the war with a communist victory.

The stakes for the battle were monumental for both the KPA and the U.N. forces. A successful North Korean breakthrough at Naktong would threaten the survival of the Pusan Perimeter, potentially cutting off U.N. troops from their supply bases in Pusan. Such a victory would force the withdrawal of U.S. and allied forces from the Korean Peninsula and allow the North Koreans to unify the country under Communist control. For the KPA leadership, winning this battle was critical to achieving their strategic objectives before U.N. forces could gather enough strength for a counteroffensive.

For the U.N. forces, the battle represented a last-ditch effort to stabilize the front. The defenders understood that if the KPA were to penetrate the perimeter, the loss of strategic locations like Taegu and Pusan would make further resistance nearly impossible. U.S. commanders redeployed artillery, tanks, and air units to reinforce key points along the Naktong River, recognizing that the battle could be the turning point of the war. Holding the line at Naktong was essential not only to preserving the Pusan Perimeter but also to buying time for reinforcements to arrive and future offensive operations to be planned. The outcome of the battle would shape the future course of the Korean War, determining whether the U.N. could remain in the fight or face defeat on the peninsula.

The Second Battle of Naktong Bulge began with a series of large-scale nighttime assaults by the KPA. Seeking to avoid U.N. air strikes during daylight hours, the KPA made use of darkness to mask their movements across the Naktong River. Multiple assault units launched coordinated crossings along various sections of the river, establishing several bridgeheads on the southern bank. The goal was to overwhelm U.N. defenses through simultaneous attacks across a broad front, forcing the defenders to stretch their forces thin.

Despite facing artillery fire and difficult river conditions, the North Koreans managed to infiltrate several weak points, creating temporary footholds on the southern side of the river. These bridgeheads became staging points for further offensives aimed at breaking through the U.N. defensive perimeter. North Korean forces from their 2nd, 4th, 9th, and 10th Infantry Divisions engaged in close combat with U.N. troops in an attempt to expand these footholds and link them into a unified front. However, the confined terrain along the riverbanks made it challenging for the KPA to fully exploit their initial successes.

Having learned from their experiences during the First Battle of Naktong Bulge, U.N. commanders anticipated the North Korean strategy and implemented new defensive measures. Artillery units were strategically positioned at pre-sighted locations, allowing for precise bombardment of the river crossings as soon as enemy troops were detected. These pre-sighted positions allowed U.N. artillery crews to launch rapid, effective strikes without the need for lengthy adjustments, making it difficult for the KPA to consolidate their gains.

In addition to improved artillery tactics, U.S. commanders moved armored units, including M26 Pershing tanks, to reinforce vulnerable points along the river. These tanks provided crucial firepower in close-quarter combat scenarios, helping to blunt the North Korean offensives. Defensive coordination between infantry, artillery, and armor was significantly improved compared to earlier battles, allowing the defenders to respond more effectively to breaches along the riverbank.

The redeployment of U.S. units also involved careful planning of supply lines and communication channels, ensuring that reinforcements and ammunition could reach the front lines quickly. South Korean infantry units, working alongside U.S. forces, played a vital role in holding strategic positions, often repelling multiple waves of KPA assaults. This combination of pre-sighted artillery, armor support, and improved coordination proved essential in slowing the North Korean advance, buying the U.N. forces valuable time to counter the initial offensives and prevent the collapse of the perimeter.

Brutal Fighting Along the Naktong River

The Second Battle of Naktong Bulge saw some of the most intense close-quarters fighting of the Korean War. Determined to expand their bridgeheads and break through U.N. defenses, KPA troops engaged in brutal hand-to-hand combat along the southern banks of the river. North Korean forces relied heavily on small-unit tactics to push forward in the confined terrain, where larger formations were ineffective. Soldiers fought with bayonets, grenades, and knives in an attempt to seize control of key positions. In several areas, the battle devolved into chaotic skirmishes, with the lines shifting frequently as both sides vied for dominance.

Despite the ferocity of the KPA's efforts, U.N. forces responded with equally aggressive counterattacks. Infantry units, supported by armor and artillery, launched repeated offensives to disrupt North Korean advances and prevent them from consolidating their bridgeheads. South Korean infantry, working closely with U.S. forces, played a crucial role in holding the line, often repelling multiple waves of KPA troops. The defenders were able to regain lost ground in several key sectors, denying the North Koreans the opportunity to solidify their positions.

U.S. air and artillery support proved decisive in countering the KPA's offensives. Although the North Koreans timed their initial assaults to avoid airstrikes, U.N. aircraft became active during daylight hours, targeting supply lines and reinforcements moving toward the front. Fighter-bombers disrupted KPA logistics, destroying vehicles and ammunition dumps, further limiting the attackers' ability to sustain their assault. The aerial bombardments also demoralized front-line troops, reducing their effectiveness in combat.

Continuous artillery fire from pre-sighted positions added another layer of defense. U.S. artillery batteries targeted KPA bridgeheads with devastating precision, cutting off reinforcements and leaving North Korean units isolated and vulnerable. The bombardments caused heavy casualties among the attackers, forcing many to retreat under fire. The combination of artillery and air support allowed U.N. forces to contain the KPA's advance, stabilizing the defensive line along the Naktong River. These coordinated efforts played a critical role in preventing the North Koreans from achieving a breakthrough, marking a key turning point in the battle.

As the KPA's offensive began to stall, U.S. and South Korean forces seized the opportunity to launch coordinated counteroffensives along the Naktong River. Drawing on lessons from earlier engagements, U.N. commanders synchronized infantry assaults with armored offensives to maximize the impact of their attacks. Tanks, including the M26 Pershing, provided essential firepower and mobility, allowing infantry units to reclaim critical positions and disrupt the remaining North Korean bridgeheads.

The combined arms approach proved decisive. U.N. tanks advanced alongside infantry squads, systematically cutting off North Korean footholds along the river. Artillery fire supported these offensives by targeting KPA positions and reinforcing the attackers' progress. South Korean infantry units played a crucial role, working in tandem with U.S. troops to encircle and overwhelm isolated KPA units. The coordinated nature of these counterattacks prevented the North Koreans from regrouping or launching effective counteroffensives of their own.

The sustained pressure from U.N. counterattacks, combined

with relentless air and artillery bombardments, inflicted devastating casualties on the KPA. Their forward units, cut off from reinforcements and supplies, were forced into disorganized retreats. As ammunition and food dwindled, many North Korean units abandoned their positions, retreating across the Naktong River under the cover of darkness to avoid further losses. The collapse of these bridgeheads marked the end of the KPA's last major attempt to break the Pusan Perimeter.

The U.N. forces capitalized on the KPA's retreat by reclaiming lost ground and securing vulnerable sectors along the river. With the perimeter stabilized, U.N. commanders were able to shift their focus to planning future operations, including the Inchon landings that would ultimately change the course of the war. The defeat of the KPA at the Second Battle of Naktong Bulge signaled a turning point, as it not only preserved the Pusan Perimeter but also marked the beginning of a shift in momentum for U.N. forces. This victory ensured the survival of the perimeter and paved the way for a counteroffensive that would push the North Korean army back toward the 38th Parallel.

Turning Point in the Korean War

The failure of the KPA's assault during the Second Battle of Naktong Bulge from September 1 to September 15, 1950 was the beginning of a shift in the Korean War. With their final attempt to breach the Pusan Perimeter thwarted, the North Korean advance lost momentum. The KPA's heavy casualties and depleted resources significantly weakened their operational capacity, limiting their ability to launch further offensives. The battle demonstrated the growing effectiveness of U.N. forces, who had adapted their strategies and strengthened their defenses since the war's early days.

The victory at Naktong gave U.N. commanders a crucial window of opportunity to shift from defensive operations to planning a counteroffensive. For the first time in the conflict, the strategic initiative began to move in favor of the U.N. forces. This battle signaled the beginning of a broader momentum shift, as North Korea's inability to break the perimeter foreshadowed the eventual rollback of their early territorial gains.

The victory at Naktong not only preserved the perimeter but also demonstrated the resilience and adaptability of U.N. forces, boosting morale across the front. Soldiers on the ground knew that holding the perimeter had paved the way for future successes. This Second Battle of Naktong Bulge was a pivotal moment that secured the survival of the U.N. effort and set the stage for the transition from *defense* to *offense*.

SACRIFICE ON THE FRONTLINE

Corporal Gordon M. Craig of the U.S. Army's 1st Cavalry Division played a critical role during the Second Battle of Naktong Bulge. On September 10, 1950, Craig's unit, part of the 16th Reconnaissance Company, was advancing on a strategic hill held by the KPA when they were pinned down by heavy North Korean machine-gun, grenade, and mortar fire. Recognizing that the enemy position had to be neutralized, Craig and a small team fought their way toward the machine-gun nest, engaging in brutal combat.

During the assault, an enemy soldier hurled a grenade at Craig's team. Without hesitation, Craig threw himself onto the grenade, absorbing the explosion with his body to save his comrades. His self-sacrifice inspired the remaining soldiers to press forward, ultimately silencing the enemy position and securing the hill. For his heroism, Craig was posthumously awarded the Medal of Honor. He died at the young age of twenty-one, and his actions remain a powerful testament to the bravery displayed by U.S. forces during this pivotal battle.

Tactical Leadership in the Assault

Major General Lee Kwon-mu, Born in 1920, was a prominent figure in the Korean People's Army during the Korean War. He commanded the KPA's 4th Division, which played a pivotal role in the Second Battle of the Naktong Bulge.

Under his leadership, the 4th Division aimed to seize critical terrain along the Naktong River, employing aggressive tactics, including night crossings to avoid U.S. artillery. Their initial successes included capturing vital positions, such as Obong-ni Ridge, bolstering the North Korean advance. However, they faced fierce counterattacks from U.N. forces, resulting in heavy casualties and disruption of supply lines. His unit was eventually forced to retreat under heavy fire, abandoning their positions across the river.

After the war, Lee resumed his position as the chief of staff of the KPA. However, by 1959, he was removed during a series of political purges initiated by Kim Il Sung aimed at consolidating power and eliminating rivals linked to Soviet and Chinese factions within the military. Following his dismissal, Lee disappeared from public life, and details about his later years remain sparse to none. The year of his death is unknown.

Lee Kwon-mu is remembered as a significant military leader whose actions during the Korean War helped shape the conflict's dynamics and its aftermath. His legacy continues to be studied in the context of North Korea's military history and political landscape.

These two soldiers—Craig, with his selfless act of heroism, and Lee, with his tactical determination—represent the personal sacrifices and leadership displayed on both sides of the Second Battle of Naktong Bulge, a confrontation that shaped the outcome of the early stages of the Korean War.

These two soldiers—Craig, with his selfless act of heroism, and Kim, with his tactical determination—represent the personal sacrifices and leadership displayed on both sides of the Second Battle of Naktong Bulge, a confrontation that shaped the outcome of the early stages of the Korean War.

Holding the Line and Turning the Tide

The battles fought along the Pusan Perimeter were grueling, defined by relentless North Korean offensives and fierce resistance by U.N. forces. Both sides endured high casualties, with each engagement demanding tactical innovation and sheer determination. Initially, U.N. forces were underprepared and overwhelmed by the speed and intensity of the North Korean advance. However, their ability to adapt, reorganize, and leverage available resources—such as terrain, artillery, and air support—became the key to their success.

The defenders used every advantage they could muster, from pre-sighted artillery positions to coordinated airstrikes, slowing and eventually halting the KPA's offensives. The rough terrain along rivers like the Naktong worked in favor of the U.N. forces, funneling enemy troops into kill zones. As the battles dragged on, U.N. commanders refined their tactics, deploying infantry and armor more effectively, reinforcing vulnerable sectors, and learning how to contain North Korean night assaults. These adaptations reflected the growing cohesion among U.S., South Korean, and other allied troops fighting to preserve the southern tip of the Korean Peninsula.

Despite the heavy toll, the U.N.'s ability to hold the Pusan Perimeter was decisive.

Had the perimeter collapsed, the North Koreans would have captured Pusan, cutting off vital supply lines and possibly ending the war with a swift communist victory. Instead, the successful defense allowed U.N. forces to regroup and plan a bold counteroffensive, forcing the North Koreans into retreat and enabling the recapture of Seoul.

These early victories highlighted the resilience and determination of U.S. and South Korean forces.

Holding the line at Pusan demonstrated that the war would not end in a quick defeat but instead would continue with growing momentum for the U.N. forces. The lessons learned from these battles—coordination between air, armor, and infantry, the importance of supply chains, and the necessity of tactical flexibility—shaped future operations and set the stage for the eventual rollback of North Korean advances, ensuring the survival of South Korea and fundamentally altering the course of the war.

THE INCHON LANDING AND
SEOUL'S LIBERATION

"We shall land at Inchon, and I shall crush them."

— GENERAL DOUGLAS MACARTHUR

By the summer of 1950, the U.N. forces were in a desperate situation, holding onto the Pusan Perimeter, the last defensive line in the southeastern tip of the Korean Peninsula. The KPA had launched relentless offensives, threatening to collapse the U.N. defenses and claim a total victory. It was clear to the U.N. Command that bold action was needed to break the deadlock and shift the momentum of the war. This is where General Douglas MacArthur proposed a daring and audacious plan that would go down in military history: an amphibious assault at the port city of Inchon.

THE INCHON GAMBLE

By late summer 1950, the U.N. forces were in a precarious position, confined to the southeastern tip of the Korean Peninsula within their defensive area—the Pusan Perimeter. This perimeter, anchored by the port city of Pusan, was the last stronghold against the relentless KPA offensive.

U.N. forces, comprising U.S., South Korean, and other allied troops, faced mounting pressure as the KPA aimed to break through the perimeter and force a total collapse of the U.N. position.

The situation was critical. If the Pusan Perimeter fell, the North Koreans would likely overrun South Korea, forcing a complete U.N. withdrawal from the peninsula. As U.N. forces fought desperately to hold the line, General Douglas MacArthur recognized the need for a bold and decisive maneuver to relieve the pressure on Pusan and turn the tide of the war. His plan focused on a surprise amphibious landing far behind enemy lines at Inchon, a port city near the North Korean capital of Seoul. By seizing Inchon, MacArthur hoped to cut off North Korean supply lines, forcing the KPA to retreat from their positions in the south, thus relieving pressure on the beleaguered U.N. forces at Pusan.

The Inchon Landing, codenamed Operation Chromite, was designed to trap the KPA between U.N. forces advancing from the north and the defenders of the Pusan Perimeter to the south. MacArthur's plan aimed not only to break the North Korean siege but also to reclaim Seoul and restore the momentum to the U.N. side. It was a high-stakes gamble, but the rewards, if successful, would be monumental.

Inchon was a daring and unconventional choice for an amphibious assault. Its strategic location, just twenty-five miles from Seoul, made it a prime target. By capturing Inchon, U.N. forces could sever critical North Korean supply and communication lines that were keeping their war effort afloat. Additionally, Inchon's proximity to Seoul, the political and administrative heart of Korea, made it a valuable prize for the U.N. forces, symbolizing the possibility of liberating South Korea from North Korean control.

However, the risks associated with attacking Inchon were enormous. The port city had extreme tidal variations—one of the highest tidal ranges in the world—making timing crucial for landing operations. The tides created a narrow window for naval landings, and if mistimed, the amphibious forces could be stranded on treacherous mudflats, exposed to North Korean fire. Additionally, Inchon's narrow channels and heavily fortified defenses made it a difficult target. North Korean forces had entrenched themselves in the city, prepared for the possibility of an attack. Military advisors warned that an amphibious assault on such a heavily defended and logistically challenging location could result in catastrophic losses.

Despite the overwhelming risks, MacArthur was resolute in his decision to attack Inchon. He believed that the very factors that made Inchon an unlikely target—its dangerous tides, fortified defenses, and narrow access—would work in his favor by catching the North Koreans off guard. He argued that the surprise element would allow the U.N. forces to land with minimal resistance, and that the boldness of the maneuver would outweigh the operational risks. MacArthur's confidence in the success of Operation Chromite was such that he famously declared, "The enemy will be caught with his pants down."

Many military advisors, including members of the Joint Chiefs of Staff, expressed reservations about the plan. They viewed the risks as too great, recommending a more conservative approach. However, MacArthur's strategic audacity and unwavering belief in the importance of seizing the initiative led to the approval of the Inchon Landing. In the end, MacArthur's gamble would prove to be one of the most brilliant tactical maneuvers of the Korean War, leading to the liberation of Seoul and dramatically shifting the balance of the conflict in favor of the U.N. forces.

U.N. Preparations and Forces Involved

The Inchon Landing, known as Operation Chromite, involved a highly coordinated multinational effort. The core of the assault force was composed of approximately 75,000 troops, with the U.S. 1st Marine Division playing a leading role in the amphibious assault. This division, known for its experience and elite status, was critical in establishing a beachhead at Inchon. In addition to the U.S. Marines, other U.N. forces, including South Korean troops and contingents from allied nations like the United Kingdom, played vital roles in the operation. South Korean forces, in particular, provided crucial ground support during the initial landings and the subsequent advance toward Seoul.

The operation's success hinged on the cooperation of these various forces, each bringing different capabilities and experiences to the battlefield. Coordination between U.S. and South Korean units helped ensure that the operation maintained momentum once the landings began. This joint effort represented a hallmark of U.N. collaboration during the Korean War, as it unified various military assets under a common strategic goal: to outflank the North Korean People's Army and force their retreat from South Korea.

One of the defining features of the Inchon Landing was the overwhelming naval and air power brought to bear by U.N. forces. The naval fleet supporting the operation was formidable, with over 260 ships in total, including aircraft carriers, battleships, destroyers, and landing craft. These ships provided crucial pre-landing bombardments that softened North Korean defenses, targeting artillery positions, fortifications, and key infrastructure along the coast of Inchon. The naval fleet's firepower helped reduce the intensity of enemy resistance during the critical early phases of the amphibious assault.

In the skies, U.N. aircraft, including fighter jets and bombers, targeted North Korean supply lines and communication networks, effectively disrupting KPA reinforcements. The air campaign, led by U.S. Navy and U.S. Air Force units, played a pivotal role in limiting the KPA's ability to respond to the surprise landing. U.N. bombers struck key transportation hubs, bridges, and roads, delaying the movement of North Korean troops to the Inchon area and ensuring that U.N. ground forces could establish their foothold with minimal interference. The combination of naval bombardments and airstrikes created a synergy that crippled North Korean defenses, contributing directly to the success of the operation.

The complexity of the Inchon Landing required meticulous planning by U.N. commanders, particularly given the logistical challenges posed by the area's extreme tidal variations and narrow approaches. The tides at Inchon varied by as much as thirty-two feet, creating a narrow window during which landing craft could safely navigate the channels. Timing was everything. U.N. planners had to ensure that the assault took place during a favorable tidal period to prevent landing forces from becoming stranded on mudflats, which would leave them vulnerable to enemy fire.

Amphibious forces underwent extensive training to prepare for the unique challenges of the Inchon assault. Rehearsals included simulating the difficult conditions they would face, ensuring that the timing, coordination, and execution of the landing were as smooth as possible. Naval, air, and ground units worked in close coordination, practicing joint maneuvers to ensure effective communication and responsiveness during the actual operation. Special attention was given to intelligence gathering, as understanding the topography, enemy positions, and tidal conditions was critical to the operation's success.

Amphibious Assault Begins

At dawn on September 15, 1950, Operation Chromite

commenced with a massive naval bombardment designed to soften the North Korean defenses at Inchon. U.N. naval forces unleashed a relentless artillery barrage, targeting coastal fortifications, bunkers, and enemy gun positions to pave the way for the amphibious landing. The bombardment was critical in disorienting North Korean troops, destroying key defensive positions, and minimizing U.N. casualties during the initial assault. As the bombardment ceased, the first wave of U.S. Marines from the 1st Marine Division approached the beaches under the cover of smoke and debris.

The landing itself, which occurred across multiple beachheads, took advantage of the element of surprise. North Korean forces were caught off guard, as they had not expected a full-scale amphibious invasion at Inchon due to the treacherous tidal conditions and fortified defenses. Despite some initial resistance, including sporadic machine gun fire and artillery shelling, U.N. forces quickly gained a foothold on the beaches. The Marines used specialized amphibious landing craft to cross the dangerous mudflats and breach coastal defenses. Their swift, decisive action allowed the U.N. troops to overwhelm the stunned North Korean defenders.

Once ashore, the 1st Marine Division moved rapidly to secure their key objectives, which included strategic infrastructure critical to supporting the U.N. advance. By the end of the first day, U.N. forces had taken control of Kimpo Airfield, an important asset that allowed them to bring in additional reinforcements and supplies. The airfield's capture was essential for establishing air superiority in the region, enabling U.N. aircraft to provide close air support during subsequent operations. Along with Kimpo, the Marines seized vital supply depots and communications hubs, cutting off the KPA's ability to resupply or communicate effectively.

Despite facing well-entrenched and fortified North Korean positions, the U.N. forces pressed inland with remarkable speed.

Urban combat followed as they moved through Inchon, neutralizing remaining enemy pockets of resistance. The quick seizure of Inchon's critical facilities, including its docks and infrastructure, allowed for an efficient logistical flow of U.N. reinforcements and equipment. Within twenty-four hours, the U.N. forces had established a secure beachhead, preparing to launch further offensives toward Seoul.

The Inchon Landing, executed with precision and speed, was a resounding success. Not only did it disrupt North Korean logistics and weaken their foothold in South Korea; it also paved the way for the eventual liberation of Seoul. The ability of the U.N. troops to secure the beaches and key objectives so swiftly demonstrated the effectiveness of MacArthur's daring plan and the impeccable coordination of air, naval, and ground forces.

Despite the initial shock of the amphibious assault, North Korean forces, particularly those entrenched in Inchon, mounted a tenacious defense. However, their response was severely hindered by disrupted communication lines and the rapid collapse of their supply networks, which were key targets of the U.N.'s bombardments and airstrikes. The North Koreans, caught off guard by the speed and scale of the landing, struggled to coordinate their counterattacks. Their ability to reinforce defensive positions was significantly weakened, allowing U.N. troops to gain ground quickly.

As U.N. forces pushed inland, they encountered pockets of fierce resistance. North Korean defenders, particularly in fortified positions near the city center, attempted to stall the U.N. advance. Nevertheless, the overwhelming firepower and coordination of U.N. forces, supported by superior logistics and reinforcements, allowed them to steadily gain the upper hand. The Marines, supported by artillery and naval bombardment, systematically cleared enemy positions. Inchon was secured within days, and the U.N. troops consolidated their positions, ready to advance toward Seoul.

One of the critical factors in the U.N. victory at Inchon was the continuous naval and air superiority they maintained throughout the battle. U.S. Navy ships, including battleships and destroyers, provided relentless bombardment of North Korean positions, neutralizing artillery batteries and disrupting troop movements. The naval presence not only softened enemy defenses before the initial landing but also continued to provide support during the inland advance, ensuring that the North Koreans could not regroup or reinforce their positions.

U.N. air power also played a decisive role in the success of the battle. Fighter-bombers from U.S. carriers and airfields targeted North Korean supply lines, bridges, and reinforcement routes, preventing fresh troops from reaching Inchon. This air superiority crippled the KPA's ability to mount an effective defense or launch counteroffensives. U.N. aircraft dominated the skies, enabling ground forces to move with relative security and reducing the effectiveness of any North Korean attempts to halt their progress.

The combination of overwhelming naval firepower and air superiority ensured that U.N. forces had the advantage at every stage of the battle. By controlling the seas and skies, they were able to neutralize North Korean reinforcements, isolate Inchon, and secure a decisive victory that opened the door to the subsequent liberation of Seoul.

RECAPTURE OF SEOUL

With Inchon firmly under U.N. control, General MacArthur wasted no time in ordering the next phase of the operation: the liberation of Seoul, the capital of South Korea, which had been under North Korean occupation since the early days of the war. The recapture of Seoul held immense strategic and symbolic significance. Militarily, it was critical for cutting off the KPA's remaining supply lines and communication routes. Politically, liberating Seoul represented the restoration of the South Korean government and a major morale boost for the U.N. forces.

On September 22, 1950, U.N. forces began their advance toward Seoul, encountering stiff resistance from North Korean troops who had heavily fortified positions in and around the city. The urban combat was brutal, with house-to-house fighting and numerous casualties on both sides. However, by September 25, after several days of intense fighting, U.N. forces successfully recaptured Seoul. The victory at Seoul not only marked a decisive turn in the Korean War but also dealt a psychological blow to the North Korean regime, weakening their control over the south and disrupting their overall war strategy.

The strategic success of the Inchon Landing and the subsequent liberation of Seoul had immediate and far-reaching consequences for the U.N. forces struggling to hold the Pusan Perimeter. By cutting off North Korean supply lines and forcing the KPA to retreat from central and southern Korea, the Inchon operation effectively ended the North Korean offensive. This dramatic shift allowed U.N. forces at Pusan to regroup and go on the offensive, pushing the weakened KPA northward.

The Inchon Landing was not just a tactical victory but a critical turning point in the war. It relieved the beleaguered U.N. forces in the south and set the stage for a broader counteroffensive that would carry the conflict into North Korean territory. The operation demonstrated the power of bold, strategic planning and transformed the war from a defensive struggle into an opportunity for U.N. forces to regain the initiative.

The Inchon Landing stands as one of the most brilliant amphibious assaults in military history, solidifying its place as a defining moment of the Korean War. The operation's success was largely due to meticulous planning, effective coordination of naval, air, and ground forces, and General Douglas MacArthur's strategic audacity. Despite the significant risks posed by Inchon's treacherous tidal conditions and the heavily fortified North

Korean defenses, the landing achieved its objectives with remarkable speed and precision.

The operation shifted the entire momentum of the war, transitioning U.N. forces from a defensive posture, desperately holding onto the Pusan Perimeter, to an aggressive counteroffensive that reversed North Korea's gains. The liberation of Seoul shortly after the Inchon Landing further demonstrated the effectiveness of the operation and its long-term strategic impact. By forcing the KPA to retreat from southern Korea, the landing not only saved the South from imminent collapse but also paved the way for U.N. advances deep into North Korean territory. This bold and decisive operation remains a textbook example of the importance of strategic planning and the ability to seize the initiative in warfare.

COURAGE UNDER FIRE

Captain William E. Barber commanded a rifle company in the 1st Marine Division during the Inchon Landing, leading his men with determination through the amphibious assault and the subsequent battle for Inchon. Barber's unit was among the first waves to hit the beaches on September 15, 1950. His leadership was pivotal in securing key objectives, including the capture of Kimpo Airfield, which played a critical role in allowing U.N. forces to bring in reinforcements and supplies.

Facing heavy resistance from entrenched North Korean forces, Barber's company engaged in intense close-quarters combat as they advanced through Inchon's urban landscape. Under his command, his men fought their way through strong defensive positions, utilizing the element of surprise and overwhelming firepower. Despite significant challenges, including difficult terrain and sporadic enemy counterattacks, Barber ensured that his unit maintained momentum. His quick decision-making and tactical prowess allowed U.N. forces to secure Inchon within days, opening the path toward Seoul.

After the Inchon Landing, Barber continued to serve with distinction throughout the Korean War. His actions during the later Battle of Chosin Reservoir, where he held a key pass against overwhelming Chinese forces, earned him the Medal of Honor. After the war, Barber continued to serve until he retired from the Marines in 1970 and lived in California, where he became a civilian-military analyst and an advocate for veterans. He passed away in 2002, leaving behind a legacy of extraordinary courage and leadership in some of the Korean War's most pivotal battles.

DEFIANT DEFENSE

Major Pak Song-chul led a battalion within the North Korean People's Army during the Inchon Landing, tasked with defending critical positions in and around the port city. As the amphibious assault began, Pak's unit faced intense naval bombardment, which disrupted communications and caused heavy casualties. Despite the overwhelming firepower of the U.N. forces, Major Pak organized his men into defensive positions, trying to stem the U.N. advance.

Pak's leadership was crucial in holding the line during the initial phases of the battle, directing his troops in guerrilla-style tactics as they sought to delay the U.N. forces pushing inland. His battalion took advantage of Inchon's urban environment, engaging U.N. forces in house-to-house fighting and counterattacks. However, the element of surprise and the superior coordination between U.N. air, naval, and ground forces made it nearly impossible for Pak's battalion to hold their ground.

As U.N. forces quickly overwhelmed Inchon, Major Pak and his surviving troops were forced to retreat. Though he fought fiercely to maintain control of key positions, the collapse of North Korean defenses in Inchon marked a major turning point in the war. Following the retreat, Pak continued to serve in the North Korean military but was severely injured during later battles as U.N. forces pressed northward. After the war, Pak rose through various military and political positions. He is remembered for his unwavering commitment to his country.

These two soldiers—Barber's relentless courage under fire and Pak's tenacity in defense—reflect the personal sacrifices and leadership displayed on both sides of the Inchon Landing, a battle that altered the course of the Korean War.

SEOUL'S LIBERATION

The city of Seoul was not only the capital of South Korea but also the political, economic, and cultural heart of the nation. Its significance transcended mere geography. Militarily, Seoul was a key logistical hub, with vital roads, railways, and communication lines that linked North Korean forces in the south to their command structures in the north. Recapturing Seoul would severely disrupt these lines, weakening the North Korean People's Army and hampering their ability to coordinate their operations in southern Korea.

From a symbolic standpoint, reclaiming Seoul was essential for both the United Nations and the Republic of Korea. Since Seoul had fallen to North Korean forces early in the war, its loss had been a major blow to South Korean morale and international confidence in the U.N. mission.

By liberating the capital, the U.N. forces would restore the seat of the South Korean government, reasserting the legitimacy of the ROK under President Syngman Rhee and undermining North Korean claims to total control over the peninsula. The recapture of Seoul would also send a powerful message to the international community about the U.N.'s ability to reverse the course of the war and provide a morale boost to the South

Korean population, which had endured months of hardship under occupation.

Following the stunning success of the Inchon Landing on September 15, 1950, U.N. forces seized a critical opportunity to capitalize on their momentum. The Inchon assault had caught the KPA off guard, cutting off their reinforcements and forcing a strategic withdrawal from southern Korea. The next logical step for the U.N. was to move inland and capture Seoul, a critical objective that would cripple the North Korean war effort.

The advance toward Seoul was led by U.S. Marines from the 1st Marine Division and South Korean units, who spearheaded the U.N.'s offensive. Despite the initial success at Inchon, the push inland toward the capital would not be easy. The North Koreans had heavily fortified positions in and around Seoul, and the KPA intended to make the battle for the capital as costly as possible for the U.N. forces.

By taking Seoul, the U.N. hoped not only to deal a major blow to the KPA's morale but also to force a North Korean retreat from the Pusan Perimeter, where U.N. forces had been holding out under siege for weeks. The capture of Seoul was seen as a key strategic move that would shift the momentum of the war, transforming the U.N. from a defensive posture to an offensive force capable of driving the North Koreans back across the 38th Parallel.

North Korean Fortifications

As U.N. forces advanced toward Seoul, they encountered heavily fortified North Korean defenses entrenched throughout the city. The KPA had taken full advantage of Seoul's urban landscape, transforming key infrastructure into defensive strongholds. Major buildings, such as government offices, factories, and apartment complexes, were converted into fortified positions. These structures provided KPA forces with elevated vantage points, enabling them to position snipers and machine gunners to rain fire on advancing U.N. troops.

Additionally, the bridges spanning the Han River, which cut through Seoul, were either heavily guarded or rigged with explosives to prevent U.N. forces from easily crossing. The KPA also established defensive lines along the narrow streets and alleyways of the city, making it difficult for armored vehicles to maneuver and turning urban spaces into deadly chokepoints. Barricades and trenches were constructed along key routes into the city to stall the U.N. advance. With their communications disrupted after the Inchon Landing, KPA commanders resorted to guerrilla tactics, relying on hit-and-run ambushes, sniper fire, and booby traps to slow U.N. progress.

Recognizing the strategic importance of Seoul, Kim Il Sung ordered his commanders to defend the capital at all costs. The KPA's approach was to make the battle as prolonged and costly as possible, forcing U.N. forces to fight for every street and building in the densely packed urban environment. These defenses, though formidable, were ultimately no match for the superior firepower and coordination of U.N. forces, but they significantly increased U.N. casualties and delayed the recapture of the city.

Understanding the complexity of urban warfare, the U.N. Command, led by General Douglas MacArthur, adopted a methodical and cautious approach to minimize civilian casualties and avoid the destruction of Seoul's infrastructure. MacArthur was keenly aware that Seoul's liberation had immense symbolic value, and preserving the city's infrastructure was essential for restoring the South Korean government and maintaining public support for the war effort.

Unlike the Inchon Landing, where overwhelming firepower was used to great effect, the Battle of Seoul required a different set of tactics. Due to the urban terrain, large-scale use of artillery and airstrikes was restricted to avoid excessive damage to the city. Instead, U.N. forces focused on infantry tactics, small arms engagements, and close-quarters combat. Specialized units, including the U.S. 1st Marine Division, the South Korean 1st Infantry Division, and the U.S. 7th Infantry Division, were highly trained in house-to-house combat and clearing fortified positions. Their expertise made them particularly effective in the intense urban warfare they encountered during the liberation of Seoul.

Artillery support was limited and highly targeted, striking only the most heavily defended KPA positions. Similarly, air support was restricted to precision strikes against key logistical points and communication hubs, rather than widespread bombing runs. This strategic restraint was aimed at preserving Seoul's infrastructure and minimizing civilian casualties, but it also meant that U.N. troops would have to engage in fierce, close-quarters combat without the extensive artillery and air support they had relied on in other battles.

The U.N. approach relied heavily on coordinated infantry assaults, with troops advancing slowly and methodically, clearing each building, street, and alleyway of KPA defenders. South Korean forces played a critical role in this effort, using their knowledge of the city's layout to navigate the dense urban environment and support the U.S. Marines as they pushed toward the city center. This approach allowed the U.N. forces to advance steadily while minimizing the risk of unnecessary destruction in the South Korean capital.

Initial U.N. Advances

The assault on Seoul began in earnest on September 22, 1950, with U.N. forces, led by the U.S. 1st Marine Division, initiating their advance from the city's outskirts toward its heavily defended center. As the first wave of U.N. troops entered the suburban areas, they encountered fierce resistance from entrenched KPA forces. The KPA had established fortified positions along the outer perimeter of Seoul, using both natural and urban defenses to slow the U.N. advance.

The 1st Marine Division, which had played a pivotal role in the Inchon Landing, took the lead in the assault. Their advance was slow and methodical, as they faced KPA forces deeply entrenched in defensive positions around key buildings, bridges, and chokepoints. Using every element of the city's infrastructure —from narrow streets to fortified high-rise buildings—to their advantage, the KPA had prepared for this confrontation. As the Marines pushed forward, they had to clear each position carefully, often under heavy fire from well-hidden snipers and machine gun nests.

To counter the KPA's defense, ROK forces fought alongside the U.S. Marines, employing flanking maneuvers to bypass the most heavily fortified KPA positions. Their intimate knowledge of the local terrain proved invaluable, as they helped guide U.S. forces through the urban sprawl of Seoul. However, progress remained slow due to the density of the urban environment and the complexity of the KPA's defense network.

As U.N. forces advanced deeper into Seoul, the battle quickly transitioned into intense urban warfare. The city's tight streets, alleyways, and dense clusters of buildings turned every block into a battlefield. House-to-house combat became the defining characteristic of the battle, as U.N. forces were forced to clear each building room by room, floor by floor. The narrow streets limited the effectiveness of U.N. armor, and tanks often became targets for North Korean anti-tank weapons.

Close-quarters fighting was brutal, with engagements taking place at street level, inside buildings, and in alleys where KPA soldiers had set up ambushes. KPA guerrilla tactics, including sniper fire, hidden explosives, and surprise attacks from behind barricades, created significant challenges for the U.N. forces. The North Koreans made effective use of the city's multi-story buildings, placing snipers in high vantage points and using the lower floors for defensive positions, which forced U.N. troops to engage in grueling firefights.

Despite these challenges, the U.N. forces, particularly the U.S. Marines, continued their slow but steady advance. They relied heavily on small arms fire and close coordination between infantry units, with artillery and air support playing a secondary role. As U.N. forces cleared neighborhoods and key streets, they faced relentless resistance, with the KPA determined to hold onto their positions for as long as possible. However, the U.N.'s superior training, equipment, and coordination gradually overwhelmed the North Korean defenders, setting the stage for the final push to liberate Seoul.

This phase of the battle demonstrated the tactical complexity of urban warfare, where traditional battlefield strategies were difficult to implement, and success depended on adaptability, discipline, and resilience in the face of an entrenched enemy.

One of the most significant tactical challenges during the Battle of Seoul was the limited use of artillery and air support. Unlike the open battlefield, where U.N. forces had successfully employed overwhelming firepower, the dense urban environment of Seoul restricted these tactics. The city was the political and cultural heart of South Korea, and both the U.N. Command and the South Korean government were determined to avoid excessive destruction to the city's infrastructure. This restriction forced U.N. forces to shift their tactics away from large-scale bombardments.

Artillery support, usually a critical component of U.N. operations, was deliberately limited to precise strikes on fortified KPA positions. Air support was similarly restricted, with U.N. aircraft primarily tasked with targeting supply lines and communication hubs outside of the city to prevent KPA reinforcements from arriving in Seoul. Though this strategy helped isolate North Korean forces in the capital, it did little to immediately assist ground troops in clearing enemy positions. Yet, U.N. troops were successful in relying more heavily on infantry and small arms fire, engaging KPA forces in grueling street-to-street and building-to-building combat.

CROSSING THE HAN RIVER

One of the most pivotal challenges for U.N. forces during the battle was the need to cross the Han River, which bisects Seoul and served as a natural defensive barrier for the KPA. The river made it difficult for U.N. forces to coordinate a unified assault on both sides of the city. The North Korean defenders had heavily fortified the bridges and established defensive positions along the riverbanks, making any attempts to cross the river perilous.

To overcome this obstacle, U.N. engineers played a crucial role. They rapidly secured key bridges while working under constant enemy fire to repair those that had been damaged or destroyed by the retreating North Korean forces. These bridges were essential for moving armor and infantry across the river and enabling the U.N. to launch a coordinated offensive on both sides of Seoul. Despite heavy fire from KPA defenders, U.N. troops, supported by South Korean forces, successfully established bridgeheads, allowing armored units to cross and continue their assault on the city.

The contribution of South Korean forces was instrumental in the success of the battle. South Korean troops were tasked with securing the southern and eastern approaches to Seoul, areas that were critical for launching coordinated assaults on enemy strongholds. Their familiarity with the terrain and their deep commitment to recapturing their capital helped galvanize U.N. efforts. South Korean forces operated in conjunction with U.S. Marines, conducting flanking maneuvers and clearing enemy positions that threatened U.N. advances from the west.

Their role in securing key roads and bridges enabled U.N. armor and infantry to make quicker progress through the city. As part of the joint U.N. effort, South Korean forces fought fiercely, often leading the charge against heavily fortified positions and bearing the brunt of casualties in the process. Their participation not only boosted morale but also demonstrated the importance of the joint U.N.-South Korean effort in reclaiming their capital.

After nearly a week of brutal urban combat, the KPA began a disorganized retreat from Seoul on September 28, 1950. The fighting had exacted a heavy toll on both sides, but the U.N. forces, led by the U.S. Marines and ROK units, had steadily pushed the KPA out of their fortified positions. The North Korean defenders, initially dug in throughout the city, could no longer maintain their foothold as U.N. forces continued their methodical advance.

The withdrawal was hastily organized and marked by a series of disjointed rear-guard actions as the KPA attempted to cover their retreat by delaying the U.N. troops. Despite these efforts, the North Koreans could not hold back the advancing U.N. forces, and their retreat quickly turned chaotic. The KPA had suffered severe casualties during the battle, with supply lines cut and reinforcements blocked, leaving them little choice but to abandon Seoul. By the end of the battle, the remnants of the North Korean forces withdrew toward the north, leaving the capital in U.N. control.

Securing the Capital

With the North Koreans in full retreat, U.N. forces moved swiftly to secure key government buildings in Seoul. The Seoul City Hall, a symbol of South Korea's political authority, was a primary target. Once captured, U.N. troops raised the South Korean flag over the building, signifying not only the military victory but also the restoration of South Korean sovereignty. The reestablishment of the South Korean government in the capital marked a critical political victory for both the U.N. and the South

Korean people, as Seoul was once again under the control of the Republic of Korea.

The fall of Seoul also signaled a broader shift in the Korean War. The KPA's retreat from the capital represented the beginning of their withdrawal from southern Korea. U.N. forces had broken the North Korean momentum, forcing the KPA into a defensive position as they withdrew north of the 38th Parallel. The liberation of Seoul not only restored the South Korean government but also set the stage for the U.N.'s counteroffensive, which would eventually carry the war deep into North Korean territory.

The loss of Seoul delivered a significant psychological and strategic blow to the North Korean People's Army. Seoul had been a symbol of North Korean dominance over the south since its capture early in the war, and its liberation shattered any pretense of KPA control over the entire Korean Peninsula. The defeat in Seoul weakened North Korean morale, as it underscored the effectiveness of the United Nations forces and highlighted the KPA's inability to hold key strategic positions.

Furthermore, the retreat from Seoul forced the KPA to abandon their positions south of the 38th Parallel, which had served as the demarcation line between North and South Korea before the war. This retreat marked a major strategic shift, as U.N. forces now held the initiative and began moving from a defensive to an offensive posture. The KPA's ability to sustain their southern campaign collapsed in the wake of the defeat, and the loss of Seoul deprived North Korea of a crucial supply line and communication hub, further hindering their war effort.

The recapture of Seoul was a turning point in the Korean War. After months of U.N. forces defending the Pusan Perimeter and enduring intense fighting, the fall of Seoul dramatically shifted the momentum in favor of the U.N. coalition. The victory at Seoul represented not only the liberation of South Korea's capital but also the restoration of South Korean political authority under President Syngman Rhee, which bolstered the morale of both the South Korean people and the U.N. forces.

Strategically, the recapture of Seoul placed U.N. forces in a position of offensive superiority. With the North Koreans retreating northward, U.N. commanders began planning for subsequent offensives that would carry the fight into North Korean territory. The battle had demonstrated the effectiveness of joint U.N. operations, particularly the coordination between infantry, armor, and air support. Now, with the KPA in retreat, the U.N. forces could press their advantage and initiate a broader campaign aimed at rolling back North Korean gains and eventually advancing toward the Yalu River on the border with China.

The fall of Seoul marked a pivotal shift in the war, transforming it from a conflict focused on defensive survival at the Pusan Perimeter to a campaign of U.N. counteroffensives, leading to a new phase of the conflict where U.N. forces sought to decisively defeat the KPA and restore peace to the peninsula.

Leading the Charge

Captain Lewis "Chesty" Puller was a highly respected officer in the 1st Marine Division, known for his leadership and tenacity during some of the toughest battles of the Korean War. During the Battle of Seoul, Puller commanded 1st Marine Regiment tasked with leading the U.N. assault through the fortified streets of the South Korean capital. With his extensive combat experience from World War II, Puller was no stranger to the challenges of urban warfare, but the fighting in Seoul presented new difficulties.

The KPA had transformed the city into a fortress, with snipers positioned in high-rise buildings, fortified bunkers, and narrow streets laced with ambushes. Puller's unit faced fierce resistance as they advanced block by block, often engaging in close-quarters combat to clear KPA soldiers from buildings and defensive positions. Despite the constant threat of ambushes, snipers, and the challenges of navigating the urban environment, Puller's leadership kept his men focused and motivated. His ability to adapt to the dynamic conditions on the ground and maintain strong discipline within his ranks contributed to the Marines' steady advance toward the city center.

At the Battle of Chosin Reservoir in December 1950, Colonel Chesty Puller earned both the Distinguished Service Cross and his fifth Navy Cross for his extraordinary heroism. Facing relentless attacks over several days, he famously remarked, "We've been looking for the enemy for some time now. We've finally found him. We're surrounded. That simplifies things." This statement became emblematic of his tenacity, as Puller led his Marines through encirclement and extreme cold, showcasing his resilience and combat leadership.

After the Korean War, Puller's legendary status within the Marine Corps only grew. He became one of the most decorated Marines in U.S. history, earning multiple Navy Crosses for his actions in Korea and other conflicts. Colonel Puller stayed in the Marines at Camp Lejeune in North Carolina until he had a stroke and retired in November of 1955.

Following his retirement, he settled in Virginia, where he became a prominent advocate for veterans' issues. He passed away on October 11, 1971, at seventy-three years old in Hampton, Virginia, leaving behind a legacy of unparalleled bravery and leadership in battle.

Defending the Capital

Major Kim Hyun-shik was a battalion commander within the KPA tasked with defending key sections of Seoul during the U.N.'s assault. A battle-hardened officer, Kim had previously led KPA forces in engagements across South Korea, but the fight for Seoul presented unprecedented challenges. As the U.N. forces, spearheaded by U.S. Marines and South Korean troops, pressed into the city, Kim was ordered to hold strategic positions near the Han River and prevent U.N. forces from crossing into the heart of the city.

Kim's battalion was heavily outgunned, facing constant bombardment from U.N. air and artillery strikes, but he remained resolute in his defense. His men, fortified in key government buildings and alleyways, used guerrilla tactics to delay the U.N. advance. Snipers, ambush teams, and rear-guard actions were employed to inflict as many casualties as possible on the attacking forces. Kim coordinated his men to conduct hit-and-run operations, using the urban environment to their advantage.

Despite his efforts, Kim's forces were steadily pushed back by the superior firepower and coordination of U.N. troops. The turning point came when U.N. forces, having secured key crossings over the Han River, launched a series of assaults on Kim's defensive lines. With communications disrupted and reinforcements unable to reach the city, Kim's battalion was eventually forced to retreat in the face of overwhelming odds. Kim and his remaining troops withdrew from Seoul on September 28, marking a significant defeat for the North Korean forces.

After the battle, Kim continued to serve in the KPA but was severely injured during the U.N. counteroffensive that followed the liberation of Seoul. After the war, Kim likely continued his career in the KPA until his death.

These two figures—Puller's aggressive command of U.N. forces and Kim's determined defense of Seoul—highlight the personal bravery and strategic challenges faced by soldiers on both sides during one of the most significant battles of the Korean War.

THE TURNING POINT OF THE WAR

The Inchon Landing and the liberation of Seoul marked a

turning point in the Korean War, reshaping the strategic landscape and giving U.N. forces the upper hand. General Douglas MacArthur's daring amphibious assault at Inchon demonstrated the value of risk-taking in warfare, utilizing the element of surprise to outmaneuver the North Korean People's Army. The operation successfully disrupted the KPA's supply lines and communication networks, forcing them into a disorderly retreat and lifting the siege at the Pusan Perimeter.

Within days of the Inchon Landing, the rapid recapture of Seoul restored the capital to the Republic of Korea and symbolized a dramatic shift in momentum. The victory boosted the morale of U.N. forces, including South Korean troops, while demoralizing the North Koreans, who had been pushed back from their significant southern gains. The success also demonstrated the importance of coordinated operations between naval, air, and ground forces, with each component playing a critical role in achieving the overall objective.

While the liberation of Seoul was a major success, it also set the stage for new challenges. The swift advance of U.N. forces northward soon brought them to the Yalu River, near the Chinese border, prompting concerns about Chinese intervention. This next phase of the war would introduce new complexities, as the Korean conflict evolved from a localized civil war into a broader geopolitical struggle involving the major powers of the Cold War.

OVERREACH AND CHINESE INTERVENTION

"Retreat, hell! We're not retreating, we're just advancing in a different direction."

— MAJOR GENERAL OLIVER P. SMITH, U.S. MARINE CORPS

After recapturing Seoul and driving North Korean forces into retreat, U.N. forces advanced beyond the 38th Parallel toward the Yalu River, the border between North Korea and China. General Douglas MacArthur was eager to end the war with a decisive victory, aiming to reunify the Korean Peninsula under South Korean control. However, the rapid advance overstretched U.N. supply lines and ignored warnings from China. The Chinese viewed the U.N. offensive as a direct threat to their national security and responded by secretly deploying troops across the Yalu River, initiating a large-scale intervention that changed the course of the war.

BATTLE OF CHOSIN RESERVOIR

By the fall of 1950, U.N. forces, led by the U.S. and commanded by General Douglas MacArthur, had achieved a string of decisive victories that pushed the North Korean People's Army (KPA) back across the 38th Parallel. Following the liberation of Seoul in late September, U.N. forces advanced deep into North Korea, with the primary objective of reaching the Yalu River, the natural border between North Korea and China. This rapid advance was motivated by the belief that the war could be swiftly concluded with the collapse of the North Korean regime. MacArthur's ambitious goal was to reunify the Korean Peninsula under the South Korean government and eliminate Communist control.

The U.N. offensive was part of Operation Chromite, which had initially involved the Inchon Landing. With the success of the operation, MacArthur sought to press the advantage and end the war decisively. However, as U.N. forces moved north, they became stretched thin over vast, rugged terrain, especially in areas like the Chosin Reservoir, where supply lines were long and difficult to maintain. Despite intelligence reports suggesting Chinese involvement, MacArthur was confident that Chinese intervention was unlikely or, if it occurred, could be easily dealt with by U.N. forces.

For China, the U.N. advance toward the Yalu River was a direct threat to its national security. Mao Zedong, the Chinese leader, feared that the presence of U.S. forces so close to China's border could eventually lead to a U.S. invasion. In response, the Chinese government made the decision to enter the Korean War on the side of North Korea, officially under the guise of the People's Volunteer Army (PVA) to avoid a formal declaration of war.

China's strategic objectives during the Korean War were focused on two primary goals. First, China sought to prevent a U.N. victory that would establish a U.S.-allied government right on its border, which could threaten its national security. Second, China aimed to ensure the survival of North Korea as a buffer state, protecting against the expansion of U.S. influence in the region and preserving a strategic zone that would promote regional stability favorable to Chinese interests. By supporting North Korea, China could maintain a degree of control over the geopolitical landscape in East Asia.

Chinese military planners devised a bold strategy to encircle and destroy U.N. forces in North Korea before they could consolidate their gains and advance to the Yalu River. The rugged, mountainous terrain of North Korea, combined with freezing winter conditions, provided a strategic advantage for the Chinese forces, who were more accustomed to the conditions. The People's Volunteer Army (PVA) intended to use stealth, night attacks, and surprise to overwhelm the U.N. forces, many of whom were unprepared for large-scale winter warfare.

The Battle of Chosin Reservoir became the focal point of China's counteroffensive. The PVA aimed to trap the U.S. Marines and other U.N. forces advancing toward the reservoir, cutting off their escape routes and inflicting a devastating defeat that would halt the U.N. advance northward.

The U.N. forces at the Chosin Reservoir were composed primarily of U.S. Marines from the 1st Marine Division, a veteran force known for its discipline and combat effectiveness. These Marines were supported by various U.S. Army units, including elements from the 7th Infantry Division, as well as smaller allied contingents from the United Kingdom and South Korea. However, the U.N. forces faced significant logistical challenges due to their dispersion in small, isolated pockets around the reservoir. The rugged, mountainous terrain of North Korea made it difficult for units to maintain communication and supply lines, with many troops already suffering from shortages of food, ammunition, and winter clothing. The freezing temperatures, which dropped to as low as −30 degrees Fahrenheit (−34 degrees

Celsius), exacerbated these difficulties, with frostbite becoming a major concern.

The Marines had advanced as far as the Chosin Reservoir in their push toward the Yalu River, unaware that Chinese forces were massing in the mountains around them. The mountainous terrain forced the U.N. troops to stretch out over a large area, with their forces split into multiple columns and vulnerable to ambushes and encirclement. Despite these challenges, the U.N. forces remained confident in their ability to continue advancing, underestimating the scale of the Chinese threat.

While U.N. forces focused on their northern advance, the PVA was quietly preparing a large-scale counteroffensive. The PVA, numbering approximately 120,000 troops, moved into the mountainous regions surrounding the Chosin Reservoir under the cover of darkness, making use of the rugged terrain to avoid detection by U.N. reconnaissance. Chinese forces had the advantage of familiarity with the harsh winter conditions and used their stealth and knowledge of the landscape to conceal their movements.

The Chinese plan was to encircle and annihilate the U.N. forces, taking advantage of the dispersed and isolated positions of U.S. and allied troops. PVA commanders intended to launch their assault in a series of coordinated nighttime attacks, exploiting the element of surprise and the U.N. forces' lack of preparation for large-scale winter warfare. The Chinese forces were lightly equipped and highly mobile, allowing them to maneuver quickly through the difficult terrain, while U.N. forces, burdened with vehicles and heavy equipment, found movement much slower.

By November 27, 1950, the PVA had completed their encirclement of U.N. forces at the Chosin Reservoir, setting the stage for one of the most brutal and decisive battles of the Korean War.

Massive Surprise Attack

On the night of November 27, 1950, the PVA launched a massive surprise assault against U.N. forces positioned around the Chosin Reservoir. The Chinese offensive was well-coordinated, with waves of infantry attacking from multiple directions, completely encircling U.N. positions and cutting off their supply lines. The U.N. troops, especially the U.S. 1st Marine Division, were caught off guard, having underestimated the scale and preparedness of the Chinese forces. The PVA used the cover of darkness and the mountainous terrain to their advantage, striking hard and fast.

The Chinese soldiers, lightly armed and equipped, over-whelmed U.N. positions through sheer numbers, despite their own limitations in firepower and equipment. The U.N. forces quickly found themselves isolated in small, scattered defensive positions, with Chinese forces pressing the attack relentlessly throughout the night and into the following days.

The Chosin Reservoir battle was fought under brutal subzero temperatures, with the thermometer plunging as low as -30 degrees Fahrenheit. U.N. soldiers faced extreme cold, which caused frostbite, frozen equipment, and difficulties maintaining basic supplies, such as food and ammunition. The freezing conditions also made movement more difficult, and vehicles often became immobile due to frozen fuel lines. Soldiers were forced to contend with not only the physical toll of the battle but also the punishing cold, which made even basic tasks dangerous.

With their supply lines severed by the Chinese encirclement, the U.S. Marines and other U.N. forces soon began experiencing ammunition shortages. They were forced to ration what little ammunition remained, even as the relentless Chinese attacks continued. The combination of intense fatigue from constant fighting, frostbite, and limited supplies made the battle a desperate fight for survival. Despite these conditions, the Marines organized a disciplined defense, holding their positions while waiting for the opportunity to break out of the Chinese encirclement.

The relentless Chinese assault tested the endurance and morale of the U.N. forces, but it also strained the PVA, which was suffering from its own supply issues and the effects of the extreme cold. Both sides endured incredible hardships, but the Chinese forces pressed their attack with the goal of completely destroying the U.N. units trapped at the reservoir.

Despite being surrounded and heavily outnumbered by Chinese forces, the U.S. Marines demonstrated extraordinary discipline and tactical skill during the Battle of Chosin Reservoir. Rather than succumbing to panic in the face of overwhelming odds, the Marines established well-coordinated defensive perimeters, relying on their superior training and leadership to hold the line. Using artillery fire and well-timed counterattacks, the Marines managed to prevent their positions from being completely overrun.

In several key engagements, the Marines inflicted heavy casualties on the attacking Chinese forces, leveraging their firepower, discipline, and terrain to outmaneuver and hold off the waves of Chinese troops. This ability to maintain cohesion and organization despite the dire circumstances was critical to their survival, as the encirclement could have easily turned into a complete rout without such tactical control.

Air support played a crucial role in aiding the surrounded U.N. forces during the Battle of the Chosin Reservoir. The U.S. Air Force and Navy provided continuous close air support with F4U Corsair fighter-bombers, F-80 Shooting Star jets, and F-51 Mustang fighters, which targeted Chinese positions, supply lines, and troop movements. Additionally, B-26 Invader light bombers and F9F Panther jets conducted bombing runs. These airstrikes disrupted Chinese assaults, delayed their advances, and bought valuable time for the Marines to regroup, preventing the Chinese from fully consolidating their forces.

In addition to airstrikes, aerial resupply missions were critical in keeping the Marines supplied with essential resources. Since land routes were cut off by Chinese forces, the Marines depended on air-dropped supplies, including ammunition, food, and medical necessities, to sustain their defense. These aerial resupplies not only kept the troops fighting but also boosted morale, showing the Marines that despite their isolation, they were not abandoned. Without this air support and resupply, the situation at Chosin Reservoir might have been far more dire for the U.N. forces.

Breaking Through Chinese Roadblocks

After realizing that they were surrounded by vastly superior Chinese forces, U.S. commanders made the strategic decision to execute a fighting retreat toward Hungnam, a port on North Korea's eastern coast, where evacuation by sea could be arranged. The retreat, conducted under constant enemy fire and in the face of some of the harshest winter conditions imaginable, has since become legendary for its discipline and effectiveness. Despite being pursued by the Chinese People's Volunteer Army, U.S. Marines and other U.N. forces broke through numerous Chinese road-blocks and fought off ambushes, ensuring their escape to the port.

This withdrawal was a masterclass in military organization and resilience. Rather than devolving into chaos, the Marines and their allied units remained disciplined, maintaining unit cohesion throughout the retreat, even as they fought in subzero temperatures and under relentless enemy pressure.

The troops involved in this grueling retreat earned the nick-name "The Chosin Few" for their legendary endurance and determination. They fought their way through Chinese ambushes, facing overwhelming numbers of enemy troops, all while suffering from frostbite, exhaustion, and dwindling supplies. Even in retreat, U.N. forces inflicted heavy casualties on the Chinese, proving their tenacity despite the dire situation.

The disciplined nature of the retreat, where U.N. forces repelled attacks and maintained their formation under extreme duress, stands as one of the most impressive military withdrawals in modern history. Though the Battle of Chosin Reservoir was technically a tactical victory for the Chinese, the successful U.N. withdrawal demonstrated the skill and resilience of the U.S. Marines and their allies.

By mid-December 1950, after weeks of intense fighting and a disciplined retreat from the Chosin Reservoir, U.N. forces reached the port city of Hungnam on North Korea's east coast. Here, one of the largest sea evacuations of the Korean War took place. Over 100,000 U.N. troops, including U.S. Marines, U.S. Army units, and South Korean soldiers, were successfully evacuated by sea. The operation also included the rescue of approximately 100,000 Korean refugees, a remarkable feat that prevented further loss of life and avoided a total military disaster. Despite the heavy Chinese pressure, U.N. forces managed to withdraw in an organized fashion, ensuring the safe evacuation of personnel and civilians. The evacuation was covered by continuous naval gunfire and air support, providing protection during the operation.

TACTICAL CHINESE VICTORY

While the Battle of Chosin Reservoir was a tactical victory for Chinese forces, who successfully drove U.N. forces out of North Korea, the price of this victory was significant. The PVA suffered heavy casualties, estimated to be in the tens of thousands. This severely slowed their ability to press farther southward and forced Chinese commanders to reassess their strategy. The heavy losses inflicted on the Chinese during the battle made it clear that while they had gained the upper hand in this engagement, maintaining such high levels of attrition would be unsustainable in the long run.

The Battle of Chosin Reservoir was a turning point in the Korean War. After this battle, U.N. forces were forced to abandon their offensive operations and retreat from North Korea. This shift marked the end of the U.N.'s push toward the Yalu River and initiated a period of defensive operations, culminating in the establishment of a new front line south of the 38th Parallel. While the battle was a tactical victory for Chinese forces, the high casualties they suffered limited their ability to press farther south, leading to a more static phase of the war. The eventual ceasefire and the establishment of the Korean Demilitarized Zone (DMZ) reflected the broader strategic implications of battles like Chosin, which altered the trajectory of the war and shaped its long-term outcome.

Leading a Disciplined Retreat

Lieutenant Colonel Raymond G. Davis commanded the 1st Battalion, 7th Marines during the Battle of Chosin Reservoir, playing a critical role in leading the U.S. Marines through some of the most intense fighting. His battalion was part of the U.N. forces that found themselves surrounded by a massive Chinese counteroffensive in late November 1950. With temperatures dropping as low as -30 degrees Fahrenheit, Davis's men faced not only the relentless Chinese assaults but also the brutal elements that led to widespread frostbite and supply shortages. When temperatures plunged to -30 degrees Fahrenheit, frostbite could occur on exposed skin within ten to thirty minutes, and sometimes faster under severe wind chills.

Davis's leadership was key to the battalion's success in breaking through the encirclement. He led his unit in the famous march to rescue a surrounded Marine company at Toktong Pass in a fierce snowstorm, a vital position that protected the main supply route to the rest of the division. Davis pushed his men through treacherous terrain, under constant enemy fire, and in freezing conditions, ensuring that his battalion held the pass and kept the division's retreat route open. His exceptional leadership and bravery during the Chosin campaign earned him the Medal of Honor.

After the war, Davis continued his military service, rising to the rank of a full general. He served in the Vietnam War and retired from the Marine Corps in 1972. Davis passed away on September 3, 2003, in Conyers, Georgia at eighty-eight years old, leaving behind a legacy of heroism and leadership that makes him one of the most revered figures in U.S. Marine Corps history.

Coordinating the Encirclement

Major General Song Shilun played a pivotal role in orchestrating the Chinese People's Volunteer Army operations during the Battle of Chosin Reservoir. Tasked with leading the 9th Army Group, Song's forces were instrumental in the surprise assault that encircled the U.N. troops, primarily targeting the 1st Marine Division and U.S. Army units. Under his command, the Chinese forces executed a series of coordinated attacks, utilizing the harsh terrain and freezing weather to their advantage. Song's strategy focused on cutting off U.N. supply lines and using human-wave attacks to overwhelm the more mechanized but isolated U.N. forces.

Despite the eventual U.N. breakout and withdrawal, Song's leadership resulted in significant damage to the U.N. forces and forced their retreat from North Korea, marking a strategic victory for the Chinese. However, the PVA also sustained heavy losses due to the extreme cold, lack of adequate winter gear, and the disciplined U.N. defense. These casualties led Chinese leadership to reassess their operational strategies in the Korean War moving forward.

After the war, Song continued to serve in the People's Liberation Army, but the staggering losses his units suffered at Chosin Reservoir haunted him. He passed away in Beijing in September 1991, remembered as a key military leader in one of China's most significant engagements of the Korean War.

THIRD BATTLE OF SEOUL

As the U.N. forces were still engaged in the fierce fighting at Chosin Reservoir, the Chinese People's Volunteer Army (PVA) launched a separate, large-scale offensive aimed at Seoul. This operation, beginning on December 31, 1950, was part of China's broader strategy to capitalize on U.N. disarray and instability following their rapid withdrawal from North Korea. Chinese forces sought to press their advantage and push the U.N. farther south, taking advantage of their thinly stretched lines.

Chinese and North Korean troops crossed the 38th Parallel with the aim of recapturing Seoul. Capturing the city would deal a significant blow to U.N. morale, disrupt logistics, and give the Chinese and North Koreans a stronger negotiating position. The offensive was designed to exploit U.N. vulnerabilities following their retreat from North Korea, as many U.N. units were still regrouping after the Battle of Chosin Reservoir and the Battle of the Ch'ongch'on River (from November 27 to December 13, 1950, and November 25 to December 2, 1950, respectively).

The combined Chinese and North Korean forces launched surprise attacks, using night assaults and mass infantry tactics to disorient U.N. troops and break through their defensive lines. The offensive was marked by its speed, as Chinese and North Korean troops advanced rapidly, aiming to catch the U.N. forces off guard and overwhelm them before they could establish new defensive positions.

U.N. Strategic Withdrawal

U.N. forces, under the overall command of General Douglas MacArthur, faced significant challenges as they attempted to regroup after the retreat from North Korea. Many U.N. units were severely depleted from earlier battles, particularly the U.S. Marines and Army divisions that had fought at Chosin Reservoir. This left U.N. forces stretched thin across a broad front, with insufficient manpower to mount a strong defense of Seoul.

Recognizing the overwhelming strength of the Chinese offensive, U.N. commanders made the difficult decision to withdraw southward to avoid being encircled. Rather than risk a devastating defeat in the streets of Seoul, they chose to preserve their remaining forces and conduct a strategic withdrawal. The decision to abandon Seoul was controversial, as the city had already changed hands once during the war and was a major symbolic and political center for both sides.

By January 4, 1951, U.N. forces had completed their withdrawal from Seoul, marking the second time in six months that the city had fallen to Communist forces. Although the retreat was seen as a tactical necessity to avoid a potential collapse of U.N. forces in South Korea, the loss of Seoul was a significant psychological blow to both the U.N. Command and the South Korean government. However, this retreat also provided U.N. forces the opportunity to regroup and prepare for a future counteroffensive, setting the stage for the next phase of the war.

The Chinese People's Volunteer Army, in coordination with the North Korean People's Army, launched a highly organized and aggressive offensive toward Seoul. The combined forces relied on overwhelming numbers to pressure U.N. troops, capitalizing on their superior manpower compared to the relatively depleted U.N. units. While the PVA led the charge, KPA units reinforced the offensive, contributing to the rapid advance.

The PVA deployed fresh reinforcements, ensuring a continuous flow of troops during the offensive. However, as they pushed farther south, the logistics of maintaining supplies, including ammunition and food, began to strain the advancing forces. These logistical difficulties, exacerbated by rough winter terrain and long supply lines, became a limiting factor, weakening the offensive's momentum as it progressed toward Seoul.

The PVA's strategy revolved around night assaults, which allowed them to exploit their familiarity with the terrain and the relative lack of night-fighting capabilities among U.N. forces. Night attacks also disrupted U.N. defensive lines and sowed confusion, enabling Chinese forces to punch through weak points and continue their rapid advance.

Speed and mobility were central to the Chinese strategy. The PVA aimed to drive U.N. forces from Seoul quickly, hoping to force the U.N. into disarray and potentially extend their gains farther south into South Korea. This focus on speed placed additional pressure on U.N. forces, which were already struggling to regroup after earlier battles in North Korea.

Outnumbered and Stretched Thin

The U.N. forces, including U.S., South Korean, and allied contingents, were spread across a wide front following heavy fighting in North Korea. Recent battles had depleted their strength, making it difficult to mount a robust defense as Chinese and North Korean troops advanced southward. U.N. troops were hampered by logistical challenges, fatigue, and a lack of reserves, which compounded their inability to form a cohesive defensive line in the face of overwhelming enemy numbers.

Efforts to establish a coordinated defense around Seoul were further hindered by the speed of the Chinese advance. The PVA, using rapid mobility and night attacks, managed to exploit gaps in U.N. positions, forcing U.N. commanders to make critical decisions to prevent a total collapse of the front.

As the Chinese and North Korean forces pressed forward, U.N. units began a series of tactical withdrawals, choosing to abandon key defensive positions north of Seoul to avoid encirclement. While the retreat was orderly and allowed U.N. forces to regroup south of the city, it resulted in the loss of vital ground, including several strategic outposts and roads leading into Seoul. This withdrawal was not without challenges, as U.N. forces had to navigate difficult terrain while facing relentless pressure from the advancing PVA. Nevertheless, these withdrawals allowed the U.N. to preserve its fighting strength for future counteroffensives, even at the cost of temporarily losing control of Seoul.

Facing overwhelming Chinese and North Korean forces, U.N. commanders were forced to make the difficult decision to evacuate Seoul by January 4, 1951. Despite efforts to mount a defense, the stretched-thin U.N. forces recognized the city's defense had become untenable. The rapid advance of Chinese and North Korean troops, combined with the logistical challenges and the threat of encirclement, left the U.N. Command with no choice but to withdraw. The fall of the capital of South Korea to Communist forces for the second time in just six months highlighted the volatility of the Korean War.

Although the capture of Seoul on January 4, 1951, represented a significant tactical victory for the PVA and KPA, it came with severe logistical difficulties. The rapid advance southward, combined with fierce resistance from U.N. forces, stretched the Chinese and North Korean supply lines to their breaking point. The mountainous terrain, harsh winter conditions, and the sheer scale of the operation created immense strain on their logistics, leaving many units undersupplied. High casualties, particularly during the push toward Seoul, further weakened the PVA's operational capacity, leading to a depletion of manpower and resources.

Instead of pressing their advantage, the PVA was forced to halt their advance soon after capturing Seoul, giving the U.N. forces time to regroup.

The fall of Seoul dealt a heavy blow to the morale of U.N. forces and the South Korean population, particularly because it marked the second time the city had fallen to Communist forces in just six months. As the capital, Seoul represented the heart of South Korean governance and national identity. The city's loss signaled a major setback in the war effort, damaging both U.N. and South Korean morale. It sparked fears of a prolonged war and raised concerns about the possibility of further Communist advances.

The repeated loss of such a critical and symbolic city weighed heavily on the U.N.'s strategic outlook and public perception of the conflict. However, U.N. leadership, led by General MacArthur, viewed this retreat as a temporary setback. Plans were already underway to regroup, reconstitute forces, and prepare for counteroffensives in early 1951 that would eventually recapture Seoul and stabilize the front lines south of the 38th Parallel, shifting the momentum of the war back in the U.N.'s favor.

FIERCE DEFENSE UNDER FIRE

Captain Harold G. Stover served as a company commander in the U.S. Army's 2nd Infantry Division during the Third Battle of Seoul. As Chinese and North Korean forces pushed southward in late December 1950, Stover's unit was part of the U.N. forces tasked with defending key positions north of Seoul. Facing overwhelming enemy numbers, Stover demonstrated remarkable leadership in holding defensive lines while covering the tactical withdrawal of U.N. forces. His company, despite being outnumbered, was instrumental in slowing the Chinese advance, allowing U.N. commanders to organize an orderly retreat from Seoul.

Stover faced significant challenges as his unit battled not only the numerically superior enemy but also the harsh winter conditions, which made resupply difficult. Ammunition shortages and freezing temperatures compounded the difficulties of defending the rapidly deteriorating front. However, through a combination of tactical ingenuity and unwavering discipline, Stover's leadership helped prevent the disintegration of his unit, earning him a Silver Star for bravery in combat.

After the war, Stover continued his military career, eventually retiring as a lieutenant colonel. He settled in Fort Bragg, North Carolina, where he became a military historian, writing extensively about his experiences during the Korean War. He passed away peacefully in 1995, remembered by his fellow soldiers as a steadfast leader during one of the war's most tumultuous battles.

Determined Assault

Colonel Song Min-jun commanded a battalion within the North Korean People's Army during the Third Battle of Seoul, playing a pivotal role in the Communist offensive to recapture the South Korean capital. Leading a combined force of North Korean and Chinese troops, Song's battalion was responsible for spearheading the assault on U.N. positions near the 38th Parallel in late December 1950. Song's leadership, particularly in the night attacks favored by Chinese and North Korean forces, was crucial in breaking through U.N. defensive lines and pushing the offensive toward Seoul.

The challenges were immense. Colonel Song and his men faced logistical hardships, with supply lines stretched thin as they advanced through rugged terrain. Despite suffering heavy casualties from U.N. airstrikes and artillery, Song maintained the momentum of the assault by using guerrilla tactics, including surprise attacks and ambushes, to disorient the U.N. forces. His battalion was among the first to enter Seoul on January 4, 1951, marking a significant propaganda victory for North Korean forces.

After the war, Colonel Song remained in the North Korean military, eventually rising to the rank of general. He became an influential figure in the post-war reconstruction efforts, focusing on the development of North Korea's defense strategy. He passed away in Pyongyang in 1974, honored as a war hero for his role in the recapture of Seoul.

A Strategic Shift

The push north toward the Yalu River represented a bold but ultimately flawed strategy for the U.N. forces. Following the successful Inchon Landing and the recapture of Seoul, U.N. commanders, particularly General Douglas MacArthur, believed that pushing north would end the war swiftly. However, this over-confidence overlooked the strategic significance of China's prox-imity to the conflict. The entry of the Chinese People's Volunteer Army (PVA) into the war dramatically altered the course of events, catching U.N. forces off guard and forcing a rapid and chaotic retreat.

The Battle of Chosin Reservoir and the Third Battle of Seoul stand as vivid examples of the cost of overreach. At Chosin, U.N. troops faced overwhelming Chinese numbers, brutal winter conditions, and a tactically superior enemy. Despite these disad-vantages, the U.S. Marines' ability to execute a disciplined retreat showcased their resilience, but it underscored the consequences of stretching U.N. forces too thin in the pursuit of a decisive victory.

In the Third Battle of Seoul, Chinese and North Korean forces leveraged their superior numbers and aggressive tactics to push the U.N. out of Seoul for the second time. The loss of the city dealt a blow to U.N. morale, but the Chinese offensive itself soon faltered under logistical strain and exhaustion, leaving both sides weakened and in need of regrouping.

These battles marked the end of the U.N.'s rapid offensives and the beginning of a new phase in the Korean War—one defined by attrition, defensive lines, and grinding engagements.

No longer was the war about swift advances or decisive victories. Instead, it became a protracted struggle where neither side could gain a clear advantage. The intervention of China shattered hopes of a quick resolution, ensuring that the conflict would drag on into a stalemate that would ultimately last until the armistice in 1953. The resilience shown by U.N. forces in retreat, however, proved to be a testament to their fighting spirit, even in the face of overwhelming odds and strategic miscalculations.

CRITICAL BATTLES AND THE FIGHT TO HOLD THE LINE

"They are not gods; they are men, and they can be stopped."

— LIEUTENANT COLONEL JAMES CARNE,
GLOSTERS, BATTLE OF IMJIN RIVER

In 1951, the Korean War shifted from fast-moving offensives to a grueling war of attrition, where defensive operations and key battles along the front lines became crucial in halting enemy advances. U.N. forces, made up of international coalitions, faced relentless Chinese and North Korean offensives in engagements that tested their resilience and tactical adaptability. Battles like Imjin River, Kapyong, and Heartbreak Ridge were marked by fierce trench warfare, intense artillery bombardments, and bloody infantry assaults.

In the midst of these battles, a significant command change underscored the shift in U.N. strategy. In April 1951, President Truman made the controversial decision to relieve General Douglas MacArthur of his command of U.N. forces due to escalating disagreements over military and political strategy in Korea. Truman's choice to replace MacArthur with General Matthew Ridgway reflected the strategic pivot from aggressive offensives to a more sustainable, defensive approach aimed at holding critical positions and preventing further Communist advances.

Under Ridgway's leadership, the U.N. command refocused efforts on fortifying defensive lines, improving troop morale, and applying tactical restraint, which were essential in the intense holding actions that came to define the war's stalemate phase. This change in command emphasized the importance of securing the line, setting the stage for the grueling battles of attrition that followed.

Despite heavy casualties on both sides, these battles were vital in preventing further enemy progress, as U.N. forces fought to hold strategic positions and wear down the Communist forces, solidifying a stalemate that would shape the rest of the war.

BATTLE OF KAPYONG

In early 1951, the Korean War entered a pivotal stage, marked by a shift in tactics and renewed offensives by Chinese and North Korean forces. After months of brutal fighting, U.N. forces, which had initially pushed the North Korean army back to the Chinese border, now found themselves on the defensive. Following China's intervention in late 1950, the conflict had transformed into a more complex and drawn-out struggle, with both sides attempting to gain and maintain control over key areas. One of the most critical locations in this phase was the South Korean capital of Seoul.

Having already changed hands twice since the start of the war, Seoul remained a top strategic objective for both sides. For the Chinese and North Korean forces, capturing the city again would not only disrupt U.N. operations but also deliver a severe psychological blow to the South Korean government and its allies. For the U.N. Command, holding Seoul became a primary objective, and its defense represented a larger effort to halt the Communist advance across the Korean peninsula.

The Battle of Kapyong, which took place between April 22 and April 25, 1951, was a key event in this struggle. This engagement demonstrated the importance of coalition warfare, as Australian, Canadian, and other Commonwealth troops played a decisive role in holding the line against overwhelming Chinese forces, ultimately preventing another fall of Seoul.

The Kapyong Valley was a vital geographical feature northeast of Seoul, west of Chunchon, strategically positioned along one of the main routes the Chinese army needed to secure in order to advance toward the South Korean capital. The valley itself was a natural defensive stronghold, with steep hills and ridges flanking the narrow passageways below. This rugged terrain made it an ideal location for defensive operations, as the high ground allowed smaller, well-positioned forces to control access and funnel enemy troops into vulnerable positions. For U.N. forces, securing the Kapyong Valley was critical in creating a defensive barrier between the advancing Chinese troops and Seoul. A breakthrough here would leave the road to the capital dangerously exposed.

Recognizing the valley's importance, U.N. Command assigned its defense to the 27th British Commonwealth Brigade, an international unit made up of Australian, Canadian, British, and New Zealand troops. This brigade had already earned a reputation for its resilience in earlier battles and was well-prepared for the type of mountainous, defensive warfare that the Korean landscape demanded. Positioned on key ridges overlooking the valley, the Australian 3rd Battalion, Royal Australian Regiment (3 RAR), and the Canadian Princess Patricia's Canadian Light Infantry (PPCLI) took up defensive positions to block the approaching Chinese forces.

The terrain gave the Commonwealth forces a significant

advantage, allowing them to effectively use artillery and defensive tactics to slow the Chinese advance. With the steep hills providing natural cover and observation points, the U.N. forces were able to hold their positions despite being heavily outnumbered by the Chinese troops. This defensive strategy played a crucial role in preventing the fall of the Kapyong Valley and, ultimately, in safeguarding Seoul from yet another attack.

CHINESE OFFENSIVE

In the lead-up to the Battle of Kapyong, Chinese forces had been steadily building their strength, preparing to launch a large-scale assault aimed at breaking through U.N. defensive lines. The Chinese People's Volunteer Army (PVA), which had entered the Korean War in late 1950, had a strategy centered around overwhelming their opponents with superior numbers and surprise tactics. By April 1951, Chinese commanders had identified the Kapyong Valley as a critical point of attack, believing that if they could break through the U.N. forces stationed there, they would have a clear path to Seoul. Their plan was to use the element of surprise, launching assaults under the cover of darkness to catch the U.N. forces off guard with over 20,000 soldiers against the U.N.'s 2,000 men.

On the night of April 22, 1951, the Chinese offensive began. Taking advantage of the rugged terrain and the element of nightfall, the Chinese troops launched a series of coordinated attacks aimed at overrunning the Commonwealth forces positioned in the valley. Thousands of Chinese soldiers, moving quickly and quietly through the hills and valleys, attempted to envelop the U.N. positions, using the cover of darkness to mask their movements and avoid detection.

The Chinese relied on their traditional strategy of mass assaults, attempting to overwhelm the smaller, more dispersed

U.N. units with sheer numbers. In several instances, Chinese forces got dangerously close to penetrating key U.N. defensive lines, creating intense and chaotic fighting in the dark as Commonwealth troops held their ground. Despite the Chinese numerical superiority, the U.N. forces were determined to prevent a breakthrough and fought fiercely throughout the night to maintain their positions.

Faced with a numerically superior and determined enemy, the U.N. forces stationed at Kapyong knew they had to rely on more than just manpower to hold the line. The 27th British Commonwealth Brigade, primarily composed of Australian and Canadian troops, had prepared a strong defensive strategy that focused on leveraging the natural terrain to their advantage. The Australian 3rd Battalion had taken up defensive positions on the high ridges overlooking the valley, giving them a commanding view of the surrounding area. This elevated ground allowed the U.N. forces to spot Chinese movements and coordinate effective artillery and mortar strikes on approaching enemy formations.

One of the key elements of the U.N. defensive plan was the use of coordinated artillery support. Despite being outnumbered, the Commonwealth forces were able to call in concentrated artillery barrages that pounded the advancing Chinese troops. These artillery strikes, coupled with close air support from U.N. aircraft, disrupted the Chinese assaults and inflicted heavy casualties, preventing them from overwhelming the U.N. positions. The Australians and Canadians, positioned in well-fortified locations, also used the terrain to create choke points, forcing the Chinese troops into narrow defiles where they became easy targets for artillery and small arms fire.

Tactical ingenuity played a major role in the U.N. forces' success. Despite their limited numbers, the Australians and Canadians used a combination of terrain, firepower, and coordination to maximize their defensive capabilities. The high ridges not only provided a strong defensive line but also allowed the U.N. forces to direct artillery fire with precision, hitting Chinese troops before they could launch full-scale attacks. The Commonwealth forces remained disciplined and cohesive, even as waves of Chinese soldiers pressed their positions. This effective use of defensive positioning, firepower, and communication ultimately allowed the U.N. forces to hold the line, repelling the Chinese offensive and preventing a breakthrough into the valley.

The Battle of Kapyong was marked by several key moments of intense fighting, where Australian and Canadian troops held their ground against overwhelming Chinese forces. One of the most notable engagements occurred on Hill 504, where the Australian 3rd Battalion, Royal Australian Regiment (3 RAR), faced relentless attacks from waves of Chinese troops. Despite being heavily outnumbered, the Australians managed to maintain their defensive positions through sheer determination, utilizing their artillery support and defensive fortifications to hold off the enemy. The close-quarters combat on Hill 504 was brutal, with Chinese soldiers repeatedly launching assaults in an attempt to overrun the Australians. However, the steadfast defense of the hill became a symbol of the Australians' resilience and tactical prowess.

At the same time, the Canadian Light Infantry (PPCLI) played a crucial role in defending a series of ridges along the Kapyong Valley. The Canadians were positioned at another key point in the valley, and like their Australian counterparts, they faced wave after wave of Chinese attacks during the night. Despite being outnumbered and facing intense pressure, the Canadians held firm, delivering effective small-arms fire and coordinating artillery strikes that devastated Chinese forces trying to advance through the valley. The stand of the PPCLI became one of the defining moments of the battle, showcasing their discipline and courage under fire. Their ability to maintain cohesion and hold their position in the face of overwhelming odds helped prevent the Chinese from breaching U.N. lines and moving farther south.

Throughout the battle, acts of valor and leadership emerged as Commonwealth troops made the most of their defensive positions. Officers and enlisted men alike displayed remarkable bravery, with many stepping up to fill leadership roles in the heat of combat. The coordination between the Australians and Canadians, combined with their effective use of artillery and defensive tactics, proved critical in withstanding the Chinese onslaught.

U.N. Victory

After several days of intense fighting, the U.N. forces at Kapyong successfully repelled the Chinese offensive. Despite being outnumbered and facing continuous attacks, the Australians, Canadians, and other Commonwealth troops managed to hold their ground and prevent the Chinese from breaking through. The turning point in the battle came as Chinese forces, exhausted and suffering heavy casualties, were unable to sustain their assaults. The combined use of artillery, defensive positions, and effective communication between coalition forces played a decisive role in the U.N. victory.

Artillery support was one of the most important factors in the successful defense of Kapyong. The ability of the Commonwealth forces to call in concentrated artillery barrages on Chinese positions disrupted the enemy's momentum and inflicted devastating losses on their troops. In addition, close air support from U.N. aircraft further weakened the Chinese forces, targeting supply lines and troop movements behind enemy lines. The strategic positioning of the U.N. forces on high ridges allowed them to direct artillery fire with precision, amplifying the effectiveness of their defense.

The Battle of Kapyong was a decisive victory for the U.N. coalition and a defining moment in the Korean War. The battle prevented a Chinese breakthrough that would have put Seoul at risk of falling for the third time during the war. Had the Chinese forces succeeded at Kapyong, the path to the South Korean capital would have been left wide open, potentially shifting the momentum of the war back in favor of the Communist forces.

The successful defense of Kapyong provided a significant boost to U.N. morale. After months of back-and-forth fighting, this victory was a much-needed reminder of the coalition's ability to hold the line against overwhelming odds. For the Commonwealth forces, in particular, the battle became a symbol of their courage and resilience. It also reinforced the importance of maintaining strong international alliances, as the cooperation between Commonwealth troops and their U.N. allies proved crucial in safeguarding South Korea from further enemy advances.

The aftermath of the Battle of Kapyong saw both sides suffering heavy casualties. While the exact number of Chinese casualties remains unclear, it is estimated that they lost thousands of troops in the failed attempt to break through U.N. lines. The Commonwealth forces also sustained losses, though their strategic defensive positions and effective use of artillery helped minimize the toll to 59 deaths and around 120 wounded. After days of intense fighting, the Chinese forces were forced to withdraw, unable to capitalize on their initial momentum. This retreat marked the end of their immediate threat to Seoul and set the stage for a more stabilized front line in the months to come.

The bravery and gallantry of the Australian and Canadian troops were widely recognized in the aftermath of the battle. Many soldiers were awarded honors for their actions, including the Military Cross and the Distinguished Conduct Medal. The contributions of the Commonwealth forces were celebrated not only within their own nations but across the broader U.N. coalition, as their role in the battle was seen as a key factor in preventing a major defeat.

The long-term consequences of the Battle of Kapyong were significant for both the U.N. and Chinese forces. For the U.N., the victory solidified their defensive capabilities and demonstrated their ability to hold key positions, even under intense pressure. It also strengthened the resolve of the coalition, proving that international cooperation could overcome even the most daunting challenges. For the Chinese, the failure to break through at Kapyong was a major setback, highlighting the limitations of their mass-assault tactics against well-defended positions. This battle underscored the difficulty of achieving decisive breakthroughs in the rugged terrain of Korea, forcing the Chinese to reconsider their approach in future engagements.

The Steadfast Defender of Kapyong

Lieutenant Mike Levy, born in Bombay in 1925 to British parents, led an unusual life marked by courage and resilience. As a young boy, his family moved to Shanghai, where he developed a passion for sports. His early experiences of conflict began in 1941 when the Japanese invaded Shanghai, leading to his internment in Lunghua Civil Assembly Camp. However, Levy escaped in 1944, embarking on a two-thousand-mile journey across occupied China to India. His knowledge of Chinese culture earned him a place in the British Special Operations Executive, where he served in Force 136, participating in guerrilla warfare and receiving a Mentioned in Despatches for his bravery.

When the Korean War erupted in 1950, Levy, now a restaurateur in Vancouver, joined Canada's Special Force as a lieutenant with the 2nd Battalion, Princess Patricia's Canadian Light Infantry (2 PPCLI). During the Battle of Kapyong on April 24-

25, 1951, Levy commanded 10 Platoon on Hill 677 as Chinese forces launched relentless assaults against the Canadian defenses. Recognizing the dire situation of D Company, Levy made a bold decision to call in artillery fire on his own position to repel the attackers. This risk proved pivotal as the New Zealand artillery rained shells down on the Chinese enemy, ultimately halting their advance without any Canadian casualties from the friendly fire.

Though Levy's heroism went largely unrecognized, his contributions during Kapyong remain a testament to his leadership and bravery. Levy married in 1951 and had four children. He retired from service in 1974 at forty-nine and passed away in 2007, leaving behind a legacy of valor in the face of overwhelming odds.

THE RELENTLESS ASSAULT LEADER

Lieutenant Park Jun-ho was a company commander in the North Korean People's Army, leading a contingent of troops assigned to support the Chinese People's Volunteer Army during the Battle of Kapyong. Park's role was to spearhead night raids and coordinate with Chinese units to outflank and overwhelm U.N. positions, focusing on exploiting gaps in the Commonwealth defenses. Tasked with navigating the rugged terrain under the cover of darkness, Park led several assaults against the Australian and Canadian forces stationed on the ridges, hoping to break their defensive line and open a path to Seoul.

The greatest challenge Park faced was the well-coordinated artillery and defensive tactics employed by the Commonwealth forces, which inflicted heavy casualties on his unit and disrupted his plans for a quick breakthrough. Despite multiple failed attempts to breach the defenses, Park demonstrated unwavering determination, rallying his troops and organizing small, targeted attacks in hopes of wearing down the U.N. defenses. However, the relentless artillery fire and air support proved insurmountable, and Park's unit was eventually forced to retreat along with the rest of the KPA forces.

After the war, Lieutenant Park Jun-ho was promoted to a training position within the North Korean military, where he taught infantry tactics and specialized in night combat operations. He continued to serve the North Korean military in various roles until his retirement in the 1970s. Park passed away in 1992 in Pyongyang, remembered by his peers as a resilient officer who led by example, even in the face of overwhelming odds.

BATTLE OF IMJIN RIVER

In April 1951, the Korean War was entering a crucial phase as the Chinese People's Volunteer Army launched its Spring Offensive, a large-scale attempt to push U.N. forces south and recapture the South Korean capital of Seoul. This offensive was a coordinated effort to overwhelm U.N. positions through a series of simultaneous attacks across multiple fronts. While Australian and Canadian forces were engaged at the Battle of Kapyong to the east, British troops of the 29th Infantry Brigade found themselves fighting a critical battle along the Imjin River, located approximately thirty miles north of Seoul. The river was a natural defensive barrier, making it a key line of defense for U.N. forces trying to prevent a Chinese breakthrough that could potentially lead to the fall of Seoul for the third time during the war.

The strategic importance of the Imjin River lay in its position as one of the last major geographical obstacles before the Chinese could advance on Seoul. If the Chinese succeeded in crossing the river and overwhelming the British forces stationed there, the road to the South Korean capital would be open, and the U.N. forces would be forced into a desperate retreat. The British 29th Infantry Brigade, made up of several distinguished regiments, including the 1st Battalion each of the Gloucestershire Regiment (Glosters), the Royal Ulster Rifles (Rifles), and the

Northumberland Fusiliers (Fusiliers), was tasked with holding the line along the Imjin River. Their mission was clear: prevent the Chinese from breaking through, delay their advance as long as possible, and allow U.N. forces farther south to regroup and establish a stronger defensive perimeter around Seoul.

THE CHINESE OFFENSIVE

The Chinese objectives during the Spring Offensive were ambitious. Having successfully pushed U.N. forces southward in previous campaigns, the Chinese leadership was determined to seize Seoul once again, hoping to inflict a major defeat on the U.N. coalition and force political negotiations on more favorable terms. The offensive, which began in late April, was part of a broader strategy to overwhelm U.N. defenses through sheer numbers and rapid, coordinated attacks. The PVA and KPA had amassed a force vastly outnumbering the British and other U.N. troops stationed along the Imjin River by roughly five to one. The Chinese strategy involved crossing the river under the cover of night and launching a surprise assault on the British positions, exploiting the element of surprise to overpower the U.N. forces before they could effectively respond.

On April 22, 1951, the Chinese launched their initial attack, focusing on multiple crossing points along the Imjin River. The PVA forces moved quickly and quietly under the cover of darkness, attempting to infiltrate British lines and bypass strong defensive positions. The 29th Infantry Brigade, though aware of the looming threat, found themselves facing overwhelming numbers, with Chinese soldiers attacking in waves and using the terrain to their advantage. The goal of the Chinese offensive was not only to break through the British defenses but also to encircle and isolate the U.N. troops, cutting them off from reinforcements and forcing a retreat that would leave Seoul vulnerable to capture. As the battle progressed, it became clear that the British forces were in for one of the most intense and critical engagements of the war.

British Defensive Strategy

The defense of the Imjin River was entrusted to the 29th Infantry Brigade, a unit composed of three, highly trained British regiments, an Irish regiment, and a Belgian and Luxemburg battalion. These forces were strategically positioned as a twelve-mile front along the river, with the aim of delaying the Chinese advance long enough for U.N. forces to regroup and strengthen defenses farther south. The rugged terrain and riverbank provided natural defensive advantages, but the overwhelming number of Chinese troops posed a severe challenge.

The British forces adopted a defensive strategy that relied heavily on well-coordinated artillery and small arms fire. Artillery units were positioned to provide supporting fire to the infantry, and forward observation posts were established to identify enemy movements and direct firepower with precision. The use of artillery was crucial in disrupting the Chinese waves of attack, softening enemy positions, and breaking up large concentrations of advancing troops. Despite being heavily outnumbered, the British forces were able to inflict significant casualties on the Chinese through these coordinated efforts.

In addition to their defensive positioning, communication with U.N. Command and neighboring forces was essential to the British strategy. The 29th Infantry Brigade's role was not only to delay the Chinese advance but also to ensure that the retreat and withdrawal southward were timed effectively to avoid being overrun. As the battle intensified, maintaining communication lines under fire became increasingly difficult, but was critical to coordinating the eventual retreat. The ability to hold out long enough while relaying vital information to U.N. commanders ensured that the Chinese advance would not go unchecked, even if the British positions were eventually overrun.

One of the most significant engagements during the Battle of Imjin River took place at Hill 235, later known as "Gloster Hill." The Gloucestershire Regiment, tasked with holding this strategic high ground, found itself isolated and surrounded by overwhelming Chinese forces. As wave after wave of Chinese soldiers attacked, the Glosters, under the command of Lieutenant Colonel James Carne, mounted a determined defense. Despite being cut off from the rest of the brigade and facing dwindling supplies, the regiment held its ground, repelling Chinese assaults for as long as possible.

The defense of Gloster Hill was marked by acts of extraordinary courage and discipline. Lieutenant Colonel Carne's leadership was instrumental in keeping morale high, even as the situation grew increasingly dire. He personally led counterattacks and ensured that his men continued to fight despite the overwhelming odds against them. The desperate fighting on Gloster Hill became a symbol of British resilience during the Korean War, as the Glosters held their position until they were left with no choice but to attempt a breakout or face capture.

The final stand of the Glosters, along with the efforts of the Royal Ulster Rifles and the Northumberland Fusiliers elsewhere along the line, delayed the Chinese advance long enough for U.N. forces to consolidate their defenses farther south. Though the Gloucestershire Regiment was ultimately surrounded and many of its members captured, their heroic defense is remembered as one of the most gallant actions of the Korean War, demonstrating the bravery and resolve of British soldiers under immense pressure. The ability of these troops to hold out despite being outnumbered contributed significantly to the broader U.N. effort to repel the Chinese Spring Offensive.

THE BRITISH WITHDRAWAL

After several days of fierce fighting along the Imjin River, it became clear to the British command that holding their positions any longer was untenable. The Chinese had committed overwhelming numbers to the assault, and despite the gallant defense by the 29th Infantry Brigade, the British forces were being steadily pushed back. Faced with encirclement and dwindling supplies, the decision was made to conduct a strategic withdrawal. While the British troops had fought valiantly, their primary objective—to delay the Chinese advance long enough for U.N. forces to regroup farther south—had been achieved.

The withdrawal was carefully coordinated, with priority given to extracting as many surviving troops as possible. Despite heavy casualties, including the loss of the Gloucestershire Regiment, the retreat was carried out in an orderly fashion. British forces made use of their defensive positions to slow down the Chinese as much as possible, even during the retreat, allowing time for the safe extraction of many soldiers. The Royal Ulster Rifles and Northumberland Fusiliers, in particular, covered the retreat, engaging the advancing Chinese troops in rear-guard actions. This disciplined withdrawal allowed the U.N. forces to regroup and consolidate their defenses farther south of the Imjin River, preventing a complete breakthrough.

Although the British forces sustained significant losses, their ability to hold out for as long as they did and execute a well-organized retreat ensured that the Chinese advance was delayed long enough for the larger U.N. forces to prepare for future engagements.

The Battle of Imjin River proved to be a strategically important action in the broader context of the Korean War. While the Chinese forces were ultimately able to push past the British defenses, the resistance put up by the 29th Infantry Brigade significantly slowed the Chinese momentum. This delay prevented an immediate break-through toward Seoul, giving U.N. forces time to regroup, reestablish defensive positions, and prepare for the next phase of the war. Without the determined stand of the 29th Infantry Brigade's troops, particularly the Gloucestershire Regiment, the Chinese might have advanced much more rapidly, potentially compromising the defense of Seoul and further threatening the U.N. position in South Korea.

The loss of the Gloucestershire Regiment, which was encircled and forced to surrender after exhausting all their ammunition and supplies, was a major blow. However, their sacrifice played a key role in preventing the Chinese from achieving a more significant victory. The regiment's heroic last stand became a symbol of British resolve and military professionalism, earning respect and admiration both within the Commonwealth and among the wider U.N. forces. Despite the regiment's capture, their efforts—along with those of the Royal Ulster Rifles, Northumberland Fusiliers, the 8th King's Royal Irish Hussars, the Belgian Volunteer Corp, and the additional ROK, Filipino, and Common Wealth soldiers in the battle—allowed the U.N. to consolidate its defenses and regroup for future operations.

In the aftermath of the battle, U.N. forces were able to stabilize the front lines, preventing the Chinese Spring Offensive from achieving its full potential. The battle also highlighted the value of coalition forces in the Korean War, demonstrating how international cooperation and coordination could lead to effective resistance against a numerically superior enemy. The Battle of Imjin River, though a tactical withdrawal for the British, was a strategic success for the U.N. coalition, as it contributed to halting the Chinese advance and maintaining the integrity of the U.N. defense in Korea.

Legacy of the Battle

The Battle of Imjin River stands as one of the most celebrated actions of the British Army during the Korean War, and its legacy has endured in both military and historical circles. The courage and resilience displayed by the British 29th Infantry Brigade in the face of overwhelming Chinese forces captured the imagination of both contemporaries and future generations. The brigade's ability to delay a vastly superior enemy force long enough for U.N. forces to regroup was a testament to the professionalism, discipline, and fighting spirit of the British Army.

The bravery and endurance of the soldiers involved did not go unrecognized. Numerous medals and honors were awarded to members of the 29th Infantry Brigade for their extraordinary conduct during the battle. Lieutenant Colonel James Carne, who led the Gloucestershire Regiment's heroic stand at Hill 235, was awarded the Victoria Cross for his leadership and gallantry, and many other soldiers received the Military Cross, Distinguished Conduct Medal, and other awards for their roles in the fierce fighting. The hill itself, later named "Gloster Hill," became a site of commemoration, with memorials established to honor the sacrifice and valor of the men who fought there.

The Battle of Imjin River became a source of pride for the British Army, showcasing its ability to hold its own within the broader U.N. coalition in Korea. The valor displayed during the battle is regularly commemorated, and the story of the Gloucestershire Regiment's final stand remains an enduring symbol of British military tradition and bravery.

GLOSTER HERO AT IMJIN RIVER

In April 1951, during the Korean War, Captain Maurice "Mike" Harvey commanded D Company in the Royal Hampshire Regiment, attached to the Gloucestershire Regiment, and played a pivotal role in the Battle of the Imjin River. Facing overwhelming numbers from the PVA, D Company defended the high ground above the Imjin. Under the cover of darkness on April 22, the

Chinese launched relentless assaults, forcing Harvey's men to fight fiercely to hold their position.

Despite initially repelling the enemy, escalating pressure and a lack of reinforcements led to an order for Harvey's company to withdraw. After forty-eight hours of intense combat, he instructed his men to destroy redundant weapons, distribute their remaining ammunition, and lead the survivors down a perilous slope strewn with fallen soldiers. Reflecting on the withdrawal, he noted, "The silence was eerie after the rattle of small arms fire and the thunder of bombs and shells in that ring of steel and fire on Gloster Hill." While navigating treacherous terrain, his men came under machine-gun fire in a narrow defile, and Harvey recognized that had the enemy concentrated their fire, none of his men would have survived.

Ultimately, Harvey and about forty other survivors from the Glosters returned to U.N. lines, although many from his battalion had been captured. Tragically, during their trek, some UN tank crews mistook his mud-covered men for enemy soldiers, resulting in friendly fire that killed six members of his company.

For his bravery, Harvey was awarded the Military Cross. After the war, Harvey continued to serve in various capacities, becoming a respected leader and consultant until his retirement in 1978. Harvey passed away in 2007, remembered for his heroism.

TACTICAL LEADER OF THE IMJIN RIVER OFFENSIVE

Colonel Ri Yong-sik, a senior officer in the North Korean People's Army, played a pivotal role in coordinating the Chinese and North Korean offensive at the Imjin River. As one of the key tactical leaders overseeing operations in the region, Ri was tasked with directing multiple waves of Chinese and North Korean forces in their attempt to break through the British defenses. His primary responsibility was managing troop movements, selecting vulnerable points along the river for night assaults, and ensuring that the supply lines remained open despite U.N. artillery strikes.

Ri Yong-sik faced immense challenges during the battle. The rugged terrain along the Imjin River made it difficult to maintain supply chains and reinforce positions, especially under the constant threat of U.N. airstrikes and artillery barrages. Despite outnumbering the British troops, Ri's forces struggled to capitalize on their numerical superiority due to the U.N. coalition's well-coordinated defense and superior firepower. Ri worked to rally his troops in the face of heavy casualties, leading from the front and personally overseeing several of the river crossings to inspire his men.

After the war, Colonel Ri Yong-sik was promoted within the NKPA and took on the role of a military instructor, training younger officers in guerrilla tactics and infantry operations. He remained a respected figure in the North Korean military until his death in 1985 in Pyongyang, remembered for his leadership during some of the most critical battles of the Korean War.

BATTLE OF BLOODY RIDGE

By mid-1951, the Korean War had shifted from a mobile conflict to a stalemate, with the front lines largely stabilizing along the 38th Parallel. Both U.N. and Communist forces found themselves entrenched in defensive positions, unable to make significant territorial gains despite continued fighting. As a result, the war increasingly focused on capturing strategically valuable terrain, particularly high ground that could provide crucial advantages for observation and artillery targeting. Control of these ridges and hills became essential for both sides, as they offered commanding views of enemy positions and allowed for more accurate artillery fire, which was vital in a war where artillery had become the dominant form of firepower.

One of the first and most brutal hill battles fought over these critical positions was the Battle of Bloody Ridge, which took place between August and September 1951. U.N. forces, primarily led by the U.S. 2nd Infantry Division, launched repeated assaults against well-entrenched North Korean troops occupying the ridge. This battle marked the beginning of a series of intense engagements where both sides would suffer heavy casualties for minimal territorial gain. The Battle of Bloody Ridge epitomized the grinding, attrition-based warfare that would come to define much of the conflict in its later stages, as both U.N. and North Korean forces fought fiercely to secure or deny control of these strategic high points.

The geographical and tactical significance of Bloody Ridge cannot be overstated. Rising sharply above the surrounding terrain, the ridge provided whoever held it with a commanding view of the battlefield, making it a key observation post for directing artillery fire and monitoring enemy movements. From this elevated position, North Korean forces could observe U.N. positions in the valley below, giving them the ability to adjust their defenses and prepare for U.N. assaults. For the U.N. forces, capturing Bloody Ridge was critical to breaking through the North Korean defensive line and gaining control of the area's high ground. Securing the ridge would not only provide better observation points but would also improve the accuracy and effectiveness of U.N. artillery strikes, which were essential in reducing North Korean fortifications.

The U.N. objective was straightforward: seize Bloody Ridge to weaken the North Korean defensive network and pave the way for further advances. However, the North Korean defense strategy was equally clear. They understood the importance of holding the ridge to prevent the U.N. from gaining the tactical advantage of high ground. The North Koreans had fortified their positions on the ridge, creating a series of bunkers, trenches, and machine-gun nests designed to make any assault costly and diffi-cult. Their determination to hold Bloody Ridge at all costs reflected the broader strategy of both sides at this point in the war—secure vital terrain, even if it meant heavy casualties, to prevent the other side from gaining a critical advantage in the war of attrition.

U.N. Offensive Strategy

The U.N. offensive at Bloody Ridge was spearheaded by the U.S. 2nd Infantry Division, a battle-hardened unit that had already played a significant role in earlier stages of the Korean War. Tasked with capturing the ridge, the 2nd Infantry Division adopted a strategy of relentless frontal assaults supported by air strikes and heavy artillery bombardments. Given the entrenched nature of the North Korean defenses, U.N. commanders knew that a sustained, multi-pronged approach would be required to dislodge the enemy from their well-fortified positions.

The offensive involved repeated direct attacks on North Korean positions, with infantry forces advancing up the ridge under cover of air and artillery fire. U.S. bombers and fighter planes were used to strike North Korean bunkers and machine-gun nests from the air, while artillery units positioned below the ridge pounded enemy positions continuously to soften up their defenses. However, the North Korean forces had taken advantage of the rugged terrain, digging into the steep hillsides and creating interconnected bunkers that were difficult to destroy even with concentrated firepower.

The challenges faced by the U.N. forces were immense. The terrain itself was a formidable obstacle, as the steep slopes of Bloody Ridge made it difficult for U.N. troops to advance without exposing themselves to heavy enemy fire. The North Koreans had heavily fortified their positions, constructing deep bunkers, trenches, and concealed machine-gun posts that allowed them to inflict heavy casualties on U.N. forces during each assault. Additionally, the North Koreans launched relentless counterattacks, often under the cover of night, in an effort to push back the advancing U.N. troops and hold the ridge. Despite superior firepower, the U.N. forces found themselves in a grinding, attritional battle where progress was slow and came at great cost.

The initial assaults on Bloody Ridge began in late August 1951, and from the outset, the U.N. forces encountered fierce resistance from the entrenched North Korean defenders. North Korean troops, who had prepared for the assault, met the U.N. attacks with intense machine-gun fire, mortar shells, and small-arms fire from well-concealed positions along the ridge. The U.N. forces, despite their superior firepower, struggled to gain a foothold on the ridge due to the rugged terrain and the sheer tenacity of the North Korean defenders.

The battle quickly escalated into brutal, close-quarters combat, as U.N. infantry units attempted to clear out North Korean bunkers and trenches one by one. The fighting was intense, with high casualties on both sides as the U.N. troops fought to secure key points along the ridge. North Korean forces, aware of the strategic value of the high ground, resisted fiercely, launching frequent counterattacks to regain lost positions. This back-and-forth struggle resulted in heavy losses, as neither side was willing to concede the vital terrain.

Air strikes, artillery, and mortar fire played a central role in the U.N. strategy to weaken the North Korean defenses. U.S. aircraft dropped bombs on fortified positions, while artillery units fired incessantly at the North Korean bunkers. Despite these efforts, many of the North Korean positions remained intact, forcing U.N. troops into deadly assaults against well-protected enemy positions. North Korean forces, though outnumbered and outgunned, displayed remarkable resilience and frequently counterattacked, often forcing U.N. troops to retreat and regroup.

The battle dragged on for weeks, with U.N. forces gradually gaining ground, but at a tremendous cost in lives. Every advance was met with fierce North Korean resistance, and the steep, rocky terrain only added to the difficulties faced by the U.N. soldiers. The grueling nature of the battle exemplified the shift toward attrition warfare, where victory was measured in inches and the price of each gain was paid in blood.

North Korean Withdrawal

After weeks of relentless and grueling combat, the U.N. forces, led by the U.S. 2nd Infantry Division, finally achieved a breakthrough at Bloody Ridge. The combination of repeated frontal assaults, concentrated artillery barrages, and sustained air support gradually wore down the North Korean defenders. Despite the determined resistance and numerous counterattacks by the North Korean forces, the sheer firepower and persistence of the U.N. troops eventually forced the North Koreans to abandon their positions. The U.N. victory, however, came at a tremendous cost, as both sides had suffered heavy casualties during the intense fighting.

Realizing that they could no longer hold Bloody Ridge without incurring catastrophic losses, the North Korean forces made the strategic decision to withdraw from the ridge and regroup at nearby Hill 931. This hill, located just a few kilometers away, made up part of Heartbreak Ridge and provided another formidable defensive position. The North Koreans quickly entrenched themselves there, preparing for the next phase of combat. Though the U.N. forces had succeeded in capturing Bloody Ridge, the territorial gain was minimal, underscoring the brutal reality of attrition warfare in the Korean War. The hard-fought victory highlighted the staggering human cost of seizing even a small patch of land in the mountainous terrain of Korea.

The Battle of Bloody Ridge became a grim symbol of the Korean War's grinding and bloody nature. Both sides sustained heavy casualties, with thousands of soldiers killed or wounded during the weeks of combat. For the U.N. forces, the capture of the ridge represented a tactical victory, but it also laid bare the limitations of such successes in the context of the broader conflict. The North Koreans, though forced to retreat, had not been decisively defeated, and their quick regrouping at Hill 931 indicated that the war of attrition was far from over.

As the war became increasingly static, with entrenched positions and fortified hills dominating the landscape, it became clear that future battles would be similarly costly and hard-fought. Gaining and holding high ground was critical, but doing so required immense sacrifices. The Battle of Bloody Ridge demonstrated the futility of seeking quick victories in such rugged terrain, as every inch gained came at a severe human cost.

The aftermath of Bloody Ridge set the stage for future confrontations, most notably the Battle of Heartbreak Ridge, which took place shortly afterward as the North Koreans fortified their positions on Hill 931. The fighting would continue with the same intensity, further emphasizing the war's brutal shift toward attrition and the high price paid by both sides in the struggle for control of Korea's strategic high ground.

LEGACY OF THE BATTLE

The Battle of Bloody Ridge came to symbolize the stalemate phase of the Korean War, during which both sides repeatedly fought over hills and ridges with little to no strategic advancement. The brutal fighting on the steep slopes of Bloody Ridge exemplified the type of attrition warfare that had come to dominate the conflict by 1951. Neither the U.N. forces nor the North Korean army could gain a decisive edge, leading to a prolonged war of endurance in which controlling even the smallest patch of high ground became a costly and difficult endeavor.

The high cost of the battle highlighted the challenges of achieving meaningful victories in the rugged Korean terrain. The terrain itself—characterized by steep ridges, thick vegetation, and narrow valleys—made it extremely difficult for either side to launch large-scale maneuvers or hold newly captured positions for long. This led to battles where both sides would endure heavy casualties for minimal territorial gains. Bloody Ridge became a testament to the futility of such battles, where lives were lost in exchange for a few yards of ground, underscoring the grinding nature of the war.

The perseverance and sacrifice of the U.S. 2nd Infantry Division, which bore the brunt of the fighting during the battle, are commemorated as a symbol of dedication and resolve. Despite facing fierce resistance, the division fought tirelessly to dislodge the North Korean forces, exemplifying the bravery and endurance required of soldiers in such a grueling conflict. Their efforts and those of their allied units left a lasting legacy in military history, serving as a reminder of the resilience required in attrition warfare.

The Battle of Bloody Ridge holds a significant place in the broader narrative of the Korean War. It epitomized the shift to attrition warfare, where battles were fought over small pieces of strategic terrain at an enormous human cost. The weeks of brutal fighting on the ridge served as a reminder of the challenges faced by both U.N. and North Korean forces as they sought to gain control over Korea's rugged landscape.

The battle demonstrated the difficulty of securing lasting victories in such an unforgiving environment. Despite their success in capturing Bloody Ridge, U.N. forces found that even tactical victories often led to little strategic gain, as the North Koreans regrouped and fortified nearby positions, setting the stage for more bloody confrontations. The legacy of Bloody Ridge serves as a reflection on the nature of attrition warfare and the immense sacrifices required to achieve even the smallest of victories in the Korean War's harsh, mountainous terrain.

Tactical Leader at Bloody Ridge

Captain Everett P. Smith, a company commander in the U.S. 2nd Infantry Division, played a critical role in the Battle of Bloody Ridge. Tasked with leading repeated assaults against the entrenched North Korean positions, Smith demonstrated exceptional tactical leadership in one of the Korean War's most grueling engagements. Under his command, his company was responsible for securing a key section of the ridge, which required them to advance up steep, heavily defended slopes while under constant enemy fire. Smith coordinated air and artillery support, directing firepower to weaken enemy bunkers before sending his men into intense close-quarters combat to clear trenches and fortified positions.

One of the greatest challenges Smith faced was the difficult terrain, which favored the North Korean defenders. The enemy had established well-concealed machine-gun nests and bunkers that withstood artillery bombardments, forcing Smith and his men into repeated, high-casualty assaults. Despite these obstacles, Smith's leadership and determination ensured that his company was able to secure several crucial points on the ridge, contributing to the eventual U.N. victory. His ability to maintain morale and cohesion in the face of overwhelming odds was a key factor in his company's success during the battle.

After the war, Captain Smith continued his service in the U.S. Army, eventually rising to the rank of colonel. He served in various capacities during the Cold War, helping to modernize U.S. infantry tactics based on his experiences in Korea. Smith retired from the military in the late 1970s and spent his later years in Seattle, Washington, where he passed away in 1994. His service at Bloody Ridge was remembered for its exemplary courage and leadership under fire.

Defenders of Bloody Ridge

During the Battle of Bloody Ridge, North Korean People's Army units, including the 6th, 12th, and 13th Divisions, led the defense of strategically crucial high ground against persistent U.N. assaults. Entrusted with delaying the UN forces, the North Korean commanders established an extensive network of bunkers, trenches, and machine-gun nests along the rugged ridge slopes. This fortified position allowed them to withstand continuous artillery and aerial bombardment while leveraging the challenging terrain to slow the advancing U.N. troops. Despite being heavily outnumbered and under near-constant fire, the KPA divisions used the ridge's natural defenses to launch counterattacks, temporarily halting the U.N. advance.

As the battle continued, the KPA divisions faced severe logistical challenges. Supply lines were under constant bombardment, making it difficult for their commanders to replenish essential resources like ammunition and medical supplies. The KPA troops were often cut off from reinforcements, which forced their leaders to ration supplies carefully and hold their ground under extreme duress. Despite these hardships, the KPA men fought tenaciously, mounting counterattacks that pushed back U.N. forces momentarily and showcased their resilience and devotion even as casualties mounted.

After weeks of grueling combat and substantial losses, the KPA commanders were forced to withdraw from Bloody Ridge to Hill 931, regrouping for future defensive actions. Their defense is remembered as a testament to the determination and sacrifice of KPA leaders in holding strategically valuable positions, despite the overwhelming odds against them.

BATTLE OF HEARTBREAK RIDGE

Following the intense fighting at Bloody Ridge, the Korean War entered a new phase of grueling hill battles, with U.N. forces and North Korean troops both vying for control of strategic high ground. One of the most significant of these engagements was the Battle of Heartbreak Ridge, fought between September 13 and October 15, 1951. Situated near the 38th Parallel, Heartbreak Ridge was a key position in the mountainous terrain of North Korea, and both sides recognized its importance for commanding the surrounding region. The ridge had become a critical defensive stronghold for the North Koreans, who used it to observe U.N. movements and direct artillery fire.

For the U.N. forces, led by the U.S. 2nd Infantry Division, the capture of Heartbreak Ridge was essential for weakening the North Korean defenses in the area and securing a tactical advantage. Controlling the ridge would provide U.N. forces with vital observation points and improve the accuracy of artillery and air strikes. Furthermore, it would open the door for future offensives, potentially allowing U.N. forces to push deeper into North Korean territory. However, capturing Heartbreak Ridge would not be easy, as the North Koreans had heavily fortified their positions, turning the battle into a grinding and costly affair. The significance of the ridge and the intensity of the fighting made Heartbreak Ridge one of the defining battles of the later stages of the Korean War.

Heartbreak Ridge held immense geographic and tactical value in the context of the Korean War. The ridge, with its steep slopes and commanding views, offered a natural defensive position for the North Korean forces. From this elevated vantage point, the North Koreans could monitor U.N. troop movements in the valleys below, giving them a significant advantage in terms of reconnaissance and artillery targeting. Holding the ridge allowed them to control access to the surrounding area and disrupt U.N. supply lines and communication networks. Its strategic location near the 38th Parallel also made it a key point in the ongoing struggle to gain control over the demilitarized zone.

For the U.N. forces, the capture of Heartbreak Ridge was a critical objective. By taking control of the high ground, the U.N. could neutralize the North Korean observation posts and gain a better position to direct artillery fire and air strikes. This would not only weaken the North Korean defensive network but also provide the U.N. with a launching point for future operations aimed at driving deeper into enemy-held territory. The battle was part of a broader U.N. strategy to break through the entrenched North Korean lines and regain momentum in the war.

On the other hand, the North Korean defense strategy was centered on holding Heartbreak Ridge at all costs. The North Koreans had constructed a network of fortified bunkers, trenches, and machine-gun nests along the ridge, making it extremely diffi-cult for U.N. forces to dislodge them. Their goal was to prevent further U.N. advances, maintain control over the region, and buy time for reinforcements to arrive. The battle for Heartbreak Ridge would become a symbol of the Korean War's shift toward attrition warfare, where both sides suffered heavy casualties in the fight to control critical, yet limited, terrain.

U.N. Offensive Strategy

The U.N. offensive at Heartbreak Ridge was primarily led by the U.S. 2nd Infantry Division, supported by the French Battalion, a highly respected unit within the U.N. forces. Together, they spear-headed the assault on the well-fortified North Korean positions atop the ridge. Given the difficult terrain and the entrenched enemy defenses, U.N. commanders understood that success would require a combined arms approach. This meant coordi-nating infantry assaults with powerful artillery barrages and precision air strikes, all working together to weaken the North Korean defenses before ground troops could advance.

The role of artillery was central to the U.N. strategy. Artillery units continuously pounded the ridge, targeting North Korean bunkers, machine-gun nests, and defensive trenches in an effort to disrupt their lines and reduce their ability to launch counterattacks. Meanwhile, U.S. aircraft conducted air strikes to hit enemy positions that were out of reach of artillery fire. The combination of air and artillery support was designed to soften the enemy before the infantry moved in, though this approach was not without its challenges.

The rugged terrain of Heartbreak Ridge had three main peaks along its spine: Hill 894, Hill 931, and Hill 851. Its steep slopes and rocky outcrops made it incredibly difficult for U.N. forces to make significant advances. Soldiers had to fight for every inch of ground, often navigating narrow, exposed pathways where they were vulnerable to enemy fire. The North Koreans had also constructed formidable fortifications, including deep bunkers and interlocking trench systems, which provided them with significant protection from artillery and air strikes. As a result, U.N. forces had to launch multiple frontal assaults, with each attack encountering fierce resistance from the well-prepared North Korean troops. This led to high casualties and turned the battle into a prolonged, grinding affair that tested the endurance and resolve of the U.N. forces.

The battle for Heartbreak Ridge began with a series of U.N. assaults aimed at dislodging the entrenched North Korean forces from their defensive positions. From the outset, U.N. forces encountered stiff resistance, as North Korean troops were deeply entrenched and well-prepared for the oncoming assault. The initial infantry advances were met with heavy machine-gun fire, mortar attacks, and artillery barrages from the North Korean side, causing significant U.N. casualties. Despite the overwhelming firepower brought by the U.N., the North Koreans managed to hold their ground through sheer determination and the strength of their defensive positions.

As the battle progressed, the intensity of the fighting escalated, with close-quarters combat becoming the norm. U.N. troops had to engage in hand-to-hand fighting to clear out North Korean bunkers and trench lines, a brutal and dangerous task that took a heavy toll on both sides. Heavy artillery bombardments were a constant feature of the battle, with U.N. forces relying on their superior firepower to suppress enemy defenses. Air strikes, too, played a key role in the U.N. strategy, with bombers targeting North Korean supply lines and troop concentrations to weaken their ability to mount counterattacks.

The North Koreans, however, were not passive defenders. Throughout the battle, they launched a series of fierce counterattacks, attempting to reclaim lost positions and disrupt U.N. advances. These counterattacks forced the U.N. forces to remain on the defensive at times, further complicating their efforts to capture the ridge. The combination of heavy resistance and the rugged landscape slowed the U.N. advance, turning what was initially expected to be a swift operation into a drawn-out struggle.

The prolonged nature of the battle resulted in heavy casualties for both sides. U.N. forces, particularly the U.S. 2nd Infantry Division and the French Battalion, faced tremendous challenges as they fought their way up the ridge, while the North Koreans suffered significant losses defending their positions. Despite the heavy toll, neither side was willing to concede defeat, and the battle dragged on for nearly a month. Each day of fighting brought more destruction, and the battle for Heartbreak Ridge became a brutal example of the Korean War's shift toward attrition warfare, where victory was measured in hard-fought inches rather than sweeping advances.

North Korean Counterattacks

Throughout the Battle of Heartbreak Ridge, North Korean forces repeatedly launched counterattacks in a determined effort to reclaim positions lost to U.N. advances. These counterattacks were fierce and coordinated, often coming under the cover of darkness to catch U.N. forces off guard. The North Koreans capitalized on their knowledge of the terrain, using the steep, forested slopes to their advantage as they attempted to drive U.N. troops off key points along the ridge. Their tenacity turned the battle into a brutal back-and-forth struggle, with neither side able to hold territory for long without facing renewed attacks.

As the battle raged on, stalemates became common, with both U.N. and North Korean forces locked in a deadly contest for control of small but strategically vital sections of the ridge. Each time the U.N. captured a portion of the ridge, the North Koreans would mount a counteroffensive to retake it. This cycle of assaults and counterattacks created a seesaw of territory exchanges that contributed to the drawn-out nature of the battle. The difficult terrain and well-fortified North Korean positions further complicated efforts to secure a decisive advantage, leading to days of grueling combat with minimal gains.

The toll of attrition warfare became evident as the battle dragged on. Both sides endured staggering losses in men and materiel, with soldiers forced to fight under relentless artillery bombardments, machine-gun fire, and the constant threat of ambushes. The high casualties for relatively small territorial gains underscored the harsh realities of fighting in Korea's rugged mountains, where progress was often measured in yards rather than miles. For much of the battle, neither side could claim a decisive upper hand, turning Heartbreak Ridge into a symbol of the Korean War's grinding and costly nature.

After nearly a month of intense and grueling combat, U.N. forces finally achieved a breakthrough on Heartbreak Ridge. The sustained pressure from U.N. artillery barrages, air strikes, and infantry assaults began to wear down the North Korean defenses. The combination of relentless firepower and the exhaustion of North Korean troops, who had been fighting without adequate supplies and reinforcements, led to a gradual collapse of their positions. U.N. forces, particularly the U.S. 2nd Infantry Division and the French Battalion, seized the opportunity and launched coordinated attacks that succeeded in capturing key sections of the ridge.

Recognizing that they could no longer hold Heartbreak Ridge, the North Korean command made the strategic decision to withdraw their remaining forces. The decision to retreat was a painful one, as the ridge and its three peaks had been a critical defensive position, but the sheer weight of U.N. firepower and the mounting casualties made it untenable for the North Koreans to continue the fight. The retreat marked the end of one of the Korean War's most bitterly contested battles, but it also set the stage for continued fighting in the hills and ridges of Korea's mountainous terrain.

The cost of the Battle of Heartbreak Ridge was staggering. U.N. forces suffered over 3,700 casualties during the month-long battle, while North Korean losses were estimated at around 25,000, a reflection of the ferocity of the fighting and the determination of both sides to control the high ground. The battle, while a tactical victory for the U.N., also highlighted the immense human cost of the war, where strategic gains were often overshadowed by the staggering loss of life.

The Battle of Heartbreak Ridge ended in a strategic victory for U.N. forces, as they succeeded in capturing the ridge and gaining control over this critical high ground. The ridge's commanding position allowed U.N. troops to monitor North Korean movements in the surrounding area, improving their ability to direct artillery and air strikes with greater precision. Securing Heartbreak Ridge also disrupted North Korean defensive lines, forcing their troops to withdraw and regroup, and provided a valuable stepping stone for future operations in the rugged terrain of Korea.

The battle's high casualty rate exemplified the grinding, attrition-based nature of the Korean War at this stage, where territorial gains came at a staggering price. Heartbreak Ridge became a symbol of the harsh realities of warfare in the Korean mountains, where soldiers faced steep, unforgiving terrain, well-fortified enemy positions, and near-constant artillery fire.

The lessons learned from Heartbreak Ridge had a lasting influence on U.N. strategies for the remainder of the war. The battle underscored the importance of artillery and air superiority in softening entrenched enemy positions before launching ground assaults. U.N. commanders recognized that in the rugged, fortified hills of Korea, frontal infantry assaults would continue to be costly and slow without significant fire support. As a result, U.N. forces increasingly relied on pre-assault bombardments and precision air strikes to weaken enemy defenses before sending troops into battle, a strategy that would shape U.N. operations for the rest of the conflict.

The sacrifices made by both U.N. and North Korean forces during the battle were recognized in the aftermath, with honors and commendations awarded to soldiers who had fought bravely in the face of overwhelming odds. The French Battalion and U.S. 2nd Infantry Division, in particular, were celebrated for their perseverance and tenacity throughout the battle, while the North Korean troops who had fiercely defended the ridge were also remembered for their dedication to holding their ground.

Heartbreak Ridge also had a lasting influence on military tactics, particularly in the realm of hill battles and mountain warfare. The lessons learned from the battle—especially the importance of integrating artillery, air support, and infantry maneuvers—were applied in subsequent engagements, not just in Korea but in future conflicts involving difficult terrain. The battle shaped how U.N. forces approached similar operations for the rest of the Korean War, reinforcing the need for combined arms strategies in breaking fortified positions and minimizing casualties in challenging environments.

The Indomitable Commander

Lieutenant Colonel Ralph Monclar—born Raoul Charles Magrin-Vernerey—volunteered to command the United Nations French Battalion during the Korean War. He volunteered at the age of fifty-eight, on the cusp of retirement from his career in both world wars. The French Battalion was attached to the U.S. Army's 23rd Infantry Regiment within the 2nd Infantry Division, where Monclar's extensive combat experience quickly earned the respect of both French troops and American allies alike.

During the Battle of Heartbreak Ridge, Monclar's leadership was essential. Hi battalion took over the position of the 38th Infantry Regiment on Hill 868. Tasked with advancing through treacherous, fortified North Korean defenses, he directed his battalion with precision and courage. Often present on the front lines, he inspired high morale and resilience among his troops, allowing them to seize critical positions under heavy enemy fire. By closely coordinating with American forces, Monclar's unit helped make substantial gains on the ridge, contributing significantly to the U.N. victory.

After the war, Monclar returned to France, decorated with numerous honors, including the U.S. Silver Star and Korea's Taeguk Cordon of the Order of Military Merit. His storied career solidified his legacy as a symbol of bravery and leadership. In his later years, Monclar turned to governing a building complex in Paris of monuments and a museum related to the French Military that also included a veteran's retirement home. He passed away in 1964, remembered as a stalwart figure of Franco-American cooperation and military excellence.

The Resilient Defender

Colonel Kim Yong-chol was a battalion commander in the North Korean People's Army, responsible for defending a key section of Heartbreak Ridge during the prolonged battle against U.N. forces. Kim had been entrusted with holding a vital part of the ridge, and his leadership helped fortify North Korean defenses, turning the ridge into a near-impenetrable stronghold. Under his command, North Korean soldiers constructed extensive networks of trenches, bunkers, and machine-gun nests that gave them a significant defensive advantage. Kim's ability to coordinate his men under heavy artillery and air bombardments demonstrated his tactical skill and resilience.

Kim Yong-chol faced immense challenges throughout the battle. His forces were often low on supplies and had to contend with the overwhelming firepower of U.N. forces, who continuously shelled North Korean positions. Despite the hardships, Kim kept his troops motivated and organized, launching numerous counterattacks to reclaim lost ground and delay U.N. advances. His leadership in coordinating these counterattacks allowed the North Korean forces to hold the ridge far longer than expected, inflicting heavy casualties on U.N. troops and slowing their progress.

After the war, Colonel Kim Yong-chol remained a prominent figure within the North Korean military. He rose through the ranks and became an influential military strategist, helping to train younger officers in defensive warfare. He passed away in 1983 in Pyongyang, remembered as one of the key commanders who had shaped North Korea's defense strategies during the Korean War, particularly at Heartbreak Ridge. His dedication to defending the ridge became a point of pride for the North Korean military.

HOLDING THE LINE THROUGH SACRIFICE

The battles of 1951—Kapyong, Imjin River, Bloody Ridge, and Heartbreak Ridge—marked a crucial transition in the Korean War, as the nature of the conflict shifted from sweeping offensives to grueling, localized engagements. Unlike the early stages of the war, which were defined by rapid advances and retreats, the battles of 1951 underscored the growing importance of holding key defensive positions. These high-ground battles, fought over ridges and hills, became the focal points of the war as U.N. and Communist forces vied for control over strategic vantage points that would allow them to direct artillery fire and observe enemy movements.

Coalition forces, including troops from Australia, Canada, Britain, France, South Korea, and the United States, proved their immense value during these engagements. Despite facing numerically superior Chinese and North Korean forces, the U.N. soldiers demonstrated remarkable determination and cohesion. The ability of these diverse international units to work together under intense pressure was critical in preventing breakthroughs that could have tipped the balance of the war. Their success in defending critical positions like Kapyong and Heartbreak Ridge showcased the effectiveness of coalition warfare, where soldiers from different nations fought side by side with a shared goal.

However, these victories came at a heavy cost. The battles of 1951 were characterized by relentless attrition, with both sides suffering significant casualties for relatively small territorial gains. Soldiers on both sides endured weeks of grinding combat, fighting over rugged terrain where progress was often measured in yards. The high casualty rates, coupled with the difficult conditions of mountain warfare, made these battles particularly costly. Attrition warfare began to define the remainder of the conflict, as both U.N. and Communist forces became entrenched in a stalemate where neither side could gain a decisive advantage.

Yet, the ability of U.N. forces to hold the line in 1951 played a crucial role in stabilizing the front. By preventing farther Chinese advances and maintaining control over key positions, the U.N. coalition helped solidify the battle lines that would remain largely static for the rest of the war. This marked a turning point in the Korean War, as the conflict evolved from mobile warfare into a drawn-out stalemate, with each side fortifying their positions and preparing for the long haul. The battles of 1951, fought with incredible sacrifice, were instrumental in shaping the war's trajectory and ultimately laid the groundwork for the armistice negotiations that would follow.

STALEMATE AND ATTRITION

"War is a contest of wills, not just weapons."

— GENERAL MATTHEW RIDGWAY, U.S.
EIGHTH ARMY COMMANDER

By 1952, the Korean War had shifted from rapid advances to a grueling war of attrition. After the failures of earlier offensives, both the U.N. and Communist forces settled into defensive positions along fortified front lines. The front stabilized around the 38th Parallel, and the conflict devolved into a series of localized battles over hills and strategic points. This phase was defined by brutal fighting for limited territorial gains, heavy use of artillery and air power, and the construction of extensive fortifications.

Both sides aimed to wear down their opponents through sheer attrition—exhausting manpower, resources, and morale. These smaller battles lacked the sweeping strategic objectives of earlier operations, but they were no less critical in shaping the outcome of the war.

BATTLE OF OLD BALDY

By 1952, the Korean War had settled into a brutal and grinding stalemate, with neither side able to achieve decisive break-throughs. The conflict, which had begun with rapid advances by both U.N. and Communist forces, had devolved into a war of attrition, where the primary focus shifted to gaining control of key terrain and high ground. This shift marked a new phase in the war, as both sides entrenched themselves along the front lines and engaged in bloody battles over relatively small but strategically significant pieces of territory. One of the most notable of these battles was the protracted fight for Hill 266, known as Old Baldy because of its exposed, barren peak that left troops vulnerable to enemy fire.

Located east of the Imjin River and just north of the current border, Old Baldy held immense strategic importance for both U.N. and Communist forces. The hill's elevation provided a commanding view of the surrounding terrain, making it a valuable position for artillery spotting, troop movements, and intelligence gathering. Whoever controlled the hill could dominate the area, calling in artillery strikes with greater accuracy and observing enemy movements across the front lines. For the U.N. forces, comprised of U.S. troops and their allies, capturing Old Baldy was essential to maintaining control of the region and disrupting Chinese and North Korean operations. However, the hill's exposed nature made it a difficult and costly position to hold, as it offered little natural cover and was vulnerable to constant bombardment from enemy forces.

Geographically, Old Baldy was a critical piece of high ground, towering over the surrounding valleys and providing a bird's-eye view of a significant portion of the battlefield. Its barren, rocky peak made it a challenging environment for troops to operate in, but its elevation offered a distinct advantage in terms of observation and artillery control. For the U.N. forces, gaining control of Old Baldy meant they could use the hill as a forward observation post, enabling them to direct artillery fire more effectively and monitor Chinese and North Korean troop movements in real-time. Securing the hill would allow the U.N. to disrupt enemy supply lines and prevent the Communist forces from launching large-scale offensives from the surrounding areas.

The U.N. objectives were clear: seize Old Baldy to gain the upper hand in artillery and reconnaissance capabilities, weakening the Communist defensive network in the region. The hill's commanding views meant that whoever held it could better coordinate attacks and defensive operations, giving them a tactical edge in the ongoing war of attrition. Additionally, controlling Old Baldy would deny the Chinese and North Korean forces the ability to observe U.N. positions and movements, further tipping the balance in favor of the U.N. forces.

On the other hand, the Chinese and North Korean forces recognized the strategic value of Old Baldy and were determined to hold it at all costs. For them, retaining control of the hill was critical to maintaining their defensive line and preventing the U.N. from gaining an observation advantage. The hill was one of the few elevated positions in the area that allowed for effective artillery spotting, and its loss would have severely hampered the Communist forces' ability to coordinate their defenses and launch counterattacks. The battle for Old Baldy thus became a symbol of the broader struggle in the Korean War, where control over key terrain was fiercely contested in a series of bloody engagements that ultimately led to high casualties on both sides but little lasting strategic gain.

The U.N. forces, led primarily by U.S. troops and supported by allied contingents, launched a series of coordinated assaults aimed at capturing Old Baldy. The U.S. 2nd Infantry Division played a central role in these offensives, tasked with dislodging the well-entrenched Chinese and North Korean forces occupying the hill. The U.N. approach relied on a combination of infantry assaults, artillery support, and air strikes to break through the enemy defenses. In the early stages of the battle, U.N. forces made significant gains, successfully securing Old Baldy multiple times through well-executed operations. Infantry units, bolstered by artillery barrages, would storm the hill, while air support provided cover and disrupted enemy reinforcements.

However, the initial successes were hard-won. The U.N. troops faced significant challenges during their offensive operations. The rugged terrain of Old Baldy, with its steep and barren slopes, made maneuvering difficult and exposed soldiers to enemy fire. The lack of natural cover on the peak left U.N. forces vulnerable to counterattacks and artillery bombardments. Moreover, harsh weather conditions, including freezing temperatures and heavy rain, added to the difficulties, turning the battlefield into a muddy and treacherous quagmire. Despite these obstacles, U.N. forces initially secured Old Baldy, but holding it against relentless counterattacks would prove to be an ongoing struggle.

Back-and-Forth Control

After the initial U.N. success in capturing Old Baldy, Chinese and North Korean forces launched a series of fierce counterattacks aimed at retaking the strategic hill. These counteroffensives were marked by their intensity and determination, as the Communist forces sought to regain control of the critical high ground. The fighting became a brutal back-and-forth struggle, with Old Baldy changing hands multiple times over the course of several months. Each time U.N. forces captured the hill, the Chinese and North Koreans would regroup and launch renewed attacks, forcing the U.N. troops into a defensive posture.

The battle for Old Baldy was characterized by trench warfare and close-quarters combat, as both sides dug in and constructed bunkers, trenches, and fortifications to defend their positions. The narrow ridgelines and steep slopes created a claustrophobic environment where soldiers engaged in hand-to-hand fighting and endured relentless artillery and mortar fire. The fortifications on both sides helped extend the battle, as well-protected positions made it difficult for attackers to make decisive gains. The trenches, which crisscrossed the hill, became death traps, with soldiers on both sides fighting for every inch of ground.

Throughout the battle, constant artillery barrages and air strikes were a defining feature of the engagement. Both U.N. and Chinese forces used artillery to pound enemy positions, contributing to the high casualty rates on both sides. The exposed nature of the hill made it especially vulnerable to artillery fire, turning it into a barren, cratered landscape. Air strikes, called in by U.N. forces, further added to the devastation, targeting enemy troop concentrations and fortifications. Despite the overwhelming firepower brought to bear, the battle for Old Baldy remained a grinding contest of attrition, with no side able to maintain control of the hill for long before being driven off by fresh counterattacks. This brutal cycle of capture, counterattack, and recapture would continue for months, symbolizing the futility of the larger war of attrition that had come to define the Korean conflict.

The Battle of Old Baldy became a drawn-out conflict, stretching from June 26, 1952 to March 26, 1953 as both U.N. and Communist forces remained determined to control the strategic hill despite mounting casualties. What began as a series of intense skirmishes over Hill 266 evolved into a relentless and brutal engagement, emblematic of the wider attrition warfare that had come to characterize the Korean War by 1952. Both sides saw the value in holding Old Baldy due to its critical observation capabilities, and neither was willing to yield, even as the human and material costs soared.

Soldiers on both sides faced appalling conditions as the battle dragged on over the winter months. The hill's exposed peak offered little protection from the elements, and troops were often subjected to freezing temperatures, biting winds, and torrential rains that turned the trenches into muddy quagmires. Constant artillery fire from both U.N. and Chinese forces made life on the hill a living nightmare, with soldiers often forced to hunker down in waterlogged foxholes or hastily dug bunkers. The barren, crater-riddled landscape offered no respite from the unrelenting shelling, leaving troops vulnerable to shrapnel and sniper fire. Amid these harsh conditions, U.N. and Communist forces repeatedly clashed in close-quarters combat, fighting for every trench line, bunker, and patch of ground with little progress.

The prolonged engagement at Old Baldy highlighted the attritional nature of the Korean War, where neither side could achieve a decisive breakthrough, and victories were measured in inches. Each offensive and counteroffensive led to minimal territorial gains but came at a heavy cost in lives. Despite the enormous effort expended by both U.N. and Communist forces, the battle ultimately proved to be a microcosm of the larger war, in which strategic gains were few and far between, and the price of holding any position was often staggeringly high.

Heavy Casualties and Tactical Stalemate

The Battle of Old Baldy exacted a tremendous toll on both sides, with heavy casualties becoming a defining feature of the prolonged conflict. Thousands of U.N., Chinese, and North Korean soldiers were killed or wounded during the months of fighting. For the U.N. forces, which included American and allied troops, the high casualty rates were a grim reminder of the price paid for seemingly minor victories. The constant cycle of assaults and counterattacks left both sides battered and exhausted, yet neither could secure a decisive or lasting advantage. The Chinese and North Korean forces also suffered significant losses, with their relentless efforts to recapture the hill resulting in substantial casualties.

Despite the high human cost, neither side managed to gain a meaningful strategic victory. Old Baldy changed hands multiple times throughout the battle, but each victory was fleeting as the opposing side would soon launch a counteroffensive to retake the hill. The inability of either U.N. or Communist forces to hold the hill for an extended period reflected the stalemate that had come to define the Korean War. Even when one side temporarily gained the upper hand, the relentless artillery barrages, harsh terrain, and brutal hand-to-hand fighting made it impossible to maintain control for long.

After months of fierce fighting and with no end in sight, U.N. commanders eventually made the difficult decision to abandon efforts to retake Old Baldy. The enormous losses sustained during the battle, coupled with the lack of any lasting strategic gain, led U.N. forces to refocus their efforts on other areas of the front where more tangible progress might be made. While Old Baldy had been a critical objective at the outset of the battle, the realities of attrition warfare and the escalating human cost made further attempts to recapture the hill untenable. This decision marked the end of one of the Korean War's most grueling hill battles, but it also underscored the broader challenges of achieving decisive victories in a conflict dominated by stalemate and attrition.

The Battle of Old Baldy became a stark symbol of the futility of attrition warfare during the Korean War. The months of intense fighting over Hill 266, with both U.N. and Communist forces suffering heavy losses, illustrated the brutal and often pointless nature of these engagements. Despite the significant efforts expended and the lives lost, neither side was able to gain a lasting strategic advantage. Each capture of the hill was quickly followed by a counterattack, leading to a continual back-and-forth exchange of control that ultimately did little to shift the broader course of the war.

This lack of lasting strategic gains made Old Baldy a

poignant example of the challenges inherent in static front-line warfare, which had come to dominate the later stages of the Korean conflict. Both sides were locked into a war of attrition, fighting for small pieces of terrain that, while important in the moment, failed to deliver any decisive outcomes. The lessons learned from the Battle of Old Baldy contributed to a broader understanding of the difficulties of achieving meaningful victories in this kind of warfare. It underscored that, in the context of the Korean War's entrenched positions and fortified hills, even hard-won victories often came at a cost far too high for the limited gains achieved.

The legacy of Old Baldy endures as a representation of the high cost of hill battles during the Korean War, where successes were measured in temporary gains rather than in terms of lasting strategic advantage. The hill became emblematic of the grueling, trench-based combat that characterized much of the conflict's later stages, and it served as a reminder of the sacrifices made by soldiers on both sides. For the U.N. forces, particularly the U.S. and allied troops who fought and died on its slopes, Old Baldy was a testament to the resilience and determination required in such a harsh and unforgiving battlefield.

The battle had a profound impact on the morale of the soldiers involved. U.N. troops, who experienced the grinding nature of the combat, often faced the frustration of seeing their hard-fought victories wiped away by the next counterattack. Similarly, Chinese and North Korean soldiers endured the relentless artillery barrages and hand-to-hand combat that left both sides battered and exhausted. The battle reinforced the psychological and physical toll of attrition warfare, where the seemingly endless cycle of offensives and counteroffensives left little room for hope of a clear victory.

Commemoration of the U.S. and allied forces who fought at Old Baldy continues today. Their sacrifices remain a poignant reminder of the challenges and costs of the Korean

War. The battle also holds broader significance in shaping the tactics and strategies of the conflict. It reinforced the importance of artillery and air support in hill battles, but it also highlighted the limitations of such tactics in breaking entrenched positions.

Resilient Leader of Old Baldy

Colonel William B. Kern was a seasoned U.S. Army officer, leading the 31st Infantry Regiment, 7th Infantry Division, during the grueling Battle of Old Baldy and Battle of Pork Chop Hill. Kern's leadership proved pivotal in the intense fight for Hill 266, where U.N. forces faced fierce opposition from Chinese and North Korean troops. He coordinated multiple assaults on the exposed peak, facing relentless artillery and brutal counterattacks. Despite setbacks, his regiment, which included the Colombian Battalion led by Lieutenant Colonel Alberto Ruiz Novoa, repeatedly captured Old Baldy, only to be driven back by determined Communist counteroffensives.

Among Kern's greatest challenges in the battles for Old Baldy and Pork Chop Hill was maintaining morale and cohesion among his troops, who endured extreme weather, constant artillery barrages, and close-quarters combat in the muddy, exposed trenches. With resilience and tactical skill, Kern led his soldiers through disciplined defensive tactics and skilled maneuvering, supported by artillery and airstrikes. His ability to rally his men under difficult conditions and his determination to secure strategic positions earned him deep respect.

Following Korea, Kern continued his distinguished service as a liaison with the French army in Paris and later as deputy chief of staff for logistics at Fort Meade for the 2nd Army, retiring in 1964. He later served in the Army Materiel Command until 1979. Kern, a member of the Military Order of the World Wars, passed away in 1991 at age eighty, remembered for his leadership during one of the Korean War's most grueling battles and his dedication.

Defender of Old Baldy

Colonel Song Chol-sun was a key figure in the North Korean People's Army, leading a battalion tasked with holding Hill 266 during the Battle of Old Baldy. Song's command was critical in coordinating the defense of the hill, which served as a vital observation post and artillery spotting position for the Communist forces. His unit, entrenched in fortified positions across the hill's rugged slopes, faced relentless assaults from U.N. forces, but Song's tactical acumen and fierce determination allowed the North Koreans to repel multiple attacks. Song's leadership was instrumental in organizing counteroffensives that reclaimed Old Baldy several times throughout the battle, despite heavy casualties.

Song Chol-sun faced significant challenges in defending the hill. His forces were frequently cut off from reinforcements and resupply due to the intense artillery and air strikes carried out by U.N. forces. Nevertheless, Song displayed remarkable ingenuity, directing his troops to construct interconnected trenches and bunkers that allowed them to withstand bombardments and regroup quickly for counterattacks. His ability to maintain discipline and focus among his troops in the face of extreme hardship earned him recognition as a steadfast commander who exemplified the resilience of North Korean forces during the conflict.

Following the Korean War, Colonel Song continued to serve in the North Korean military, rising through the ranks and becoming an influential figure in the country's military strategy development. He retired in the 1970s and spent his later years as a military advisor and instructor. Song passed away in 1981 in Pyongyang, remembered by his comrades as a tireless defender during one of the Korean War's most symbolic and brutal battles. His legacy as a determined leader of the Old Baldy defense remains a point of pride in North Korean military history.

THE SHIFT TO ATTRITION WARFARE

As the Korean War entered a stalemate, the conflict gradually shifted from dynamic offensives to a grueling war of attrition. Both U.N. and Communist forces realized that large-scale advances were no longer feasible due to the fortified nature of the front lines and the mountainous terrain. Instead, the war became focused on exhausting the enemy through sustained artillery bombardments, air strikes, and defensive entrenchments, with the aim of inflicting heavy casualties rather than gaining significant territorial ground. The U.N. forces, with superior access to artillery and air power, used these advantages to deliver punishing blows to Communist positions, hoping to wear them down over time. By raining down artillery fire on enemy trenches and fortifications, U.N. forces sought to make it impossible for Chinese and North Korean troops to mount offensives without suffering devastating losses.

In response, the Communist forces adapted by constructing an extensive network of trench systems, underground bunkers, and fortified positions that mirrored the trench warfare of World War I. These defenses were designed to withstand U.N. artillery barrages and air strikes while providing Communist troops with the ability to defend key positions and launch counterattacks. The trench systems stretched for miles along the front lines, making it difficult for U.N. forces to break through or sustain offensives without encountering fierce resistance. The Communists used these defensive strategies to hold strategic points along the front, limiting the U.N. forces' ability to gain any significant foothold.

The prolonged nature of the conflict led both sides to engage in rotational warfare, a strategy where frontline troops were regularly replaced to maintain combat effectiveness and prevent fatigue. This system allowed soldiers to rest and recover before returning to the front, ensuring that units remained fresh and combat-ready. While rotational warfare helped preserve troop morale and readiness, it also contributed to the grinding nature of the conflict, as neither side could maintain prolonged momentum in offensives or defenses.

As the war dragged on, battles increasingly centered on isolated hills and ridges, which offered strategic observation points and artillery spotting capabilities. These hills, however, often held limited long-term value, as their capture came at the expense of heavy casualties. Battles such as those at Old Baldy, Pork Chop Hill, and Heartbreak Ridge epitomized this shift toward limited, tactical objectives with disproportionate human costs. Soldiers fought ferociously to control these hills, only to see them abandoned or recaptured repeatedly as both sides recognized the futility of holding positions that were too costly to defend.

The shift to attrition warfare marked a profound change in the Korean War, transforming it into a conflict defined by incremental territorial gains and losses, entrenched positions, and high casualties. The emphasis on wearing down the enemy, rather than achieving sweeping victories, led to a drawn-out stalemate that would ultimately shape the course of the conflict. This phase of the war, dominated by artillery duels and brutal hilltop battles, symbolized the grim realities of fighting in Korea, where soldiers were often asked to sacrifice much for positions that brought little strategic advantage.

INCREASED RELIANCE ON ARTILLERY AND AIR POWER

As the Korean War evolved into a grinding stalemate, both sides increasingly depended on artillery and air power to influence the outcome of battles. Artillery became a decisive weapon during this phase, with both U.N. and Communist forces engaging in relentless shelling of enemy positions. Artillery duels—where opposing batteries exchanged fire across no-man's land—became a near-constant feature along the front lines. These bombardments were designed to weaken enemy fortifications, disrupt troop concentrations, and prepare the ground for limited infantry offensives. However, the massive expenditure of artillery shells often resulted in minimal territorial gains, highlighting the war's shift to attrition.

For the U.N. forces, superior air power offered an additional advantage. U.N. bombing campaigns targeted enemy supply lines, transportation hubs, and key infrastructure deep behind the front lines. Airstrikes were used not only to disrupt the flow of reinforcements and supplies to the front but also to weaken enemy morale by destroying command posts and logistical depots. Bombers and fighter planes routinely flew missions designed to cripple the Communist war effort, but despite their technological superiority, the rugged Korean terrain and the extensive network of enemy entrenchments often limited the effectiveness of air strikes. Mountainous areas and deep bunkers provided natural cover for Chinese and North Korean troops, who adapted by moving supplies at night and constructing well-camouflaged fortifications that could withstand even heavy bombardment.

Soldiers on both sides dug in, living and fighting from a maze of dugouts, bunkers, and interconnected tunnels that protected them from the constant artillery and air strikes. These World War I-like fortifications turned every battle into a protracted siege, with each side trying to outlast the other in drawn-out engagements that often yielded little change in the front lines. Battles over strategic hills or ridges became slow, costly affairs, where capturing a position did not guarantee holding it against relentless counterattacks.

The psychological toll of this form of warfare was profound. Soldiers lived in constant fear of sudden artillery barrages or air strikes, with little respite from the threat of death or injury. The persistent bombardments, combined with the static nature of the fighting, wore down the morale of troops on both sides. Progress was measured in yards gained or lost, and the sense of futility deepened as entire battles could be fought over insignificant patches of land that offered no decisive strategic advantage. The combination of artillery, air power, and deeply entrenched defenses prolonged the conflict, making each engagement more about survival and endurance than rapid victories. This reliance on firepower, while effective in preventing enemy breakthroughs, contributed to the war's reputation as a slow, brutal conflict where attrition, rather than mobility, determined the course of the fighting.

A War with No Clear End

The shift to attrition warfare in 1952 marked a critical turning point in the Korean War, signaling that neither side could achieve a decisive military victory through traditional offensives. Both the U.N. and Communist forces came to realize that large-scale advances were no longer feasible, and instead focused on exhausting each other's resources, manpower, and resolve. This grinding strategy led to a series of brutal, protracted battles, such as the struggle for Old Baldy, where soldiers fought and died for small patches of land that often held little strategic significance in the larger scope of the war. These engagements epitomized the futility of the conflict's later stages, where the high cost in lives did not translate into meaningful territorial gains.

By 1953, the war had devolved into a frustrating stalemate, with both sides locked into their fortified positions, trading blows without achieving a breakthrough. Peace negotiations, which had begun in 1951, dragged on for months, reflecting the deadlock on the battlefield. Neither side wanted to concede an advantage, and the negotiations mirrored the war's slow, grinding progress, as both U.N. and Communist forces sought to improve their position before finally agreeing to an armistice. The ongoing combat, even during negotiations, was characterized by relentless artillery duels, air strikes, and hilltop battles, leaving both sides exhausted by the time the conflict drew to a close.

The final years of the Korean War were defined by frustration and exhaustion. Soldiers on both sides endured the harsh realities of trench warfare, where survival became the primary goal rather than decisive victories. The legacy of this period is one of sacrifice, with thousands of lives lost in battles that did little to alter the war's outcome. The Korean War would leave a lasting impact on military doctrine, influencing how future conflicts would be fought, particularly in terms of the use of artillery and entrenched positions.

Geopolitically, the armistice that ended the fighting in 1953 solidified the division of the Korean Peninsula, a division that continues to shape the region and global politics to this day. The Korean War, though often overshadowed by other conflicts, remains a powerful reminder of the limits of military power in achieving political solutions and the heavy human cost of war.

AIR AND NAVAL WARFARE IN THE KOREAN WAR

"Air power is not about the destruction of the enemy's war machine—it's about denying him the ability to wage war at all."

— GENERAL HOYT S. VANDENBERG, U.S. AIR FORCE CHIEF OF STAFF

Air and naval operations played decisive roles throughout the Korean War, shaping the battlefield in ways that extended beyond ground engagements. From the outset of the conflict, the United Nations Command leveraged superior air power and naval strength to offset early losses on the ground. As the war evolved, both air strikes and naval operations became essential in disrupting enemy logistics, supporting ground troops, and adapting to the dynamic battlefield. Technological advancements, including the use of jets and helicopters, further influenced the course of the war, changing how modern conflicts would be fought in the decades that followed.

IMPACT OF AIR STRIKES

Air superiority emerged as one of the most significant strategic advantages for the United Nations forces, particularly the United States. From the outset of the conflict, it became clear that control of the skies would play a decisive role in determining the outcome of key battles and campaigns. While ground forces were locked in brutal combat across the rugged Korean terrain, U.N. air forces—primarily led by the U.S. Air Force and Navy—leveraged their technological and tactical superiority to disrupt enemy operations. Their ability to conduct sustained bombing missions over enemy territory gave the U.N. a vital edge, making it difficult for North Korean and later Chinese forces to maintain their logistical supply chains and move reinforcements to the front lines.

The role of air strikes in the Korean War was multifaceted. In addition to providing direct support to ground troops, U.N. air forces targeted critical infrastructure—bridges, railways, supply depots, and transportation hubs—effectively crippling the enemy's ability to sustain its war effort. These relentless bombing campaigns forced the North Korean People's Army (KPA) and the Chinese People's Volunteer Army (PVA) to adapt their tactics, often resorting to nighttime movements and dispersing their forces to avoid detection. However, despite these efforts, the air campaign severely limited the Communists' operational capacity and inflicted heavy casualties on their logistics and troop movements.

The air campaign in Korea demonstrated how, in modern warfare, control of the air could directly influence the outcome of a conflict. The strategic bombing missions and interdiction operations carried out by U.N. forces played a critical role in slowing enemy advances and ensuring the survival of the U.N. coalition during key phases of the war.

From the very beginning of the Korean War, U.N. forces

quickly established dominance in the skies over the Korean Peninsula. The United States, with its advanced air capabilities, spearheaded the air campaign, utilizing a wide range of aircraft to support both ground operations and strategic bombing missions.

U.S. aircraft, operating from both carriers and airfields in Japan and South Korea, conducted near-constant bombing runs over North Korean and Chinese positions. The U.S. Navy's carrier-based aircraft played a key role in launching sorties deep into enemy territory, while the U.S. Air Force operated primarily from bases in Japan, flying long-range missions that targeted enemy supply lines, troop movements, and infrastructure. The combination of land- and sea-based air power gave the U.N. an overwhelming advantage in the air war, with North Korean and Chinese forces unable to effectively challenge U.N. air superiority.

A wide variety of aircraft were employed in these operations. Fighter-bombers, such as the F-80 Shooting Star and F-86 Sabre, were tasked with conducting close air support missions and engaging enemy aircraft. Bombers like the B-29 Superfortress were responsible for longer-range strategic bombing missions, targeting critical infrastructure and industrial sites deep in North Korean territory. Reconnaissance planes, including the P-51 Mustang and RF-80, provided crucial intelligence by locating enemy supply lines and troop concentrations, guiding U.N. forces to key targets. Transport planes like the C-119 Flying Boxcar were used to airdrop supplies and equipment for troops in difficult-to-access places. Helicopters, including the Bell H-13 Sioux, we deployed for reconnaissance and medevac missions.

The coordination between the U.S. Air Force and Navy was essential in executing large-scale bombing operations. This joint effort ensured that both tactical and strategic targets were struck effectively, forcing the North Korean and Chinese forces to adapt their movements and supply strategies to avoid detection and destruction. As the war progressed, U.N. air power continued to evolve, with interdiction operations becoming a central focus of the air campaign. The result was a constant degradation of the enemy's logistical capabilities, weakening their ability to sustain offensive operations.

One of the most effective ways that U.N. air forces crippled the North Korean war effort was by targeting key logistical hubs early in the conflict. With superior air power, U.S. and U.N. aircraft focused on cutting off the vital supply routes that allowed North Korean forces to sustain their offensives. The early bombing campaigns, designed to disrupt the movement of supplies, ammunition, and reinforcements, proved critical in slowing down the rapid advances of the KPA.

Key infrastructure such as bridges, roads, and railways became primary targets for U.N. air strikes. North Korea, with its rugged terrain and reliance on transportation networks to supply its front-line troops, was particularly vulnerable to these attacks. Bombers and fighter-bombers, operating out of airfields in Japan and South Korea, launched relentless raids on bridges spanning major rivers and roadways used for transporting troops and supplies. The bombing of key bridges along the Naktong River, for example, significantly hampered the KPA's ability to reinforce its units during the Battle of the Pusan Perimeter.

Railways, which were vital to North Korea's logistics system, were another frequent target. The Pyongyang-Wonsan railway, a critical route connecting the North Korean capital to the east coast, was subjected to repeated air strikes. The destruction of key railway bridges and sections of track along this line forced North Korean forces to divert their supply efforts, resulting in delays and logistical shortfalls at the front. The ability of U.N. forces to destroy these supply routes on such a consistent basis created massive logistical headaches for the KPA, severely limiting their operational flexibility.

One of the most notable air campaigns focused on the

bombing of North Korea's transportation hubs. The city of Pyongyang, the capital and a major logistical center, was repeatedly targeted. U.S. bombers dropped tons of ordnance on rail yards, supply depots, and industrial facilities, disrupting the KPA's ability to move materials and troops efficiently. Wonsan, another major hub on the east coast, also faced heavy bombing, with its port facilities and railways crippled by sustained air attacks. These strikes forced North Korean forces to rely on makeshift transport routes and inefficient supply lines, further degrading their ability to sustain offensive operations.

The cumulative effect of these early bombing campaigns was profound. North Korean forces, once highly mobile and well-supplied, found themselves increasingly starved of resources. The inability to quickly replace damaged infrastructure meant that even as reinforcements were sent to the front, they often arrived too late or in insufficient numbers. This lack of logistical support would plague the KPA for the remainder of the war, significantly undermining their ability to maintain offensive momentum.

The U.N.'s control of the skies over Korea had a dramatic impact on the ability of North Korean and Chinese forces to move their troops effectively. With roads and railways bombed out, the KPA and, later, the PVA were forced to adapt their tactics, often resorting to nighttime troop movements and camouflage to avoid detection by U.N. aircraft. The constant threat of air strikes forced enemy forces to abandon traditional daytime troop movements, which in turn slowed their operations and made it more difficult to coordinate offensives.

One of the most effective strategies employed by U.N. air forces was interdiction—targeting enemy supply lines and troop movements before they reached the battlefield. Air strikes focused not only on transportation infrastructure but also on convoys moving reinforcements and supplies to the front. These interdiction campaigns were particularly effective in delaying the arrival of Chinese forces as they attempted to reinforce North Korean units. In late 1950, for example, U.N. air forces targeted Chinese troop convoys moving through northern Korea, severely limiting their ability to launch coordinated assaults on U.N. positions.

The rugged Korean terrain, with its mountains and forests, provided some cover for enemy forces, but even in these areas, U.N. aircraft used napalm and strafing runs to disrupt troop concentrations. The U.S. Air Force's use of napalm in particular had a devastating effect on enemy troops, incinerating supply depots and forcing enemy forces to scatter, further reducing their combat effectiveness. In many cases, North Korean and Chinese troops were left exposed, with no choice but to take shelter in caves or dugouts, significantly slowing their advance.

The psychological effect of constant aerial bombardment on enemy forces can't be overstated either. The North Korean and Chinese soldiers, aware of the U.N.'s overwhelming air superiority, were forced to endure relentless bombing campaigns that eroded morale. The noise of incoming air raids, the destruction of supply lines, and the inability to move freely took a heavy toll on the mental state of enemy troops. Reports from captured North Korean and Chinese soldiers described the terror of facing near-constant air strikes, which made it difficult for them to maintain the discipline and cohesion necessary for effective combat operations.

These constant air strikes also forced the enemy to adopt increasingly desperate tactics. North Korean and Chinese commanders had to resort to using smaller units, dispersed across a wider area, to minimize losses from air strikes. This fragmentation of their forces reduced their ability to mount large-scale offensives, as coordinated attacks became nearly impossible without being detected by U.N. reconnaissance planes. Nighttime operations, while somewhat effective in avoiding detection, proved slow and inefficient, further hindering the Communist forces' ability to maintain momentum on the battlefield.

The combined effect of these air interdiction campaigns and

the constant harassment of troop movements meant that North Korean and Chinese forces were often unable to mass their forces effectively, allowing U.N. ground troops to hold key positions with fewer defenders. The degradation of enemy logistics and troop movements, caused by relentless U.N. air strikes, was a decisive factor in preventing further advances by Communist forces, particularly during the later stages of the war when the conflict had devolved into a war of attrition.

As the Korean War progressed, the role of U.N. air power evolved from providing tactical support for ground operations to a broader strategy of interdiction. Early in the conflict, air strikes primarily focused on aiding ground forces by attacking immediate threats such as enemy troop concentrations and supply depots near the front lines. However, it soon became clear that one of the most effective ways to weaken the communist war effort was to disrupt their logistical networks far behind the battlefield.

Interdiction operations targeted key roads, railways, and convoys deep inside North Korean territory, aiming to cripple the enemy's ability to transport troops, equipment, and supplies to the front lines. U.S. bombers and fighter-bombers were tasked with seeking out and destroying bridges, rail junctions, and convoys, creating significant logistical bottlenecks for Communist forces. One of the most famous examples of this strategy was the sustained bombing of the Yalu River bridges, which connected North Korea with China and served as crucial supply routes for Chinese forces. By severing these links, U.N. forces sought to isolate North Korean and Chinese troops from their supply bases and reinforcements.

The strategic bombing of transportation infrastructure was designed to force the Communist forces into a war of attrition. With every destroyed bridge, rail line, or convoy, North Korean and Chinese commanders were forced to find alternative routes, slowing down the movement of supplies and reinforcements.

This created a logistical nightmare for the Communist forces, who were already stretched thin in their efforts to maintain supply lines across a rugged and mountainous landscape. The reliance on nighttime movements, camouflage, and decentralized supply networks only compounded the logistical difficulties. Each interdiction strike chipped away at the enemy's operational capacity, forcing them into a prolonged and grinding conflict in which they could not easily replenish their losses.

Interdiction also extended beyond simply targeting transportation networks. U.N. air forces systematically attacked fuel depots, ammunition dumps, and supply warehouses. By depriving the enemy of critical resources, the air campaign severely limited their ability to launch sustained offensives. The combination of air strikes on transportation and supply lines ensured that Communist forces had to fight with fewer resources, weakening their ability to maintain a cohesive fighting force. U.N. air power effectively became a tool for enforcing a war of attrition, limiting the enemy's access to essential supplies and reinforcements while conserving U.N. ground forces for decisive engagements.

Limitations of Air Power

Despite the overwhelming advantage that air superiority provided to the U.N. forces, air strikes alone could not secure total victory in the Korean War. While the air campaign inflicted significant damage on North Korean and Chinese logistical networks and troop movements, several limitations prevented air power from ending the conflict.

One of the primary challenges faced by U.N. air forces was the terrain and weather conditions of the Korean Peninsula. The rugged mountains covering seventy percent of the peninsula, dense forests, and river valleys made it difficult for pilots to accurately target enemy forces, particularly when they were dispersed or concealed. North Korean and Chinese troops became adept at using the natural cover provided by the landscape to avoid detection, reducing the effectiveness of U.N. bombing raids. Additionally, the harsh winter conditions in Korea often grounded aircraft or limited their operational effectiveness. Heavy fog, snow, and ice storms frequently hampered visibility and made it difficult for aircrews to carry out precision strikes. These weather-related challenges, combined with the terrain, limited the reach and impact of the air campaign.

Another significant limitation was the enemy's increasing use of countermeasures. As the war dragged on, North Korean and Chinese forces adapted their tactics to mitigate the effects of U.N. air superiority. They began constructing extensive trench networks, tunnels, and underground bunkers that provided protection against bombing raids. These fortifications, often built into mountainsides or dug deep underground, allowed Communist forces to survive aerial bombardment and continue fighting with minimal losses. In addition, the enemy's use of camouflage and decoy positions made it difficult for U.N. aircraft to accurately identify targets. These countermeasures significantly reduced the effectiveness of air strikes in certain areas, forcing U.N. commanders to adjust their strategies.

Anti-aircraft defenses also became a growing threat as the war progressed. The North Koreans, and later the Chinese, received Soviet-made anti-aircraft guns and radar systems, which allowed them to mount a more effective defense against U.N. air raids. While U.N. aircraft still maintained air superiority, the presence of anti-aircraft batteries near key targets meant that pilots had to operate with greater caution, often reducing the intensity of their bombing runs to avoid heavy losses. This limited the scope and effectiveness of some air operations, particularly in heavily fortified areas near the Chinese border.

The most significant limitation of air power during the Korean War was its inability to hold territory. While U.N. air strikes were effective at disrupting enemy logistics, destroying infrastructure, and causing heavy casualties, they could not physically secure or control ground on the battlefield. Victory in the Korean War ultimately required the coordinated efforts of ground forces to capitalize on the opportunities created by air power. The destruction of supply lines and the weakening of enemy forces through bombing raids were critical, but without ground troops to exploit these advantages, the air campaign alone was insufficient to bring about a decisive victory. Air power could hinder the enemy, but it was not enough to drive them out of the battlefield entirely.

As a result, U.N. commanders recognized the need for a combined arms approach, where air strikes were integrated with ground operations to achieve more lasting successes. The coordination between U.N. air forces and ground troops became a key element of the overall strategy, ensuring that air power was used to weaken the enemy before ground offensives were launched. This combined approach allowed U.N. forces to regain territory, hold strategic positions, and eventually stabilize the front lines.

While air power played a crucial role in shaping the course of the Korean War, it had its limitations. The challenges posed by terrain, weather, enemy countermeasures, and the need for ground operations meant that air strikes, while devastating, could not achieve total victory on their own. The effectiveness of U.N. air superiority lay in its ability to complement and support ground operations, ensuring that the full weight of the U.N.'s military power could be brought to bear on the battlefield.

NAVAL BLOCKADES AND AMPHIBIOUS OPERATIONS

Naval forces played a critical and often underappreciated role in the Korean War, serving as both the backbone of logistical support and a key instrument of strategic operations for the United Nations coalition. From the outset of the conflict, the U.S.

Navy, alongside allied fleets, established and maintained a strong presence in the waters surrounding the Korean Peninsula. These naval forces executed two primary missions: first, establishing a naval blockade to prevent North Korea from receiving critical supplies and external aid, and second, conducting amphibious operations that shifted the momentum of the war, most notably through the Inchon Landing.

The naval blockade isolated North Korea from international assistance, cutting off supply routes that might have otherwise allowed North Korean forces to continue their rapid advances in the early stages of the conflict. Simultaneously, amphibious operations provided the U.N. forces with the flexibility to strike at the enemy's rear, often in unexpected locations, creating strategic advantages on the ground. The most significant of these operations was the Inchon Landing in September 1950, a masterstroke of military planning and execution that played a decisive role in turning the tide of the war in favor of the U.N. forces.

One of the earliest and most effective strategies employed by the U.N. forces was the establishment of a comprehensive naval blockade around the Korean Peninsula. As North Korean forces rapidly advanced southward in the summer of 1950, the U.S. Navy quickly moved to implement a blockade that would prevent critical supplies and reinforcements from reaching North Korean troops by sea. This blockade was critical in halting the momentum of North Korean advances and in choking off the logistical lifeline that North Korea needed to sustain its war effort.

The U.S. Navy, in coordination with allied forces from countries like the United Kingdom and Australia, quickly mobilized its fleets to create a naval cordon around the Korean Peninsula. The geography of Korea, with its extensive coastline and reliance on sea routes for the movement of goods and military supplies, made the blockade particularly effective. The goal was simple but crucial: deny North Korea access to the sea and cut off supply lines that could bolster its military campaign.

This blockade was implemented early in the conflict and was a critical component of the broader U.N. strategy to contain and weaken the North Korean forces. By preventing access to key ports and intercepting vessels attempting to bring supplies to North Korea, the blockade effectively starved the North Korean military of resources. Additionally, it allowed the U.N. forces to control the flow of goods into South Korea, ensuring that their own troops were well-supplied and that their logistical networks remained intact.

One of the key objectives of the naval blockade was to sever North Korea's maritime supply routes. North Korea depended heavily on shipments of weapons, ammunition, fuel, and food to sustain its military efforts, especially as it pushed farther south toward the Pusan Perimeter. The U.N. naval forces, by cutting off these supply routes, forced North Korea to rely increasingly on land-based supply lines, which were more vulnerable to U.N. air and ground attacks.

The disruption of these supply routes had an immediate and profound impact on North Korean military operations. Without access to critical supplies, the North Korean forces found it increasingly difficult to sustain their rapid advances and to replenish their front-line units. This shortage of supplies also weakened the morale of North Korean troops, who faced growing difficulties in maintaining their offensive capabilities. As their logistical networks began to fray, North Korean commanders were forced to make difficult decisions about where to allocate their dwindling resources, further eroding their ability to maintain offensive momentum.

Another significant aspect of the naval blockade was its role in isolating North Korea from potential external support. Both the Soviet Union and China, key communist allies of North Korea, were providing various forms of aid to the North Korean regime. However, the naval blockade made it extremely difficult for either power to deliver supplies by sea. This isolation was particularly effective in limiting the delivery of Soviet and Chinese military equipment, which was vital to the North Korean war effort.

By denying North Korea access to maritime routes, the U.N. forces prevented large-scale deliveries of weapons, ammunition, and other critical supplies that could have otherwise bolstered the North Korean forces. This isolation also had a broader diplomatic impact, as it underscored the U.N.'s ability to effectively contain the spread of communism on the Korean Peninsula. Without the ability to receive external aid by sea, North Korea became increasingly reliant on overland supply routes, which were themselves vulnerable to interdiction by U.N. air forces.

The naval blockade was a key element in the U.N. strategy to isolate and weaken North Korea. By cutting off access to the sea, disrupting supply routes, and preventing additional external aid from reaching North Korea, the blockade significantly undermined the North Korean war effort. This, combined with ongoing air and ground operations, played a major role in slowing the North Korean advance and creating the conditions necessary for U.N. forces to mount a successful counteroffensive later in the war.

One of the most vital contributions of naval forces during the Korean War was their ability to execute amphibious operations, which provided U.N. forces with strategic flexibility and the element of surprise. Amphibious assaults, reinforcements, and evacuations were critical in shaping the course of the war, allowing U.N. commanders to adapt to the fast-changing dynamics of the conflict. With North Korean forces rapidly advancing across South Korea in the early months of the war, the ability to strike back along the Korean coastline became essential to halting the Communist momentum and regaining lost ground.

Naval forces enabled U.N. troops to bypass heavily fortified inland positions by launching amphibious assaults from the sea, landing behind enemy lines and disrupting the North Korean war effort. These operations provided a degree of tactical flexibility that allowed U.N. forces to remain on the offensive, even when their positions on the ground were threatened. In addition to assaults, amphibious capabilities also allowed for rapid reinforcement of ground troops in coastal areas and facilitated crucial evacuations when ground defenses were overrun.

The Inchon Landing

The most famous and consequential amphibious operation of the Korean War was the Inchon Landing, which took place on September 15, 1950. Planned and executed by General MacArthur, the operation was designed to retake Seoul and reverse the momentum of the war, which at the time was overwhelmingly in favor of the North Korean forces. The success of the Inchon Landing hinged on its execution and the element of surprise, as Inchon itself was an extremely difficult location for an amphibious assault.

The planning of the Inchon operation involved careful consideration of several significant challenges. Inchon, located on South Korea's west coast, was known for its difficult tides, rocky archipelago, narrow approaches, and mudflats, making it an unlikely target for an amphibious landing. Additionally, the city was heavily defended by North Korean forces, with strong coastal fortifications guarding the harbor. However, MacArthur's bold decision to attack at Inchon took advantage of these challenges, as the North Koreans did not expect an assault in such a difficult location.

On the morning of September 15, U.S. and U.N. naval forces launched a surprise assault on Inchon, supported by naval gunfire and air strikes. The attack caught the North Korean forces off guard, and in less than two weeks, U.N. troops had recaptured Seoul, cutting off North Korean supply lines and forcing their troops to retreat. The Inchon Landing was a decisive turning point in the war, as it allowed U.N. forces to break out of the Pusan Perimeter and shift from a defensive to an offensive strategy. The recapture of Seoul not only provided a psychological boost to the U.N. coalition but also weakened North Korean control over the south, marking the beginning of their retreat northward.

The strategic significance of the Inchon Landing cannot be overstated. It was a masterclass in amphibious warfare, demonstrating how naval forces could be used to achieve surprise, disrupt enemy defenses, and secure key objectives. The success of Inchon effectively reversed the course of the war, placing North Korean forces on the defensive and allowing U.N. forces to regain the initiative.

While the Inchon Landing is the most well-known amphibious operation of the war, it was by no means the only one. Throughout the Korean War, the U.S. Navy and allied naval forces conducted several additional amphibious operations to reinforce ground units, support offensive campaigns, and evacuate troops when necessary.

One of the most notable examples of an amphibious evacuation occurred after the Battle of Chosin Reservoir in late 1950. After suffering significant losses in the face of overwhelming Chinese forces, U.N. troops, including the U.S. Marines, were forced to retreat to the port of Hungnam on the east coast. The U.N. naval forces played a critical role in this evacuation, ensuring that over 100,000 troops, as well as civilians and equipment, were safely evacuated by sea. The evacuation of Hungnam stands as a testament to the importance of amphibious capabilities in providing flexibility during wartime, allowing U.N. forces to regroup and fight another day.

In addition to evacuations, naval forces conducted several smaller-scale amphibious assaults throughout the war, targeting

North Korean coastal defenses and supply routes. These operations served to harass enemy forces, secure key coastal regions, and provide direct support to ground offensives by inserting troops behind enemy lines. The ability to launch amphibious assaults at multiple points along the Korean coastline kept North Korean and Chinese forces off balance, forcing them to divert troops and resources away from their main fronts to defend against potential landings.

Naval Logistics and Support

Beyond amphibious operations, the naval forces provided crucial logistical support that sustained U.N. ground operations throughout the Korean War. Naval fleets ensured that U.N. troops had the supplies, fuel, and medical aid they needed to continue fighting, particularly during the early stages of the war when supply lines were under constant threat from North Korean advances. The ability to transport large quantities of supplies by sea gave U.N. forces a logistical advantage, allowing them to quickly resupply units and maintain combat readiness.

Naval fleets played a key role in protecting the flow of supplies to U.N. troops fighting on the Korean Peninsula. U.S. Navy vessels, along with allied ships, escorted supply convoys from Japan and other bases to ports in South Korea, ensuring that critical materials reached the front lines. This logistical lifeline allowed U.N. forces to maintain a steady stream of reinforcements, ammunition, food, and medical supplies, preventing the collapse of ground defenses in key battles such as the Pusan Perimeter.

In addition to delivering supplies, naval forces provided medical evacuations for wounded soldiers, using hospital ships stationed off the coast of Korea. These ships offered essential care to troops who had been injured in battle, stabilizing them before they could be transported to hospitals in Japan or the

United States. Without naval support, the U.N. ground forces would have failed to maintain their strength and operational capacity, particularly during the most intense phases of the war.

Naval gunfire was another vital component of the support provided by U.N. forces. Throughout the Korean War, naval artillery played a key role in softening enemy positions, supporting amphibious assaults, and providing close fire support for ground offensives. U.S. battleships, cruisers, and destroyers stationed off the coast of Korea frequently used their heavy guns to bombard North Korean and Chinese positions, creating opportunities for U.N. ground forces to advance.

One of the most significant instances of naval gunfire support occurred during the Inchon Landing, where naval artillery was used to destroy North Korean coastal defenses, clear mines, and prepare the way for the amphibious assault. This combination of air strikes and naval bombardments was instrumental in ensuring the success of the operation. Similarly, during the retreat from the Chosin Reservoir, naval gunfire provided covering fire for the evacuating U.N. forces, helping to hold back pursuing Chinese troops and ensuring the safe withdrawal of tens of thousands of soldiers.

Naval gunfire support also played a crucial role in battles along the east coast of Korea, where U.N. forces conducted operations to push back enemy troops and secure vital supply routes. The ability of naval forces to deliver precise, long-range artillery fire provided U.N. commanders with a flexible and powerful tool to support their ground operations, making naval gunfire an integral part of the overall military strategy during the Korean War.

Despite the success and strategic value of naval operations during the Korean War, the U.S. Navy and its allied fleets faced significant challenges throughout the conflict. These obstacles came not only from the enemy's countermeasures but also from the difficult geography and harsh environmental conditions of the Korean Peninsula. Naval forces had to continually adapt to overcome these challenges and maintain their operational effectiveness.

From the outset of the war, North Korean forces attempted to defend their coastlines and disrupt the U.N. naval blockades. These efforts included fortifying key coastal positions and deploying coastal artillery to target U.N. ships conducting bombardments or supporting amphibious operations. Although North Korea's naval capabilities were limited, they sought to exploit their knowledge of local waters and geographical advantages to counter the superior U.N. fleets.

One of the primary threats to U.N. naval dominance came from Soviet-supplied submarines. While North Korea did not have an advanced submarine fleet, Soviet submarines posed a considerable risk, particularly in the early stages of the conflict when U.N. ships were operating close to North Korean waters. Submarine activity, along with the presence of mines and other anti-ship defenses, made coastal operations more perilous. The U.S. Navy had to deploy anti-submarine warfare (ASW) measures, including sonar-equipped destroyers, to counter these underwater threats.

Coastal artillery also proved a significant challenge. The North Korean and, later, Chinese forces positioned heavy artillery along the coast to engage U.N. ships. These guns, often hidden in rugged terrain or fortified positions, could inflict serious damage on U.N. vessels, especially during close-in naval bombardment operations. Naval forces had to neutralize these positions with air strikes and long-range naval gunfire, but the threat of coastal artillery remained a constant concern, particularly during amphibious operations.

The geography of the Korean Peninsula presented its own set of challenges for naval operations. Korea's rugged coastline, characterized by jagged cliffs, narrow inlets, and shallow waters, made navigation difficult, especially for larger vessels. These geographic features created natural choke points, where ships could be vulnerable to mines, coastal defenses, or submarine attacks. Navigational challenges were especially pronounced during amphibious operations, such as the Inchon Landing, where the unique tidal patterns and shallow mudflats added another layer of complexity.

Extreme weather conditions also posed a significant challenge to naval forces. Korea's harsh winters, marked by freezing temperatures and heavy snow, made naval operations difficult and dangerous. Ice buildup on decks and equipment could reduce the operational effectiveness of ships and aircraft, while storms and rough seas complicated supply missions and amphibious assaults. In the summer, monsoons brought heavy rains and strong winds, further hampering naval activity and making it difficult to maintain a consistent presence off the Korean coast.

These environmental and logistical difficulties required U.N. naval commanders to develop creative solutions. Amphibious landings had to be timed perfectly to account for tides, weather, and terrain, while resupply missions had to be flexible enough to adapt to sudden changes in conditions. Despite these challenges, the naval forces managed to maintain their operational tempo throughout the war, showcasing their resilience and adaptability.

While naval dominance helped turn the tide of the war in favor of the U.N. forces, it also contributed to the eventual stalemate that characterized the later stages of the conflict. By maintaining control of supply lines and conducting amphibious operations, the U.N. was able to prevent the North Korean and Chinese forces from gaining a decisive victory. However, naval power alone could not bring about a final resolution to the conflict, as the war devolved into a grinding stalemate along the 38th Parallel.

In the final stages of the war, naval forces played a crucial role in maintaining the balance of power. The ability to resupply U.N. ground troops, conduct coastal bombardments, and support amphibious operations helped ensure that the U.N. coalition could hold its defensive lines, even as the frontlines remained relatively static. While the naval operations did not directly lead to a military victory, they were instrumental in preventing further advances by Communist forces and maintaining the U.N.'s strategic position.

THE ROLE OF HELICOPTERS

The Korean War marked a critical turning point in the evolution of modern warfare, serving as the first major conflict in which helicopters and jet aircraft played a prominent role on the battlefield. Before Korea, air power had already proven its value in World War II, but the technological advancements seen during the Korean War signaled the beginning of a new era in military tactics and battlefield logistics. Helicopters and jets, both relatively new to warfare at the time, significantly altered the dynamics of combat, introducing unprecedented mobility and aerial superiority that changed the way battles were fought and supported.

Helicopters, such as the Bell H-13 "Sioux," became indispensable tools for medical evacuation (medevac) and troop transport. For the first time, wounded soldiers could be swiftly evacuated from the battlefield to field hospitals, dramatically improving survival rates and reducing fatalities from otherwise treatable injuries. Beyond medical evacuations, helicopters provided logistical support by delivering troops and supplies to remote or otherwise inaccessible areas, overcoming the rugged terrain of Korea, which often made traditional troop movements difficult or slow.

The advent of jet aircraft, like the U.S. F-86 Sabre, transformed air combat. Dogfights between U.N. jets and Soviet-supplied MiG-15s over "MiG Alley" marked the first sustained jet-to-jet aerial combat in history. These high-speed engagements introduced new challenges and required new tactics, as traditional propeller-driven planes were quickly outmatched by the maneuverability, speed, and firepower of jet fighters. In addition to air superiority, jet aircraft provided crucial close air support for ground troops, targeting enemy positions with precision and reshaping how air power was integrated into tactical ground operations.

The use of helicopters for medical and logistical purposes, combined with the dominance of jet aircraft in air combat, represented a transformative shift in battlefield dynamics during the Korean War. These innovations not only enhanced the U.N. forces' ability to respond to challenges but also laid the foundation for modern military doctrine, which continues to rely heavily on aerial mobility and firepower.

One of the most revolutionary uses of helicopters during the Korean War was in the field of medical evacuation, or medevac. Before the widespread use of helicopters wounded soldiers often had to wait hours or even days to be transported to field hospitals, especially in remote or mountainous regions. This delay frequently resulted in the deaths of soldiers who might otherwise have survived had they received prompt medical attention. With the introduction of helicopters like the Bell H-13 Sioux and Sikorsky H-5, this paradigm shifted dramatically.

The Bell H-13, small and agile, was capable of landing in tight, difficult terrain, making it ideal for extracting wounded soldiers from the battlefield. Its role as a medevac helicopter meant that injured troops could be transported from the front lines to medical facilities within minutes or hours, greatly improving their chances of survival. Helicopters reduced the average time it took to evacuate a wounded soldier by more than half, and the increased speed of medical care significantly lowered mortality rates from battlefield injuries.

During the Battle of the Pusan Perimeter in late summer 1950, helicopters, like the Sikorsky H-5, played a pivotal role in saving countless lives through medical evacuations, a development that marked a turning point in military medical logistics. One particularly notable instance involved First Lieutenant Paul W. van Boven, a veteran B-17 pilot, who now flew the H-5 helicopter for the 3rd Air Rescue Squadron.

On September 4, 1950, his team received an urgent call: a pilot, Captain Robert E. Wayne, had gone down behind enemy lines. With no official protocol for such a rescue, command left the decision to his pilots. Van Boven volunteered without hesitation. Determined, he climbed into his unarmed, vulnerable H-5 with Corporal John Fuentez as his paramedic.

These helicopters, though unarmed and unarmored, were small nimble enough to navigate the rugged terrain and fly low to avoid enemy anti-aircraft fire.

Flying east along the coastline, van Boven slipped behind enemy lines and quickly spotted smoke from the downed Mustang. With four remaining F-51s providing cover, he skimmed low over the ground, dodging enemy fire as he closed in on the rice paddy where Captain Wayne lay, badly burned and surrounded. The rescuing F-51s circled above, strafing North Korean forces and buying van Boven precious seconds.

Van Boven maneuvered his helicopter to the field's edge, disregarding bullets striking the fuselage. Wayne, catching sight of the approaching H-5, ran through excruciating pain, his white undershirt waving like a surrender flag. As North Korean troops closed in, one soldier took aim at the wounded pilot. However, in a precise pass, an F-51's .50-caliber fire neutralized the threat just yards away.

Reaching Wayne, Fuentez pulled him aboard, and van Boven lifted off amid enemy gunfire, steering toward safety. Damaged but operable, the H-5 reached the Pusan Perimeter, delivering Captain Wayne to medical care. Through bravery and skill, van Boven completed one of the first combat rescues by helicopter in history, paving the way for countless lives saved.

The impact of helicopter evacuations during the Pusan Perimeter not only saved lives but also boosted the morale of U.N. troops. Soldiers knew that if they were injured, they had a significantly higher chance of survival because of the helicopters. This confidence allowed them to fight harder, knowing they wouldn't be left on the battlefield for extended periods like in previous conflicts.

First Lieutenant van Boven's actions during the battle would go on to symbolize the critical role of air power in medical logistics, and his bravery earned him commendations for his service. The lessons learned during these early helicopter missions at Pusan shaped the future of military medical evacuations, which became a standard practice in wars to come.

Beyond medical evacuation, helicopters played a critical role in troop transport and logistics, providing a level of flexibility and mobility that was essential in the challenging Korean terrain. The mountainous geography, combined with Korea's narrow valleys and harsh weather conditions, made it difficult for ground convoys to transport troops and supplies quickly and efficiently. Helicopters became a game-changer in overcoming these logistical hurdles.

In addition to troop transport, helicopters were used to deliver supplies, ammunition, and reinforcements to forward positions, where ground convoys would have been too slow or vulnerable to enemy attacks. During operations in Korea's rugged terrain, helicopters often ferried supplies to troops engaged in battle on mountain ridges or in isolated valleys, maintaining their fighting capability and ensuring that they could sustain operations without being cut off from support. The increased mobility and logistical support provided by helicopters allowed U.N. forces to conduct operations that would have been impossible otherwise, enhancing their strategic and tactical flexibility.

Helicopters also served as crucial tools for reconnaissance and battlefield coordination, providing real-time intelligence that could be used to guide artillery strikes, air support, and troop movements. The aerial vantage point offered by helicopters allowed U.N. forces to observe enemy movements and positions more effectively than ground-based reconnaissance. Helicopters could quickly scout the battlefield, identify enemy positions, and relay that information to ground commanders, improving decision-making and the overall coordination of combat operations.

In addition to reconnaissance, helicopters were used to direct artillery and air strikes with greater precision. By hovering over the battlefield, helicopter crews could mark enemy positions for targeted bombardments, ensuring that U.N. firepower was applied where it was most needed. This integration of helicopters into battlefield coordination enhanced the effectiveness of U.N. firepower and reduced the likelihood of friendly fire incidents.

Helicopters fundamentally changed battlefield operations in the Korean War, offering new capabilities in medical evacuation, troop transport, logistics, and reconnaissance. Their ability to operate in challenging terrain, deliver rapid mobility, and provide real-time battlefield intelligence made them an indispensable asset to U.N. forces, reshaping the dynamics of combat and enhancing the overall effectiveness of military operations in Korea.

INTRODUCTION OF JET FIGHTERS

The Korean War was the first major conflict where jet aircraft took center stage, representing a significant leap in aviation technology and air combat tactics. Prior to the Korean War, most aerial engagements relied on propeller-driven planes, which had dominated the skies during World War II. However, with the introduction of jet-powered aircraft, both the speed and intensity of air combat evolved dramatically. The transition from propeller-driven aircraft to jet fighters had a profound impact on the overall dynamics of the war, as control of the skies became essential for both offensive and defensive operations.

One development during the Korean War was the introduction of jet fighters by both U.N. and Communist forces. The U.S. Air Force deployed the F-86 Sabre, a cutting-edge fighter that represented the height of American aviation technology at the time. The F-86 was renowned for its speed, maneuverability, and its six, powerful .50-caliber machine guns, which made it a formidable opponent in aerial combat. Its swept-wing design allowed it to achieve greater speeds than previous aircraft, making it an ideal choice for intercepting enemy jets and providing close air support to ground forces.

On the Communist side, the Soviet Union supplied North Korea and China with the MiG-15, a highly advanced fighter jet that quickly became a cornerstone of their air forces. One of its most significant advantages was its ability to fly at altitudes of up to 51,000 feet, giving it a distinct edge over many U.N. aircraft, which struggled to operate effectively at such heights. This altitude advantage allowed the MiG-15 to launch attacks from above and retreat to higher altitudes, making it difficult for U.N. aircraft to engage effectively.

The MiG-15 was also heavily armed compared to its U.N. counterparts. It carried one 37mm Nudelman N-37 cannon and two 23mm NR-23 cannons, which were designed to inflict maximum damage on enemy aircraft, especially the large U.S. bombers like the B-29 Superfortress. The 37mm cannon, in particular, had a lower rate of fire but could deal devastating blows with just a few rounds, often crippling enemy aircraft with a single hit. The 23mm cannons complemented this with a higher rate of fire, giving the MiG-15 a versatile and lethal armament package.

The introduction of the MiG-15 and the opposing U.S. F-86 Sabre, revolutionized air warfare in Korea. Both aircraft became the central players in the battle for air superiority, but the MiG-

15's combination of high-altitude performance and powerful cannons made it a serious threat to U.N. air operations. Its presence forced U.N. forces to adapt their strategies and aircraft capabilities to counter the MiG's advantages, shaping the nature of aerial combat throughout the war.

THE FIRST JET DOGFIGHTS

A key battleground for jet fighters during the Korean War was a region known as "MiG Alley," located in the northwestern part of North Korea near the Yalu River, which bordered China. MiG Alley was the site of some of the first jet-on-jet dogfights in history, as U.N. pilots in their F-86 Sabres squared off against Communist pilots flying MiG-15s. These aerial battles marked a new era in air combat, as the speeds and altitudes at which the jets operated were far beyond what had been experienced in previous wars.

The F-86 was faster at lower altitudes, more agile in dogfights, and ultimately had a better kill ratio against the MiG-15, thanks in part to superior U.S. training and radar targeting capabilities. However, the MiG-15's high-altitude performance and armament kept it a formidable opponent, particularly in areas such as Mig Alley. Once U.N. pilots became accustomed to the MiG-15's strengths and weaknesses, and as improved F-86 models entered the theater to minimize the altitude gap, the U.S. established air superiority by the end of the war.

The air battles over MiG Alley were fierce, with U.N. pilots tasked with defending bombing missions, intercepting enemy jets, and maintaining air superiority to protect ground forces from enemy air attacks. MiG Alley was a hotly contested zone because it was near the main supply routes leading from China into North Korea, making it a strategic location for both sides. U.N. forces sought to disrupt these supply routes by bombing bridges, railways, and convoys, while Communist forces, including Soviet and Chinese pilots flying the MiG-15s, tried to protect them.

Notable aces emerged from these dogfights, with U.S. pilots such as Captain Joseph McConnell and Major James Jabara becoming legendary for their victories over MiG-15s. McConnell, who shot down sixteen MiG-15s, became the top U.S. ace of the war. On the other side, Soviet pilots, who often flew covertly as "volunteers," also achieved success, though their involvement was officially denied by the Soviet government at the time. These dogfights were not only significant for their tactical impact but also for the broader Cold War implications, as they represented direct, though unofficial, combat between U.S. and Soviet forces.

Air superiority played a critical role in shaping the outcome of the Korean War, as control of the skies allowed U.N. forces to carry out essential operations without fear of significant opposition from the enemy air force. The ability to conduct bombing raids, supply drops, and reconnaissance missions with minimal interference from North Korean or Chinese aircraft gave the U.N. a distinct advantage on the battlefield. U.N. jets, led by the F-86 Sabres, provided cover for B-29 bombers conducting strategic bombing raids deep into enemy territory, targeting supply depots, factories, and transportation networks crucial to the North Korean war effort.

The dominance of U.N. air power also ensured that ground forces received critical close air support during key battles. U.N. aircraft were able to target enemy positions, artillery, and bunkers with precision, significantly weakening Communist defenses and allowing ground forces to advance more effectively. The strategic importance of air superiority meant that U.N. ground operations were often closely coordinated with aerial bombardments, providing a multi-dimensional approach to combat that enhanced the overall effectiveness of military campaigns.

The Korean War also saw a major shift in how air power was

integrated into ground operations, with close air support (CAS) becoming a central element of U.N. military strategy. Jet aircraft, particularly fighter-bombers, were deployed to provide immediate, on-demand air strikes in support of ground troops. This integration of air and ground forces led to the development of new tactics that maximized the capabilities of both, resulting in more fluid and responsive battlefield operations.

Fighter-bombers like the F-80 Shooting Star and the F-84 Thunderjet played a pivotal role in close air support missions. These aircraft were designed to strike enemy targets with precision, using bombs, rockets, and machine guns to eliminate threats such as bunkers, artillery positions, and enemy troop concentrations. The ability to deliver these strikes with pinpoint accuracy made fighter-bombers an indispensable tool for ground commanders, who relied on them to break through heavily fortified positions and to suppress enemy fire during critical engagements.

Close air support missions were crucial in many battles during the Korean War, allowing U.N. ground forces to hold their lines and avoid potentially devastating defeats. A real example of this can be seen during the Battle of the Pusan Perimeter in August 1950, where U.N. forces were pushed to the brink by advancing North Korean troops. One key figure in these air missions was Major Louis J. Sebille of the 67th Fighter-Bomber Squadron, who earned a medal of honor for his heroic actions on August 5, 1950.

As North Korean troops established a bridgehead across the Naktong River, threatening Taegu, Sebille led a flight of three F-51 Mustangs to attack an armored column spotted near Hamchang-eup. Despite facing heavy anti-aircraft fire, he bravely dove into the fray, loaded with bombs and rockets. On his first attack, Sebille released only one bomb due to an unbalanced load, narrowly missing the target.

As he turned to make a second run, North Korean flak heavily damaged his aircraft, injuring him severely. Though advised to head for safety, Sebille refused, famously stating, "No, I'll never make it. I'm going back and get that bastard." He dove back toward the North Korean armored personnel carrier, firing his remaining rockets and machine guns before deliberately crashing his F-51 and its remaining bomb into the convoy. His selfless act destroyed a significant number of enemy troops and vehicles but cost him his life.

Sebille's actions exemplified the critical role of close air support in the Korean War, showcasing how airpower could turn the tide against a numerically superior enemy. Despite initial criticism and comparison to the WWII kamikaze, Sebille's brave action was later recognized posthumously with the Medal of Honor, underscoring the sacrifices made by airmen during the Battle of the Pusan Perimeter and future conflicts in the war. The coordination of air and ground forces was essential in preventing a U.N. collapse at the Pusan Perimeter, enabling a counteroffensive that would eventually reshape the war's trajectory.

Sebille's legacy lives on, not just in the honor he received but also in the vital role he played in protecting U.N. troops during one of the war's most challenging periods. His story is a testament to the bravery and dedication of those who served in the Korean War.

INTEGRATION OF AIR AND GROUND FORCES

One of the most significant tactical shifts during the Korean War was the integration of airstrikes with ground operations, creating a more cohesive and adaptable battlefield strategy. U.N. commanders developed new tactics that allowed for real-time coordination between air and ground units, using jets and helicopters to scout enemy positions, direct artillery fire, and provide immediate close air support when needed. This close integration enabled U.N. forces to respond quickly to changing conditions on the battlefield, whether it was repelling an enemy attack or launching an offensive of their own.

Helicopters and jets worked together in many of these coordinated operations. While helicopters provided reconnaissance and troop mobility, jets delivered the firepower needed to neutralize enemy defenses. This combination of mobility and firepower gave U.N. forces a significant tactical advantage, particularly in the rugged and mountainous terrain of Korea, where traditional ground-based tactics were often slow and cumbersome.

The introduction of helicopters and jets during the Korean War fundamentally changed traditional battlefield strategies. Helicopters allowed for rapid deployment of troops and supplies, enabling U.N. forces to outmaneuver their opponents and respond more quickly to threats. Meanwhile, jets provided the speed, firepower, and air superiority needed to dominate the skies and deliver precise, high-impact strikes on enemy positions.

Close air support missions, which became a staple of the war, allowed for immediate, on-the-spot firepower that could turn the tide of battles. The shift from conventional troop movements to more flexible, rapid deployment tactics meant that U.N. forces could adapt more easily to Korea's challenging terrain and the unpredictable nature of the conflict. As a result, air power became an essential component of U.N. military strategy, setting the stage for the use of helicopters and jets in future conflicts, most notably in Vietnam.

The emergence of jet aircraft and helicopters in the Korean War not only transformed the nature of air combat but also reshaped how wars were fought on the ground. These advancements provided the U.N. forces with new tools and strategies that would continue to influence military doctrine for decades to come.

NAVAL AND AIR POWER AS GAME CHANGERS

In a conflict where control over rugged terrain and narrow battle-fronts often resulted in a brutal war of attrition, the United Nations' ability to dominate the air and seas gave it a decisive strategic advantage. While Communist forces, particularly North Korea and China, relied on traditional land-based tactics and manpower, U.N. forces capitalized on their technological and logistical superiority, wielding naval and air power as tools that reshaped the course of the war.

Naval power, particularly through the implementation of blockades and amphibious operations, played a pivotal role in disrupting North Korean and Chinese supply lines. The U.S. Navy, along with allied fleets, successfully cut off North Korean access to the sea, preventing vital supplies and reinforcements from reaching Communist forces. Naval blockades crippled North Korea's ability to sustain its military offensives, while amphibious operations such as the Inchon Landing turned the tide of the war. Inchon exemplified how naval forces could be used not just to defend supply lines but also to launch surprise assaults that broke through enemy defenses and recaptured key strategic positions.

Air power, meanwhile, introduced a new dimension to modern warfare. The introduction of jet fighters such as the F-86 Sabre and the MiG-15 marked the dawn of jet-to-jet combat, where aerial dogfights over MiG Alley became a defining feature of the conflict. Control of the skies allowed U.N. forces to dominate not only the air but also the ground, with close air support missions and strategic bombing campaigns providing the firepower needed to weaken entrenched enemy positions. The use of fighter-bombers and jets to deliver precision strikes on enemy bunkers, artillery, and supply routes was a game-changer, enabling ground forces to advance where they would have otherwise been stalled.

In addition to their combat roles, helicopters became a life-line for U.N. forces operating in Korea's rugged terrain. The Bell H-13 Sioux and Sikorsky H-5 helicopters revolutionized battle-field logistics and medical evacuation (medevacs), ensuring that wounded soldiers were transported to field hospitals in record time. Helicopters also enhanced mobility for ground troops, bypassing Korea's challenging mountains and valleys and enabling swift reinforcements and supply deliveries. The ability of helicopters to navigate difficult terrain and provide real-time reconnaissance gave U.N. forces a critical edge in a war fought in some of the most inhospitable conditions imaginable.

INTELLIGENCE AND STRATEGY

"Every Battle Is Won Before It Is Ever Fought."

— SUN TZU, THE ART OF WAR

The Korean War was not only a battle of soldiers and artillery. It was a war of intelligence, deception, and strategic maneuvering. Both sides—U.N. forces and the Communist coalition—relied heavily on espionage, code-breaking, propaganda, and psychological operations to gain tactical and strategic advantages. However, despite these efforts, coordination challenges between the U.S., U.N., and South Korean forces often complicated operations, revealing the complexities of managing a multinational coalition in the heat of war.

ESPIONAGE AND CODE-BREAKING EFFORTS

Intelligence and espionage played a crucial, though often overlooked, role in shaping the outcomes of key battles during the Korean War. Both the United Nations forces, led primarily by the

United States, and the Communist forces of North Korea and China relied heavily on intelligence gathering to guide their military strategies and adjust to the rapidly changing dynamics of the war. As with previous conflicts, signals intelligence (SIGINT) and code-breaking efforts proved invaluable in providing insight into enemy operations. However, the Korean War presented unique challenges for both sides due to its rugged terrain, unpredictable weather, and the varied nature of communications.

For the U.N. forces, intelligence efforts focused on intercepting North Korean and Chinese communications to preemptively disrupt their operations. Signals intelligence units, listening posts, and code-breaking teams worked tirelessly to gather and analyze intercepted messages, which often provided early warnings of impending attacks or troop movements. Although these efforts didn't garner the same attention as similar operations during World War II, such as the famous ULTRA program, they were nonetheless critical in allowing U.N. forces to stay one step ahead of their adversaries.

On the other hand, North Korea and China employed their own espionage tactics, deploying spies, informants, and infiltrators to gather valuable information on U.N. troop deployments, logistical operations, and defensive positions. Early in the war, Communist espionage efforts were particularly successful, exploiting weaknesses in the U.N.'s hastily organized defenses, especially around the Pusan Perimeter. However, both sides faced substantial challenges in intelligence collection, from the rugged and mountainous Korean terrain to the use of rudimentary communication methods, such as runners or verbal commands, which made traditional interception more difficult.

Signals Intelligence (SIGINT)

One of the main pillars of U.N. intelligence gathering was SIGINT, which involved intercepting North Korean and Chinese military communications to monitor troop movements, supply lines, and battlefield tactics. Listening stations, located in Japan and South Korea, worked around the clock to capture enemy radio transmissions. These stations used a variety of methods, including radio frequency scanning and direction-finding equipment, to identify and record enemy broadcasts.

SIGINT operations allowed U.N. forces to gain valuable insights into enemy plans, particularly as Chinese forces began entering the conflict in late 1950. By listening in on Chinese and North Korean communications, U.N. intelligence units could determine where enemy forces were massing and when they planned to launch new offensives. This allowed U.N. commanders to reposition their forces, reinforce vulnerable positions, and prepare for impending attacks, often mitigating the impact of Communist offensives.

However, these operations were not without their limitations. The rugged, mountainous terrain of Korea posed significant challenges for radio wave transmission and interception. The geography often caused radio signals to be blocked or distorted, making it difficult to capture clear transmissions. Moreover, North Korean and Chinese forces were aware of the U.N.'s SIGINT capabilities and frequently employed basic communication methods to avoid interception, including verbal messages relayed by couriers or low-tech radio systems that were more difficult to track.

During the Korean War, the efforts of U.N. code-breaking units played a pivotal role in uncovering enemy strategies and movements. One notable figure in these operations was Colonel John "Jack" Singlaub, a U.S. Army officer who led a covert intelligence unit responsible for intercepting and decoding enemy communications. Working alongside a team of skilled cryptographers, Singlaub's unit focused on decrypting messages from North Korean and Chinese military commanders.

In late 1950, during the Chinese intervention, U.N. forces

were taken by surprise as tens of thousands of Chinese troops entered the war, launching a series of coordinated offensives. The Chinese were using sophisticated radio encryption methods to conceal their plans and troop movements. Singlaub's team, operating out of Tokyo, intercepted a series of encrypted communications from Chinese commanders to their front-line units, revealing plans for a massive attack aimed at encircling U.N. forces near the Ch'ongch'on River.

By carefully analyzing the Chinese codes, Singlaub's team managed to decrypt key sections of the messages. These decrypted communications revealed that Chinese forces were planning to outflank U.N. positions and overwhelm them with a pincer movement. Armed with this critical intelligence, U.N. commanders, including General Almond, were able to reposition their troops and bolster defenses along the vulnerable sectors of the front line. As a result, U.N. forces were able to retreat in a more orderly fashion, avoiding complete encirclement and buying valuable time to regroup.

The success of Singlaub and his code-breaking team provided U.N. forces with a much-needed advantage at a critical moment in the war. By intercepting and deciphering Chinese communications, U.N. commanders gained a clearer picture of enemy movements, supply routes, and attack strategies, helping them avoid catastrophic defeats and adjust their tactics accordingly. These efforts underscored the crucial role that intelligence, particularly code-breaking, played in maintaining the balance on the battlefield during the Korean War.

Both SIGINT and code-breaking operations were heavily influenced by the unique challenges posed by the Korean terrain. The mountains and valleys that interfered with radio transmissions led U.N. forces to develop innovative solutions, such as placing listening stations on high ground or using specialized equipment to amplify weak signals. Even so, the terrain remained a significant obstacle throughout the war.

Another challenge was the use of rudimentary communication methods by North Korean and Chinese forces. Unlike in World War II, where highly encrypted electronic communications were common, many messages during the Korean War were delivered verbally through human couriers or relied on pre-arranged verbal codes that were difficult to intercept or decipher. These basic methods were difficult to intercept and often bypassed traditional intelligence-gathering techniques altogether. This forced U.N. forces to adapt their intelligence efforts and integrate multiple forms of intelligence, including aerial reconnaissance, human intelligence (HUMINT), and traditional SIGINT, to build a complete picture of enemy operations.

U.N. intelligence and code-breaking efforts during the Korean War were critical in providing strategic advantages over Communist forces despite the numerous challenges posed by Korea's geography and the low-tech nature of the enemy's communications. The ability to intercept and decrypt enemy messages allowed U.N. commanders to anticipate enemy movements and prepare for attacks, contributing to key battlefield successes. However, the limitations faced by these efforts highlighted the evolving nature of intelligence work in the post-World War II era and set the stage for future advancements in military intelligence gathering.

Communist Espionage and Intelligence

While U.N. forces developed sophisticated methods of gathering intelligence, North Korea and China employed their own espionage strategies, leveraging spies and informants to infiltrate U.N. operations and collect valuable information on troop movements, supply lines, and defensive positions. The Communists' approach to intelligence, though less technologically advanced than the U.N.'s SIGINT efforts, was effective in several key ways, particularly during the early stages of the war. By embedding operatives within U.N.-controlled areas and exploiting vulnerabilities in U.N. supply chains, North Korea and China were able to gather critical intelligence that shaped their military strategy.

Spies and informants were strategically deployed to infiltrate U.N. operations and gather intelligence, particularly during the chaotic early months of the war when U.N. forces were still organizing their defenses around the Pusan Perimeter. This human espionage provided vital information on U.N. troop movements, supply routes, and defensive plans, allowing the Communist forces to adapt their strategies and exploit weaknesses in the U.N.'s positioning.

In the early stages of the war, the U.N. was caught off guard by the sheer scale and intensity of the North Korean invasion. With U.N. forces scrambling to establish a cohesive defense, North Korean and Chinese intelligence operatives were able to gather valuable information with relative ease.

During the defense of the Pusan Perimeter, the North Korean People's Army employed various espionage tactics to undermine U.N. operations. One significant strategy involved infiltrating U.N.-controlled areas by utilizing civilian disguises, such as refugees, defectors or laborers, to gather crucial intelligence. This enabled NKPA agents to observe and report on U.N. troop movements, supply routes, and logistical operations.

Agents would frequent key logistical hubs, like the port city of Pusan, where they could blend in with dockworkers and access sensitive areas. By monitoring the flow of supplies and reinforcements, they gathered detailed information about the timing, types, and destinations of supply convoys heading to the front lines, and even morale within U.N. ranks. This intelligence was vital for identifying vulnerabilities in U.N. defenses.

In early September 1950, for example, intelligence gathered about a key supply route led to a coordinated surprise attack by North Korean forces. Armed with knowledge of U.N. logistics, the KPA launched ambushes on convoys, resulting in significant losses and hindering the resupply efforts for U.N. troops. Such disruptions had a considerable impact on U.N. operations during critical phases of the battle.

These tactics demonstrated the significant role that espionage and intelligence-gathering played in shaping the course of the Pusan Perimeter defense, demonstrating how the KPA leveraged both covert operations and local networks to enhance their military effectiveness against U.N. forces.

In addition to professional spies, Communist forces also relied heavily on informants—locals sympathetic to the North Korean or Chinese cause, who were often coerced or persuaded to provide information on U.N. operations. These informants would pass along details about troop movements, supply convoys, and even the location of key infrastructure, such as bridges or roads, that the Communist forces could target to disrupt U.N. operations.

Beyond gathering information on troop movements and defensive positions, North Korea and China also focused heavily on U.N. logistical operations, recognizing that disrupting supply lines could cripple the effectiveness of U.N. forces. The Korean War's logistical challenges were immense, with U.N. troops needing to be supplied with food, ammunition, fuel, and medical supplies across difficult and often inaccessible terrain. Communist intelligence operatives worked tirelessly to gather intelligence on these logistical operations, targeting supply routes and convoys as a way to weaken U.N. forces.

The mountainous terrain of Korea made U.N. supply lines particularly vulnerable, as convoys were often forced to navigate narrow roads and passes, which were easily monitored or ambushed by Communist forces. Spies and informants played a key role in identifying the routes taken by U.N. supply convoys, allowing North Korean and Chinese forces to stage ambushes or set up roadblocks that disrupted the flow of supplies to the front lines.

One of the most significant impacts of Communist espionage on U.N. supply security occurred during the Battle of Chosin Reservoir. Communist forces, aided by intelligence gathered on U.N. logistical movements, were able to launch coordinated attacks on U.N. supply routes, cutting off vital supplies to troops engaged in battle. The harsh winter conditions, combined with the disruption of supply lines, made the situation for U.N. forces at Chosin Reservoir even more dire. While U.N. troops eventually managed to break out of the encirclement, the logistical challenges they faced were exacerbated by the success of Communist espionage efforts, leading to an increase in casualties and frostbite.

In response to these infiltration efforts, U.N. forces had to make tactical adjustments to improve the security of their supply lines. This included altering convoy routes, increasing security around key infrastructure, and employing aerial reconnaissance to monitor for potential ambushes. Despite these measures, Communist espionage continued to pose a significant threat to U.N. logistical operations throughout the war, forcing the U.N. to adapt continually to maintain the flow of supplies to their troops.

Technology in Espionage and Code-breaking

While both sides relied on human intelligence to gather critical information during the Korean War, technology also played a key role in espionage and code-breaking efforts. The U.N., with its more advanced military technology, utilized sophisticated tools for intercepting and decoding enemy communications. While North Korea and China often relied on simpler, low-tech communication methods to evade interception, they did use encrypted electronic messaging for much of their communications.

On the U.N. side, the use of signals intelligence (SIGINT) was crucial in gathering information on North Korean and

Chinese troop movements, supply lines, and attack plans. The U.S. Military, in particular, employed cutting-edge technology developed during World War II to intercept and decode enemy communications. Listening stations in Japan and South Korea worked around the clock to monitor enemy radio transmissions, using sophisticated radio direction-finding equipment to pinpoint the location of Communist forces.

The success of SIGINT operations depended heavily on the cryptography experts who worked tirelessly to decrypt enemy messages. Many of these experts had honed their skills during World War II, where they had worked on projects like ULTRA, which decrypted German communications. These same cryptographers applied their skills to the Korean War, helping U.N. forces stay ahead of their adversaries by providing crucial information about upcoming attacks or changes in enemy strategy.

However, despite these technological advances, SIGINT had its limitations. The rugged terrain of Korea, combined with the relatively rudimentary communications systems used by the North Korean and Chinese forces, made it difficult to intercept reliable signals. Additionally, the U.N.'s reliance on technology sometimes led to blind spots in their intelligence gathering, as the enemy increasingly turned to low-tech methods of communication to avoid detection.

In some cases, North Korean and Chinese commanders would give verbal orders to their troops in person, further complicating U.N. efforts to gather intelligence. These orders were often delivered just before an attack, leaving U.N. forces with little time to react. Additionally, when radios were used, they were often basic and operated on frequencies that were harder to track, making it difficult for U.N. forces to capture the transmissions.

The reliance on these primitive communication methods provided Communist forces with a significant advantage in evading U.N. SIGINT efforts. While the U.N. excelled at intercepting and decoding radio transmissions, the simplicity of the Communists' communication network often allowed key messages to slip through undetected. This forced the U.N. to rely more heavily on human intelligence and other forms of reconnaissance to fill the gaps left by SIGINT.

In conclusion, the combination of technological advancements and low-tech tactics defined the espionage and intelligence efforts on both sides of the Korean War. While the U.N. leveraged cutting-edge SIGINT and code-breaking tools, North Korea and China countered with simple yet effective communication methods, creating a unique intelligence battle that shaped the course of the conflict.

That said, the U.N. forces, particularly the U.S. Military, achieved significant intelligence successes throughout the Korean War, often through a combination of SIGINT and code-breaking efforts. One of the most notable victories in intelligence gathering came from the U.N.'s ability to intercept and decrypt enemy communications, providing critical insights into North Korean and Chinese military strategies. This information frequently gave U.N. commanders a strategic advantage, allowing them to anticipate enemy movements and plan counteroffensives accordingly.

One of the most prominent examples of successful intelligence gathering by the U.N. occurred during the Inchon Landing, which relied heavily on SIGINT to monitor North Korean communications. By intercepting and decoding enemy messages, U.N. intelligence was able to confirm that the North Koreans were unprepared for an attack on the western coast. This information proved crucial in the decision to proceed with the Inchon operation, which ultimately turned the tide of the war by recapturing Seoul and forcing North Korean forces into retreat. The success of this operation is a testament to the importance of timely and accurate intelligence in military strategy.

Other examples of U.N. intelligence successes include the

interception of Chinese communications during their intervention in the war. By decrypting messages between Chinese commanders, U.N. forces were able to anticipate several key offensives, giving them time to reinforce vulnerable positions and counterattack. These intelligence breakthroughs helped prevent complete disaster for U.N. forces during the harsh winter months of 1950–51, when Chinese troops launched a series of powerful offensives.

On the Communist side, both North Korea and China experienced their own intelligence triumphs, particularly in the early stages of the war. One of the key successes of Communist espionage was their ability to gather valuable information about U.N. defenses during the critical period around the Pusan Perimeter. In the summer of 1950, as U.N. forces hastily organized their defensive line around the perimeter, North Korean spies were able to infiltrate U.N. operations and relay important details about troop positions, logistical vulnerabilities, and weak points in the defensive line. This intelligence allowed North Korean forces to plan coordinated attacks that nearly breached the perimeter, forcing U.N. commanders to allocate reinforcements and reconfigure their defensive strategies.

Another early intelligence success for Communist forces came during China's intervention in the war. Chinese spies and informants were able to gather intelligence on U.N. troop movements and supply lines, providing Chinese commanders with the information they needed to plan their massive surprise offensive in October 1950. The success of this offensive, which caught U.N. forces off guard and forced them into retreat, can be attributed in part to the effective intelligence gathered by Chinese operatives on the ground.

Despite their successes, both the U.N. and Communist forces faced significant intelligence failures and missed opportunities during the Korean War. These failures often resulted from inaccurate or incomplete information, leading to tactical missteps or missed chances to capitalize on enemy weaknesses.

For the U.N., one of the most notable intelligence failures occurred early in the war when their code-breaking efforts proved inadequate in anticipating North Korea's invasion in June 1950. Although U.N. forces were aware of escalating tensions on the Korean Peninsula, their intelligence failed to detect the full scope and timing of North Korea's planned offensive. As a result, U.N. forces were caught unprepared for the invasion, leading to the rapid collapse of South Korean defenses and a scramble to organize an effective counteroffensive.

This mistake was repeated when initial intelligence reports underestimated the scale of Chinese troop deployments. This miscalculation led to the devastating surprise offensive that forced U.N. forces into rapid retreat during the winter of 1950–51.

The intelligence operations conducted during the Korean War provided valuable lessons that would shape future conflicts. The use of SIGINT and code-breaking in Korea underscored the importance of advanced signals intelligence capabilities in modern warfare. This era saw the beginning of substantial developments in electronic warfare, which would later expand during the Cold War as both sides developed more intricate interception, jamming, and countermeasures. For example, by the 1960s, the Soviet Union engaged in widespread radio jamming to censor information, demonstrating the increasing role of electronic warfare as technology advanced.

The evolving tactics of low-tech communication methods used by Communist forces highlighted the need for better counter-espionage measures. The Korean War demonstrated the critical importance of human intelligence (HUMINT), particularly in the form of spies and informants. Both the U.N. and Communist forces relied heavily on HUMINT to gather real-time information about enemy movements, logistical operations, and battlefield conditions. This reliance on human intelligence would continue to be a key component of military strategy in subsequent conflicts, as nations around the world worked to improve their intelligence-gathering capabilities.

PSYCHOLOGICAL OPERATIONS AND PROPAGANDA

Psychological operations (**PSYOP**) and propaganda were essential tools used by both the United Nations and Communist forces during the Korean War. While the battles raged on the ground, an equally important war for hearts and minds was fought through messaging, aimed at influencing the morale of soldiers and civilians alike. For the U.N., psychological operations were designed to weaken the resolve of North Korean and Chinese troops, encouraging them to defect or surrender. Similarly, Communist forces relied heavily on propaganda to demonize U.N. forces and rally support from their soldiers and civilian populations.

The use of psychological warfare in the Korean War went beyond mere persuasion; it aimed to manipulate perceptions, create confusion, and disrupt enemy cohesion. On both sides, **PSYOP** and propaganda became pivotal in shaping not only the morale and decision-making of the troops but also the political will of the civilian population. By disseminating targeted messages through leaflets, broadcasts, and re-education programs, both the U.N. and Communist forces sought to create psychological pressure that could shift the course of the war in their favor.

The United Nations forces, led by the U.S., implemented a range of psychological operations designed to disrupt enemy morale and encourage defections. These operations included large-scale leaflet campaigns, loudspeaker broadcasts, and targeted psychological efforts aimed at weakening the authority of Communist leaders. Through these tactics, the U.N. sought to create internal discord among North Korean and Chinese troops while sowing seeds of doubt about the leadership and overall objectives of the Communist war effort.

One of the primary tools in the U.N.'s psychological operations arsenal was the widespread use of leaflets, which were dropped over North Korean and Chinese lines. These leaflets carried a variety of messages, ranging from offers of safe passage to defectors to encouraging enemy soldiers to surrender in exchange for humane treatment. By playing on the fears and uncertainties of Communist soldiers, these leaflets aimed to undermine their willingness to fight.

The messages on the leaflets were carefully crafted to exploit the psychological vulnerabilities of the enemy. For example, some leaflets highlighted the dire conditions on the front lines, emphasizing the scarcity of food and supplies among North Korean and Chinese forces. Others promised defectors that they would receive warm meals, medical care, and shelter if they surrendered. These types of appeals to basic human needs often proved effective, with thousands of Communist soldiers defecting to U.N. lines over the course of the war.

The impact of these leaflet campaigns was significant. Not only did they lead to defections, but they also had a demoralizing effect on the broader ranks of Communist troops. By constantly reinforcing the idea that there was an alternative to fighting, the U.N. undermined the resolve of enemy soldiers, leading to cases where entire units surrendered or retreated rather than face continued bombardment and psychological pressure.

In addition to leaflets, U.N. forces also made extensive use of loudspeaker broadcasts along the front lines to demoralize enemy troops. These broadcasts were designed to project messages directly to the soldiers in their trenches and bunkers, delivering real-time psychological pressure that could weaken their will to fight.

The content of these broadcasts often included U.S. military success stories, news of Communist losses, and promises of safe surrender. By broadcasting the latest battlefield victories of U.N. forces, the U.S. sought to create the impression that the Communist cause was doomed to fail. Additionally, broadcasts would sometimes highlight the dire consequences for those who continued to fight, creating a sense of inevitability about eventual defeat.

These loudspeaker operations had a profound psychological effect on Communist troops, especially when combined with other forms of harassment such as artillery bombardments. For soldiers already worn down by the physical demands of combat, the constant barrage of demoralizing messages further eroded their resolve. The repetitive nature of the broadcasts, which played on soldiers' fears of being abandoned or killed, often led to increased rates of desertion and surrender.

The U.N.'s psychological operations were not limited to lower-ranking soldiers; they also aimed to undermine the authority of North Korean and Chinese military leaders. By specifically targeting commanders and political officers through leaflets and broadcasts, U.N. forces sought to create doubt about the leadership capabilities of enemy commanders. These efforts were designed to weaken the chain of command and introduce confusion among the enemy ranks.

For example, during certain operations, U.N. psychological units would broadcast messages that suggested discontent or incompetence among enemy leadership. These broadcasts often implied that leaders were either sacrificing their men needlessly or were too far removed from the battlefield to understand the hardships faced by their troops. By sowing discord within the enemy's command structure, U.N. psychological operations hoped to weaken the cohesion of North Korean and Chinese units, making them more susceptible to defeat.

COMMUNIST PROPAGANDA AND PSYCHOLOGICAL WARFARE

While the U.N. employed a variety of psychological tactics to weaken Communist forces, North Korea and China also waged their own psychological warfare campaigns. Communist propaganda was designed to galvanize both troops and civilians, portraying the U.N. as imperialist invaders intent on subjugating Korea and China. These messages aimed to boost the morale of Communist troops, maintain civilian support, and foster hatred for U.N. forces.

The cornerstone of Communist psychological warfare was its anti-U.S. and anti-imperialist propaganda. North Korea and China framed the Korean War as a struggle for national liberation, positioning themselves as defenders of Korean sovereignty against U.S. imperialism. The U.N. forces, particularly the U.S., were portrayed as foreign aggressors whose only goal was to impose their capitalist agenda on the Korean people.

This messaging was disseminated through a variety of means, including posters, pamphlets, and radio broadcasts. Communist forces used these materials to depict U.N. soldiers as cruel, barbaric invaders who had no respect for Korean culture or the lives of civilians. By emphasizing the foreign nature of the U.N. forces, Communist propaganda sought to create a strong sense of national unity among both soldiers and civilians, reinforcing the idea that they were fighting for the independence and dignity of Korea.

The psychological impact of this propaganda was significant, particularly among Communist troops. By framing the war as a defensive struggle against imperialist invaders, Communist leaders were able to maintain high levels of morale among their forces, even in the face of heavy casualties. This ideological conditioning was further reinforced by political officers embedded within military units, who continuously reminded soldiers of their duty to defend their homeland from foreign domination.

Communist forces also attempted to use propaganda to sway South Korean civilians, hoping to erode their support for the U.N. and the government of Syngman Rhee. Pamphlets and radio broadcasts emphasized themes of reunification, promising that a victory for the Communists would bring peace and prosperity to the Korean Peninsula. The Communists' messaging sought to convince South Koreans that their government was corrupt and that they were being exploited by foreign powers.

However, the effectiveness of these efforts was limited. Despite the widespread distribution of Communist propaganda in South Korea, the majority of the civilian population remained loyal to the U.N. and the Rhee government. The strong anti-communism sentiment in South Korea, combined with the material support provided by the U.N., made it difficult for Communist propaganda to gain significant traction among the civilian population.

In addition to using PSYOP to influence soldiers on the battlefield and civilians, both U.N. and Communist forces focused heavily on prisoners of war (POWs) as a key target for psychological manipulation. POWs were not just viewed as captives but as potential assets who could either be re-educated or influenced to provide valuable information or intelligence. Both sides implemented programs aimed at indoctrinating their POWs, with varying degrees of success.

For the U.N. forces, particularly the United States, the goal of their re-education programs was to encourage defection among captured North Korean and Chinese soldiers and expose them to capitalist ideologies. The hope was that, through a combination of better treatment and indoctrination into democratic values, POWs would reject communism and align themselves with the U.N. cause.

The U.N.'s methods included offering POWs access to better

living conditions than they might have expected, including suffi-cient food, medical care, and humane treatment. This stood in stark contrast to the harsher, often dire conditions they faced in their own armies, and the U.N. sought to exploit this disparity. POWs were also exposed to literature and ideas that portrayed capitalism and democracy as superior to the Communist system. This was done through organized lectures, discussions, and even the distribution of reading materials designed to undermine Communist ideology.

The success stories from these efforts were notable, with some POWs choosing to defect to the U.N. side and provide valuable intelligence on North Korean or Chinese military strategies. These defectors often shared insider knowledge about troop deployments, supply lines, and tactics that proved beneficial to U.N. military operations. In some cases, POWs who defected even contributed to the psychological warfare campaigns them-selves, helping to create propaganda materials targeted at their former comrades.

However, not all Communist POWs were swayed by these re-education efforts. The deep-seated ideological commitment of many North Korean and Chinese soldiers, who had been indoc-trinated from an early age, often presented a barrier to U.N. attempts to convert them. Despite this, the program still managed to secure a number of defectors who contributed to the overall U.N. intelligence-gathering and PSYOP efforts.

On the other side, North Korean and Chinese forces imple-mented their own re-education programs targeting U.N. soldiers captured during the war. The goal of these programs was to weaken the prisoners' loyalty to the U.N. and its democratic values and instead instill a sense of solidarity with the communist cause. Communist re-education efforts were rigorous, often relying on a combination of isolation, indoctrination, and relent-less propaganda to break down the prisoners' psychological resistance.

One of the most well-documented instances of U.S. soldiers enduring intense ideological conditioning occurred with Sergeant Edward S. Dickenson, an American POW during the Korean War. Captured by Chinese forces during the Battle of Unsan in November 1950, Dickenson was subjected to a brutal combination of psychological and physical pressure aimed at breaking his spirit and loyalty to the United States. His experience highlights the extent of communist indoctrination efforts on U.N. prisoners of war.

Upon his capture, Dickenson was marched through harsh conditions to a Chinese-run POW camp, where he was possibly isolated from his fellow American soldiers. This isolation was a deliberate tactic used by the Chinese to prevent the captured men from supporting one another and maintaining their morale. Most POWs were held in group camps rather than being isolated, although efforts were made to control group dynamics to prevent solidarity among prisoners. Dickenson, like many others, became the target of intense Communist ideological conditioning and propaganda aimed at reshaping his beliefs.

The Chinese interrogators, well-trained in psychological warfare, began a relentless campaign of indoctrination. Dickenson was subjected to daily propaganda sessions where Chinese officers and civilian instructors lectured him on the supposed evils of U.S. imperialism and the righteousness of the communist cause in Korea. These sessions were often supplemented by radio broadcasts filled with anti-American rhetoric and stories of U.S. atrocities, designed to erode the POWs' beliefs in the legitimacy of the U.S. government's involvement in Korea.

One of the most grueling aspects of Dickenson's captivity was the forced participation in written confessions. The Chinese captors coerced him and his fellow POWs into writing false statements denouncing the U.S. government and expressing sympathy for the communist cause. These confessions were a powerful propaganda tool for the Chinese, who used them to demonstrate to the world that even captured U.S. soldiers were willing to condemn their own government. Dickenson was made to publicly sign statements asserting that he no longer supported U.S. intervention in Korea and that he had come to see the war as a colonialist invasion. The pressure to comply with these demands was enormous, as any resistance was met with physical punishment and extended isolation.

Despite the intense indoctrination, Dickenson's story took a controversial turn. Unlike many other POWs, who resisted the propaganda and maintained their loyalty to the United States, Dickenson became one of twenty-one American POWs who initially refused repatriation after the war, a decision that sparked outrage back home. After the armistice in 1953, these soldiers were given the choice to return to the U.S. or stay in China or North Korea. Dickenson's refusal to return initially led many to believe he had been fully indoctrinated by his captors.

However, in January 1954, Dickenson changed his mind and returned to the United States. His return was met with mixed reactions—some saw him as a victim of severe brainwashing, while others viewed him with suspicion. Upon his return, he was court-martialed and found guilty of collaboration with the enemy, though his sentence was later reduced due to the extreme conditions he had endured. His story remains a stark reminder of the brutal psychological warfare tactics employed by Communist forces during the Korean War and the lasting impact they had on U.N. soldiers.

Dickenson's experience highlights the broader Communist strategy of using POWs as tools in a propaganda war. Through isolation, forced confessions, and intense ideological conditioning, the Chinese attempted to break down the prisoners' loyalty and reshape their worldview. Though the majority of American POWs resisted these efforts, the experience left deep scars, both psychologically and politically, for those involved.

Despite these instances, the success of Communist re-education was limited in scope. While a handful of U.N. soldiers were considered "turncoats" after these programs, the vast majority of POWs maintained their loyalty to the U.N. and their home countries.

One of the main difficulties encountered by the U.N. in conducting **PSYOP** against North Korean and Chinese troops was the language barrier. Leaflets, broadcasts, and other forms of communication had to be translated accurately and convincingly to make an impact on the target audience. Mistranslations or cultural misunderstandings could lead to **PSYOP** materials being ineffective or even counterproductive. This meant that careful consideration had to be given to the nuances of language and cultural context when crafting messages intended to undermine the morale of Communist forces.

Another significant challenge for U.N. psychological operations was the deeply ingrained communist indoctrination that many North Korean and Chinese soldiers had undergone before the war. These soldiers had been exposed to communist ideology from a young age, and their commitment to the cause often made it difficult for U.N. leaflets and broadcasts to sway them. In some cases, the enemy soldiers viewed U.N. **PSYOP** efforts with suspicion or outright hostility, dismissing them as imperialist propaganda.

The effectiveness of leaflets and loudspeaker broadcasts also varied depending on the specific combat zone. In areas where Communist forces were winning or where morale was high, these **PSYOP** materials had little to no effect. Conversely, in regions where U.N. forces had the upper hand or where food and supplies were scarce, psychological operations were more successful in creating doubt and fear among enemy troops.

Challenges for Communist Propaganda

Communist propaganda, while effective in maintaining morale

among North Korean and Chinese soldiers, struggled to achieve its desired impact on South Korean civilians and U.N. troops. One of the primary limitations faced by communist propagandists was the strong U.N. support that South Korean civilians enjoyed. The material aid, military protection, and ideological alignment provided by the U.N. made it difficult for communist messages of liberation and anti-imperialism to resonate with the general population. Most South Koreans remained loyal to the U.N. and the government of Syngman Rhee, rendering much of the Communist propaganda ineffective.

Communist efforts to undermine the morale of U.N. forces encountered significant obstacles. The U.N. troops were well-supported logistically, and their governments provided ideological backing for the intervention in Korea. The morale of U.N. soldiers was bolstered by the sense of fighting for a just cause, as they saw themselves as defending South Korea from communist aggression. This made it difficult for communist psychological operations to create any lasting impact on the morale of U.N. forces.

Communist propaganda helped maintain the resolve of North Korean and Chinese soldiers, even when facing overwhelming U.N. air and artillery superiority. By framing the war as a defensive struggle against imperialist invaders, Communist leaders were able to rally their troops and keep morale high, especially during periods of intense fighting.

Propaganda efforts also influenced the civilian populations of both North and South Korea. In North Korea, the regime's messaging helped maintain unity and resistance against U.N. forces, while in South Korea, U.N. propaganda reinforced loyalty to the government of Syngman Rhee and the broader U.N. mission.

Globally, the psychological operations of both sides shaped international opinion about the war. U.N. efforts to portray the conflict as a fight for democracy against communist expansion resonated with Western audiences, while Communist propaganda aimed at portraying the U.N. as an imperialist aggressor found sympathetic ears in parts of the developing world and among leftist movements.

The psychological operations and propaganda were essential components of the Korean War. Both the U.N. and Communist forces leveraged these tools to influence troops, civilians, and prisoners of war, with varying degrees of success. The impact of these efforts extended beyond the battlefield, shaping global perceptions of the conflict and providing important lessons for future military engagements in the Cold War and beyond.

COORDINATION CHALLENGES BETWEEN U.S., U.N., AND SOUTH KOREAN FORCES

The Korean War exposed significant difficulties in coordinating military operations among a coalition of forces with different national priorities, command structures, and military capabilities. The United States led the overall effort under the United Nations flag, but the coalition included contingents from over twenty nations, including the Republic of Korea (South Korea), the United Kingdom, Australia, Canada, Turkey, France, the Philippines, New Zealand, Thailand, Ethiopia, Greece, Colombia, Belgium, South Africa, the Netherlands, Luxembourg, and others. Each of these countries brought its own unique strengths, strategies, and operational procedures, but the diversity of forces created logistical and communication challenges that complicated battlefield operations.

In addition to these coalition forces, the Republic of Korea (ROK) army was a critical part of the war effort, tasked with defending its own territory from invasion. However, at the onset of the war, South Korean forces faced significant challenges in terms of training, equipment, and organization. Many ROK units were ill-prepared for the full-scale invasion launched by

North Korea on June 25, 1950, and they relied heavily on U.S. and U.N. support for both equipment and leadership. These factors, combined with the complex command structure of the multinational coalition, created a highly challenging coordination environment throughout the war.

One of the most significant early examples of coordination difficulties occurred during the defense of the Pusan Perimeter in the summer of 1950. After the North Korean invasion pushed South Korean and U.N. forces back to the southeastern corner of the peninsula, the defense of Pusan became critical to preventing a total North Korean victory. In the desperate rush to hold the line, U.S. commanders were forced to rapidly integrate South Korean forces with newly arriving U.N. contingents, often deploying units with little knowledge of one another's tactics, command protocols, or even language.

This lack of coordination led to confusion on the battlefield. Communication barriers, especially between English-speaking U.N. forces and South Korean troops, hampered the ability to conduct joint operations effectively. Moreover, some U.N. commanders were unfamiliar with the capabilities and limitations of their South Korean counterparts, leading to unrealistic expectations and occasional breakdowns in command and control. For instance, South Korean units, still undertrained and under-equipped at the time, were sometimes given responsibilities they were not yet ready to handle, resulting in gaps in the defensive lines that had to be hastily plugged by U.S. and other U.N. forces.

Language differences compounded these challenges, with soldiers from various countries unable to effectively communicate in the heat of battle. In some cases, commanders had to rely on translators or rushed communication systems, which slowed down the transmission of orders and delayed coordinated efforts during critical moments. Additionally, each nation had its own operational priorities. While the U.S. prioritized pushing North Korean forces back beyond the 38th Parallel, other U.N.

members, especially those from countries like Britain and France, were more cautious, wary of escalating the conflict and provoking China's intervention.

Another key challenge in coordination stemmed from the varying military capabilities and tactical approaches of the participating nations. U.S. forces, particularly the Army and Marine Corps, were equipped with modern tanks, artillery, and air support, which allowed them to execute large-scale operations with relative precision. In contrast, some U.N. allies, though experienced, had limited access to advanced equipment, forcing them to adapt to a war that required modern combined arms tactics.

For example, British forces, including the 29th Infantry Brigade, were highly experienced in infantry tactics and had a history of effective battlefield discipline. However, they lacked the same level of mechanized support that U.S. forces could provide, leading to occasional friction over how best to coordinate joint operations. Similarly, Australian and Canadian contingents were well-trained but also faced limitations in terms of heavy equipment, leading to disagreements over their roles in key engagements. These disparities in military capability sometimes resulted in poorly coordinated assaults, particularly in the early months of the war, where confusion and miscommunication led to tactical setbacks.

The South Korean army, though fighting on home soil, was initially in no position to lead large-scale operations. At the beginning of the war, the ROK forces were largely composed of lightly armed infantry units with minimal armor or artillery support. As a result, they were often relegated to secondary roles or assigned to hold defensive positions rather than participate in offensive operations. This created tension between ROK commanders and their U.N. counterparts, as South Korean leaders sought to prove their forces' capabilities and defend their nation with greater autonomy.

Despite the significant challenges, coordination between U.S., U.N., and South Korean forces gradually improved as the war progressed. U.N. commanders, led by General MacArthur and later General Matthew Ridgway, developed new systems and strategies to better integrate allied units into cohesive military operations. Joint planning became more formalized, with multinational staff meetings and coordinated briefings ensuring that U.N. units had clear objectives and understood their roles in upcoming operations.

One of the most notable examples of improved coordination was the success of the Inchon Landing, which demonstrated that U.N. forces could operate effectively as a coalition, overcoming earlier coordination challenges to execute a complex military maneuver that turned the tide of the war.

As South Korean forces gained more experience and received better equipment and training, they began to play a more active and independent role in the war. By late 1951, ROK forces had become a crucial part of the U.N. war effort, capable of leading their own offensives and holding key positions on the front lines. South Korean soldiers, fighting to reclaim their homeland, adapted quickly and demonstrated considerable resilience, which helped to ease some of the earlier tensions between U.N. and ROK commanders.

While early challenges in communication, command integration, and varying military capabilities created friction on the battlefield, the coalition gradually adapted, improving its ability to conduct joint operations. The war not only strengthened the military capabilities of South Korean forces but also provided lasting lessons in coalition warfare that would guide U.S. and allied operations in future conflicts.

By the end of the war, the U.N. coalition had become a more cohesive and capable force, with the ability to operate effectively despite the challenges of multinational military cooperation.

INTELLIGENCE, STRATEGY, AND THE COMPLEX NATURE OF WAR

The Korean War, often remembered for its fierce battles and dramatic turning points, was equally defined by the invisible threads of intelligence gathering, strategic maneuvering, and psychological warfare that shaped its course. Beyond the gunfire and artillery, both U.N. and Communist forces relied heavily on espionage, code-breaking, and psychological operations (**PSYOP**) to gain an edge in a conflict that was as much about outmaneuvering the enemy off the battlefield as it was about direct confrontation.

The integration of intelligence and strategy during the war proved essential in shaping tactical and operational decisions. U.N. forces, spearheaded by the U.S., utilized signals intelligence (**SIGINT**) and code-breaking to anticipate North Korean and Chinese troop movements, disrupt supply lines, and plan counteroffensives, such as the pivotal Inchon Landing. These efforts helped turn the tide in key moments of the war, illustrating the importance of gathering and analyzing information in modern warfare. Conversely, the Communist forces, including North Korea and China, relied on espionage to infiltrate U.N. operations, gather intelligence on troop movements, and target supply chains. The back-and-forth successes and failures of these intelligence efforts underscored the complexity of the conflict, where information was a crucial weapon in its own right.

One of the defining characteristics of the Korean War was the sheer difficulty of coordinating a multinational coalition under the U.N. banner. The U.S. led a diverse group of allies, including the U.K., Australia, Turkey, Canada, and South Korea, each with its own command structures, operational priorities, and military capabilities. This diversity, while a strength in terms of global solidarity, also introduced significant challenges. Language barriers, differences in military doctrine, and logistical issues sometimes resulted in confusion on the battlefield. For example, the early defense of the Pusan Perimeter revealed the complexities of coordinating a coalition effort, as last-minute decisions to deploy multinational forces created friction among commanders and soldiers. These coordination challenges were further compounded by the need to integrate under-equipped and under-trained South Korean forces, whose capabilities were initially limited but improved as the war progressed.

However, despite these difficulties, the U.N. coalition adapted and grew stronger over time. By developing systems for better communication and joint planning, U.N. forces became more cohesive, with greater coordination between allied units in subsequent operations. South Korean forces, initially overwhelmed, rapidly gained experience, proving to be a crucial part of the U.N. war effort as they reclaimed territory and took on a more prominent role in the fight against Communist forces.

Psychological operations also played a significant role in the Korean War, influencing both troop morale and civilian perceptions. Leaflet drops, loudspeaker broadcasts, and propaganda campaigns targeted enemy soldiers with messages designed to weaken their resolve, encourage defections, and create confusion among Communist ranks. Meanwhile, Communist forces used anti-imperialist propaganda to frame U.N. forces as foreign invaders and mobilize their troops with messages of unity and liberation. While these psychological efforts were not always immediately visible in terms of battlefield results, they contributed to the broader war effort by shaping attitudes, morale, and decision-making on both sides.

Ultimately, the intelligence, strategy, and coordination efforts during the Korean War laid the groundwork for significant developments in modern military doctrine. The ability to gather, analyze, and act on intelligence became a cornerstone of U.S. military strategy in subsequent conflicts such as Vietnam and the Gulf War.

THE WAR'S FINAL STAGES AND ARMISTICE NEGOTIATIONS

"Truce is the only victory we can hope for now."

— GENERAL MARK W. CLARK

As the Korean War entered its final stages in 1953, the conflict reached a stalemate, with neither side able to secure a decisive victory. The fighting continued primarily along the established frontlines near the 38th Parallel, punctuated by battles of symbolic importance.

Meanwhile, political efforts to end the conflict intensified, leading to the signing of an armistice that established the Demilitarized Zone (DMZ). Though the fighting ceased, the war's toll on soldiers, civilians, and the Korean Peninsula was immense, leaving political tensions that persist to this day.

ESTABLISHMENT OF THE DMZ

The peace talks at Panmunjom, which began in July 1951, became one of the most prolonged and contentious diplomatic efforts of the Korean War. Negotiations between the U.N. forces, led primarily by the United States, and the Communist side, represented by North Korea and China, were fraught with political complexities that mirrored the military stalemate on the battlefield. Both sides were determined to negotiate from a position of strength, which led to continued offensives and tactical skirmishes throughout the war's final years.

One of the most significant sticking points in the talks was the issue of prisoner of war (POW) repatriation. The U.N., particularly the United States, insisted on the principle of voluntary repatriation, arguing that prisoners should have the right to decide whether they wanted to return to their home countries. This stance was largely influenced by the thousands of North Korean and Chinese POWs who expressed a desire to defect rather than return to their respective regimes. On the other hand, North Korea and China demanded the forced repatriation of all prisoners, fearing the loss of control over their citizens and the potential propaganda victory it would hand to the U.N. The impasse over this issue prolonged the peace talks, and it became one of the most emotionally charged aspects of the negotiations.

Throughout the two years of talks, fighting on the Korean Peninsula continued, though on a smaller scale than during the earlier phases of the war. Both sides launched periodic offensives, not with the intention of breaking the military deadlock, but to influence the negotiations. High-profile battles, like those fought along the 38th Parallel, were designed to provide leverage at the bargaining table. The battles, while tactically significant, ultimately did little to shift the overall strategic situation and served to prolong the suffering on both sides.

By the summer of 1953, after months of deadlock and increased international pressure for a ceasefire, both sides made concessions. On July 27, 1953, the armistice was signed at Panmunjom by representatives from North Korea, China, and the UN, though no ROK representative ever signed it. The agreement called for a ceasefire and established the Demilitarized Zone, a 2.5-mile-wide buffer zone that stretches approximately 160 miles across the Korean Peninsula, largely along the 38th Parallel. The DMZ was created to serve as a neutral area, preventing either side from crossing into the other's territory and acting as a de facto border between North and South Korea.

The armistice also included provisions for the voluntary repatriation of prisoners of war under an arrangement facilitated by a neutral agency. The POW exchange, known as "Operation Big Switch," saw thousands of prisoners from both sides either return home or seek asylum in the country of their choice. From August 5 to September 6, 1993, almost 76,000 Communist soldiers and civilians returned to their favored regime (North Korea, China, or the Soviet Union), and 7,900 ROK soldiers, 3,600 U.S. servicemen, and 1,400 people from other nationalities returned to UNC control. The issue of voluntary repatriation, while resolved, left a lingering bitterness between the North Korean and U.N. negotiators, as it highlighted the ideological divisions that remained at the heart of the conflict.

Although the signing of the armistice marked the official end of hostilities, it did not result in a formal peace treaty, meaning that North and South Korea technically remain in a state of war to this day. The DMZ, though established as a buffer to prevent further conflict, is still one of the most militarized borders in the world, symbolizing the unresolved tensions between the two Koreas. For decades now after the armistice, the DMZ stands as a physical and symbolic representation of the Cold War divisions, not only between North and South Korea but also between the communist and non-communist worlds.

The legacy of the peace talks at Panmunjom and the establishment of the DMZ is complex. On one hand, the armistice successfully brought an end to open warfare on the Korean Peninsula, preventing further loss of life. On the other hand, the DMZ lingers as a reminder of the unresolved political conflict, and the divisions that the Korean War crystallized remain entrenched. While the ceasefire has held for over seven decades, the Korean Peninsula remains divided, and the specter of renewed conflict continues to loom over the region.

LIVES LOST, CITIES DESTROYED, AND POLITICAL CONSEQUENCES

The human toll of the Korean War was staggering. Over the course of three years and a month, it is estimated that 5 million people lost their lives, including approximately 2.5 million civilians, making it one of the most devastating conflicts of the twentieth century. Soldiers from South Korea, North Korea, China, the U.S., and other U.N. countries were among the military casualties, but it was the civilian population that bore much of the suffering. Both sides bombed towns and cities indiscriminately, and widespread artillery shelling ravaged entire regions. The war left countless Korean families shattered, as they were forced to flee their homes, and many remained permanently separated due to the division of the peninsula along the 38th Parallel.

Seoul, which had changed hands four times during the war, became a symbol of the destruction. The city was repeatedly subjected to bombardment, leaving much of its infrastructure in ruins. Streets were reduced to rubble, bridges destroyed, and critical services like water and electricity rendered unusable. Similar devastation was seen in cities like Pyongyang and Inchon, where constant air raids and ground offensives obliterated large sections of urban landscapes. Villages across Korea were also devastated, with entire communities uprooted. The war displaced millions of people, many of whom ended up as refugees either within Korea or fleeing to neighboring countries, their homes and livelihoods destroyed.

Beyond the physical devastation, the division of Korea into two ideologically opposed states—communist North Korea and capitalist South Korea—created deep psychological and emotional scars. Families who had lived together for generations were suddenly torn apart by the rigid border that followed the 38th Parallel, unable to reunite due to the heavily fortified Demilitarized Zone (DMZ). This separation became one of the most painful and enduring legacies of the war, as loved ones on either side of the border were left in limbo, with no certainty of reunion.

The political consequences of the war were equally far-reaching. For North Korea, the war reinforced the legitimacy of Kim Il-sung's regime, which used the conflict as a rallying point for the nation's continued struggle against external "imperialist" forces. Kim's government built a personality cult and cemented North Korea as a militarized, isolated state focused on self-reliance (Juche). The devastation of the war allowed Kim to instill a sense of permanent crisis in the country's political culture, portraying the U.S. as a perpetual enemy and using this narrative to justify the regime's totalitarian control over society.

In the South, the war entrenched U.S. military and political influence. The United States established a permanent military presence in South Korea, a strategy designed to deter future aggression from the North and to safeguard against the spread of communism throughout Asia. The U.S.-South Korean alliance that emerged from the war set the foundation for decades of close cooperation, with South Korea becoming a crucial ally in the Cold War. The South Korean government, initially authoritarian, later evolved into a thriving democracy, but the lingering threat from the North and the memory of the war's devastation have continued to shape its defense policies and national identity.

Internationally, the Korean War underscored the importance of the U.S. policy of containment—the belief that communism must be contained to prevent its spread into non-communist countries. The conflict solidified the U.S. commitment to intervene in future Cold War conflicts, as seen in subsequent decades in Vietnam and other regions where communist insurgencies emerged. The war also marked the beginning of China's emergence as a major military power, with Chinese intervention on behalf of North Korea demonstrating its willingness to assert itself on the global stage.

The establishment of the DMZ as a buffer zone between the two Koreas became one of the most militarized borders in the world, symbolizing the unresolved conflict. This division cemented Korea as a flashpoint in Cold War geopolitics, a situation that continues to influence global diplomacy to this day. This left both Koreas with a deep sense of mistrust and an enduring divide, with families, economies, and political systems split along ideological lines that have proven nearly impossible to bridge in the decades since. The war's impact on the broader Cold War strategy, U.S. foreign policy, and the political dynamics of East Asia would shape the region for generations.

A WAR WITHOUT RESOLUTION

The Korean War ended in a way that reinforced its complex and unresolved nature. Unlike many conflicts, which conclude with clear winners and losers, the Korean War came to a halt not with a decisive victory but with an armistice that froze the conflict in place. The armistice of July 27, 1953, halted the fighting, but it did not provide a formal end to the war. Instead, the two sides agreed to a truce that left the central issue—the reunification of Korea—unresolved. The creation of the Demilitarized Zone (DMZ), a heavily fortified buffer zone stretching across the peninsula, symbolized the enduring divide between North and South Korea. This border, defined along the 38th Parallel, did not represent peace, but a tense, fragile standstill that persists to this day.

The unresolved state of the Korean War has left the peninsula in a prolonged condition of uneasy peace, where tensions flare periodically but never boil over into full-scale conflict. Both North and South Korea, along with their respective allies, remain locked in a political and military standoff, with the DMZ standing as a constant reminder of the war's unfinished business. Over the decades, attempts at reconciliation and reunification have been thwarted by ideological differences, geopolitical interests, and the militarization of the region.

The legacy of the war extends beyond the Korean Peninsula. For the U.S. and its allies, the Korean War imparted critical lessons about the limits of military force, particularly in conflicts where political objectives are unclear or divided. It highlighted the challenges of coalition warfare, where diverse nations and military forces must coordinate strategies and operations, often with competing goals. The Korean War also exposed the difficulty of waging a limited war, where the use of force is constrained by political considerations, leaving military commanders with the task of achieving strategic objectives without escalating the conflict into a broader, potentially catastrophic war, especially as nuclear weapons entered the equation during the Cold War.

For military leaders, the Korean War became a case study in the difficulty of fighting wars with no clear resolution in sight. The war demonstrated that military-might alone cannot always solve political and ideological divisions, especially when external powers with competing interests are involved. The U.S. policy of containment, designed to prevent the spread of communism, was tested in Korea, and while the U.N. coalition successfully prevented the fall of South Korea, it was unable to achieve reunification or resolve the core conflict between the North and South.

For Korea, the war left deep scars—physical, psychological, and political—that continue to shape the region's present and future. The destruction of infrastructure, the loss of millions of lives, and the permanent division of families remain powerful memories that color the way both Koreas view their shared history. The continued presence of U.S. troops in South Korea and the North's development of nuclear weapons have ensured that the conflict's shadow extends far beyond its original timeline.

Ultimately, the Korean War remains a conflict without resolution. The armistice put an end to the bloodshed but left the central questions of the war unanswered. As North and South Korea remain divided, and as geopolitical tensions in the region simmer, the legacy of the Korean War is a stark reminder that some conflicts do not end cleanly. Instead, they leave behind unresolved tensions and a fragile peace that can endure for decades.

LEGACY AND LESSONS OF THE KOREAN WAR

"The Korean War made clear that future wars would be fought not only with soldiers and weapons, but with alliances, strategy, and endurance."

— GENERAL MATTHEW RIDGWAY, U.S. ARMY

Though often overshadowed by World War II and the Vietnam War, the Korean War had a profound and lasting impact on military doctrine, Cold War strategy, and geopolitical relations. The conflict shaped U.S. policy toward communism and significantly influenced how future wars were fought. From the lessons learned in attrition warfare and terrain exploitation to the evolving dynamics between the U.S., China, and the two Koreas, the Korean War remains crucial in modern military history.

IMPACT ON MILITARY DOCTRINE AND COLD WAR STRATEGY

The Korean War had a profound influence on U.S. military doctrine and Cold War strategy, forcing military planners to adapt to a new kind of conflict: limited war. Unlike the total wars of the past—such as World War II—the Korean War had to be fought with constrained objectives to avoid triggering a larger, potentially nuclear, global conflict. The U.S. Military, working under the umbrella of the United Nations, had to navigate this delicate balance, focusing not on total victory but on preventing the spread of communism, a strategic shift that became known as the policy of containment. This doctrine of containment would shape U.S. military and foreign policy for decades, becoming the cornerstone of America's Cold War engagements in places like Vietnam, Laos, and various proxy wars around the globe. Rather than seeking to destroy the enemy outright, U.S. strategy focused on maintaining geopolitical stability by preventing communist expansion.

The Korean War also revolutionized the way the U.S. Military conducted operations, particularly in terms of combined arms tactics. The war showcased the importance of coordinating air, ground, and naval forces in joint operations to achieve strategic objectives. Airpower, especially the use of jet aircraft like the F-86 Sabre, was crucial for providing close air support to ground troops, maintaining air superiority, and conducting reconnaissance. Helicopters, which were used extensively for medical evacuations and troop transport, became a vital tool in modern warfare, allowing for rapid mobility and enhanced logistical support on the battlefield. The amphibious landing at Inchon demonstrated the effectiveness of joint naval and ground operations, highlighting the importance of strategic surprise and maneuverability in limited war contexts. These lessons on the integration of air, ground, and naval forces laid the foundation for how the U.S. Military would fight in future conflicts, particularly in Vietnam.

Rotational warfare was another significant tactical development that emerged from the Korean War. To maintain combat readiness and prevent troop fatigue, frontline units were regularly rotated in and out of combat zones. This system, which tried to prevent soldiers from being overextended and gave them time to recover between engagements, was a major departure from earlier conflicts where units would remain on the front for extended periods. This practice not only preserved the effectiveness of the fighting force but also reduced the psychological toll on individual soldiers. The rotational system would become a standard practice in future U.S. military operations, particularly in prolonged engagements like the Vietnam War and later, the wars in Iraq and Afghanistan.

The Korean War also highlighted the complexities of coalition warfare. For the United States, leading a U.N. coalition presented both challenges and opportunities. The U.S. had to coordinate with forces from multiple nations, including South Korea, the United Kingdom, Australia, Canada, and Turkey, among others. Integrating these diverse forces required new levels of diplomatic and military cooperation, as well as logistical coordination to ensure that all units operated effectively within the U.N. Command structure. While coalition warfare posed challenges, such as differing military doctrines, communication barriers, and varied levels of training and equipment, it also reinforced the importance of alliances in Cold War strategy. The Korean War experience provided a practical model for future multinational military cooperation, directly influencing the creation and operations of alliances like NATO, where the U.S. would continue to lead multinational forces in collective defense efforts.

Moreover, the conflict underscored the importance of flexibility in Cold War-era military strategy. While the overarching goal was containment, the U.S. and its allies had to constantly adapt to changing conditions on the ground and in diplomatic negotiations. The Korean War illustrated that military force could be used to achieve limited political objectives without escalating into a global war. This became a central theme of U.S. military involvement throughout the Cold War, where the threat of nuclear escalation loomed large over every conflict. The lessons of Korea were therefore not just tactical but also deeply strategic, influencing U.S. policymakers to approach future conflicts with a more measured and cautious hand.

In summary, the Korean War reshaped U.S. military doctrine by emphasizing the necessity of limited war, coalition warfare, and combined arms operations. It taught the U.S. Military how to fight under the constraints of Cold War geopolitics, where the objective was not total victory but preventing the expansion of communism while avoiding global conflict.

INFLUENCE ON U.S.-CHINA AND NORTH-SOUTH KOREA RELATIONS

The Korean War profoundly shaped the long-term dynamics between the United States and China, as well as between North and South Korea. The war marked the first direct military confrontation between the U.S. and Communist China, setting the stage for a tense and complex relationship that would define much of the Cold War. China's intervention in late 1950, when it sent hundreds of thousands of "volunteer" troops to aid North Korea, shocked U.S. military planners and forced a significant reassessment of U.S. strategy in Asia. China's entry into the war demonstrated its willingness to assert itself militarily and protect its Communist allies, signaling its emergence as a major regional power. The U.S., in turn, had to recalibrate its approach to the region, recognizing that China would be a formidable player in East Asian geopolitics for the foreseeable future.

For China, the Korean War was a defining moment that solidified its position as North Korea's primary ally and protector, a relationship that continues to shape the security dynamics of the region today. The war fostered a deep sense of shared struggle between the two nations, with China taking on the role of North Korea's lifeline in terms of economic aid, political support, and military backing. Even after the war, China remained North Korea's most crucial ally, providing essential resources and diplomatic protection, especially in international forums like the United Nations. The strong bond forged during the Korean War has helped North Korea maintain its regime stability and defy international sanctions, even as its relations with the wider world, particularly with the U.S. and its allies, remain hostile.

For the U.S., the Korean War highlighted the importance of maintaining a strong military presence in Asia. The conflict underscored the threat posed by the spread of communism in the region, leading the U.S. to establish permanent military bases in South Korea, Japan, and other Pacific nations. This military presence became a cornerstone of U.S. strategy aimed at containing not only North Korea but also China and, later, the Soviet Union. The U.S. commitment to defend South Korea was formalized through a mutual defense treaty signed in 1953, ensuring that American forces would remain in the region as a deterrent against further aggression. This enduring presence has since been a key pillar of U.S. influence in the Asia-Pacific region, reinforcing alliances with Japan, South Korea, and other regional partners.

In North and South Korea, the war deepened the ideological, political, and economic divide between the two nations—a division that has persisted and hardened over the decades. North Korea, under Kim Il-sung's leadership, emerged from the war as a deeply militarized state, focused on survival through a policy of self-reliance and military strength. The war reinforced the regime's emphasis on loyalty, unity, and resistance against external threats, particularly from the U.S. and its allies. This survivalist mentality led North Korea to prioritize its military-industrial complex, culminating in the development of nuclear weapons in later years. Isolated from the international community and heavily dependent on Chinese support, North Korea's economic struggles only deepened, leaving it cut off from the prosperity seen in much of the world, including South Korea.

In contrast, South Korea, devastated by the war, rebuilt itself with extensive U.S. economic and military support. Over the next few decades, South Korea transformed from a war-torn, authoritarian state into a thriving democracy and an economic powerhouse. The U.S. Military's presence provided a security umbrella under which South Korea could focus on economic development, eventually emerging as one of Asia's leading economies by the late twentieth century. The stark contrast between the two Koreas —one impoverished and isolated, the other prosperous and globally integrated—became a defining feature of the peninsula's post-war history. South Korea's evolution into a democratic state also underscored the broader ideological victory for the U.S. and its allies in the Cold War, demonstrating the success of containment of communism and the spread of capitalist democracy.

Despite these divergent paths, the unresolved nature of the Korean War continues to cast a long shadow over the peninsula. The Demilitarized Zone (DMZ), established in 1953 as a buffer between the North and South, remains one of the most heavily militarized borders in the world. The DMZ symbolizes the deep ideological and political divide that the war solidified, and periodic military skirmishes and diplomatic crises have kept the region on edge ever since. Incidents like the 2010 shelling of Yeonpyeong Island and the North's continued nuclear and missile tests remind the world that the Korean War never truly ended. South Korea, officially the Republic of Korea (ROK), claims that the entire Korean Peninsula is the ROK, not just what's south of the DMZ, and so the two Koreas remain technically at war. Diplomatic efforts, including summits and talks aimed at denuclearization and reunification, have seen little lasting success, with the peninsula remaining a flashpoint for regional and global tensions.

The Korean War's legacy continues to shape the U.S.-China relationship as well. The war positioned China as the protector of the North Korean regime, making any resolution to the Korean conflict dependent on China's involvement. As China's global influence has grown, its role in maintaining the status quo on the peninsula has complicated U.S. efforts to diplomatically or militarily resolve the North Korean nuclear issue. The U.S.-China rivalry, which emerged during the Korean War, has evolved into a broader strategic competition for influence in the Asia-Pacific, and the Korean Peninsula remains a focal point of this competition. The Korean War thus laid the groundwork for many of the geopolitical tensions that still define the region today.

The Korean War's long-term influence on U.S.-China relations and the ongoing division of the Korean Peninsula continues to shape the political and security landscape of East Asia. The war entrenched North Korea's reliance on China and cemented the U.S. Military's presence in South Korea, creating a regional balance of power that has endured for over seven decades. Despite various diplomatic efforts, the deep scars left by the war have prevented a true resolution, leaving the region in a state of perpetual tension and uncertainty.

INSIGHTS INTO MODERN WARFARE

The Korean War offered critical lessons in the nature of modern warfare, particularly in terms of attrition, terrain exploitation, and the evolution of airpower. As one of the first major conflicts of the Cold War era, it was not only a test of military strategy but also a precursor to many of the tactical and technological developments that would define subsequent conflicts in the twentieth and twenty-first centuries.

One of the most significant insights was the role of attrition warfare, where victory was sought not through decisive battles but through the gradual wearing down of the enemy's forces and resources. The Korean War, especially after the front lines stabilized in 1951, became a grinding conflict of attrition. Iconic battles like those at Old Baldy and Heartbreak Ridge epitomized this form of warfare. In these brutal hill battles, both U.N. and Communist forces fought for control of strategic high ground, resulting in heavy casualties on both sides. Victory in these engagements was often measured in small, incremental gains, with hills and ridges changing hands multiple times. The focus on attrition meant that troop morale, logistics, and the fortification of defensive positions became essential elements of strategy. Commanders had to ensure their forces could endure prolonged engagements, supply lines remained intact, and defensive works were robust enough to withstand repeated assaults. This emphasis on attrition highlighted the psychological and logistical demands of modern warfare, where battles stretched on for weeks or months with no immediate resolution.

Terrain exploitation was another key takeaway from the Korean War, as both sides used the Korean Peninsula's rugged, mountainous geography to their advantage. The war forced military planners, particularly those from the U.N. coalition, to adapt to unfamiliar and challenging environments. The steep hills, narrow valleys, and harsh weather conditions made traditional mechanized warfare difficult, pushing commanders to rely heavily on infantry and artillery. The use of high ground became a defining feature of the conflict, as hills and ridges were ideal for observation posts, defensive fortifications, and artillery positions. Control of high ground often dictated the outcome of battles, as it allowed forces to observe enemy movements, call in accurate artillery strikes, and deny the enemy the same advantages. At battles like Pork Chop Hill and Bloody Ridge, securing high ground became the primary objective, leading to protracted and bloody confrontations. The Korean War underscored the importance of understanding and exploiting terrain in warfare, a lesson that would be applied in future conflicts in theaters where geography played a critical role, such as Vietnam's jungles or Afghanistan's mountains.

Perhaps one of the most transformative aspects of the Korean War was its advancement of airpower, which became central to modern military doctrine. The conflict saw the widespread use of jet fighters, such as the F-86 Sabre and MiG-15, in dogfights over "MiG Alley," marking the first large-scale jet-versus-jet combat in history. Air superiority became crucial for controlling the skies and protecting ground forces, setting the stage for future conflicts where dominance in the air would be a decisive factor. Beyond air-to-air combat, the Korean War also demonstrated the importance of airpower in close air support and strategic bombing campaigns. U.N. forces, particularly the U.S. Air Force, conducted extensive bombing campaigns against North Korean infrastructure, targeting supply lines, bridges, and railways in an effort to disrupt the enemy's logistics and war-making capabilities.

Helicopters also played a revolutionary role, particularly in the areas of medical evacuation (medevac) and troop mobility. The Korean War marked the first major use of helicopters in combat, with aircraft like the H-13 Sioux evacuating wounded soldiers from the front lines to field hospitals in a matter of minutes. This capability drastically reduced mortality rates and underscored the growing importance of air mobility in modern warfare. Additionally, helicopters were used to transport troops and supplies to areas that were otherwise inaccessible due to Korea's rugged terrain. The ability to move forces quickly and efficiently in difficult environments would later become a hallmark of U.S. military operations, especially in Vietnam, where helicopter-based air mobility played a central role.

The integration of airpower with ground operations became a key aspect of combined arms warfare, demonstrating that coordinated air strikes could significantly enhance the effectiveness of ground forces. This development influenced military doctrine well beyond Korea. In later conflicts like the Vietnam War and the Gulf War, airpower would be central to the U.S. Military's strategy, with precision strikes, air superiority, and air mobility shaping the outcome of battles and campaigns.

The war demonstrated that modern conflicts would be characterized by prolonged engagements, the need to adapt to difficult and varied terrains, and the growing importance of controlling the skies. These lessons became critical in shaping U.S. military doctrine as the Cold War intensified and new conflicts emerged across the globe. The innovations in warfare tactics and technology from Korea continue to influence military operations to this day.

The war also underscored the challenges of managing limited conflicts, where objectives were constrained by broader geopolitical considerations. In Korea, the U.S. and its allies sought to contain the spread of communism without triggering a wider war with China or the Soviet Union, leading to a conflict that was more about preserving the status quo than achieving outright victory. The strategic necessity of maintaining this balance—using military force to achieve political objectives while avoiding escalation into a global war—became a cornerstone of U.S. foreign policy throughout the Cold War. It provided a template for future conflicts where similar constraints on military objectives played a central role.

Air and naval power also emerged as critical elements of modern warfare during the Korean War. The extensive use of airpower for close air support, bombing campaigns, and air superiority operations set new precedents for how future wars would be fought. The successful coordination of air, ground, and naval forces demonstrated the growing importance of combined arms operations, where each branch of the military worked in unison to achieve strategic objectives. This integration of forces, along with innovations in helicopter mobility and jet technology, provided the U.S. Military with valuable lessons that were reflected in tactical planning in conflicts like the Vietnam War, the Gulf War, and beyond.

However, the most lasting impact of the Korean War is its unresolved outcome that we see in the ongoing tensions between North and South Korea. The armistice signed in 1953 froze the conflict but did not resolve the core issue of Korean reunification, leaving the peninsula divided along the 38th Parallel. The Demilitarized Zone, established as a buffer between the two Koreas, remains one of the most militarized borders in the world, a stark reminder of the war's unfinished business. The political and military tensions between the North and South, which have flared up periodically over the decades, continue to shape the geopolitics of East Asia, affecting not only the Korean Peninsula but also the broader region, including U.S.-China relations and global security dynamics.

For the U.S. Military, the war reinforced the need for preparedness in facing unconventional and difficult terrain, the importance of adaptability in military strategy, and the value of maintaining long-term alliances. The experience of fighting in Korea also highlighted the limitations of military force when political objectives are unclear or constrained by global considerations. These insights have been deeply ingrained in U.S. military doctrine, shaping training, leadership development, and planning for future conflicts. The war's focus on balancing military operations with diplomatic goals continues to inform U.S. strategies in complex modern conflicts, where political considerations often drive military engagements.

The Korean War was a conflict defined by extremes—harsh

climates, rugged terrain, intense ideological battles, and unimaginable human suffering. Soldiers fought not only against a determined enemy but also against searing summer heat and brutal subzero winters. They traversed treacherous mountains, rivers, and frozen reservoirs, often with inadequate supplies and harsh conditions that were as deadly as enemy fire. Battles like the Chosin Reservoir and Heartbreak Ridge became infamous for the extraordinary hardships soldiers endured, testing their endurance, resilience, and resolve.

For the soldiers who fought, the war was a test of not just physical endurance but also mental toughness and adaptability. The harsh conditions at battles like the Chosin Reservoir, where temperatures plummeted below −30 degrees Fahrenheit, forced soldiers to endure freezing conditions while facing fierce enemy resistance. These battles, fought in brutal conditions, demanded incredible perseverance and ingenuity. Similarly, at Heartbreak Ridge, where steep hills became the focal points of protracted and bloody engagements, the war transformed into a grueling battle of attrition. Soldiers on both sides were pushed to their limits as they fought for control of key terrain, where even small gains came at enormous cost.

The war tested the resilience and adaptability of military forces, teaching valuable lessons in leadership, perseverance, and teamwork under extreme conditions. These experiences provided a blueprint for future U.S. military engagements, where endurance, strategic coordination, and the ability to adapt to challenging environments became critical components of military doctrine.

GLOBAL POLITICS AND MILITARY STRATEGIES

The Korean War shaped the course of the Cold War and established patterns of confrontation that would persist for decades. It solidified the U.S. policy of containment, a strategy aimed at

preventing the spread of communism through military intervention. This approach, initially devised by U.S. diplomat George
Kennan, became the cornerstone of American foreign policy
throughout the Cold War, beginning with Korea and later influencing U.S. involvement in conflicts such as the Vietnam War, the
Cuban Missile Crisis, and various proxy wars in Africa, Latin
America, and the Middle East. The Korean War provided the
first real test of this policy, and the U.S. response—direct military
intervention to protect South Korea from Communist expansion
—set a precedent for future engagements where Communist
forces sought to gain ground.

The war also marked the beginning of a permanent U.S.
military presence in South Korea, which remains a central
element of U.S. strategy in Asia. In the aftermath of the
armistice, the U.S. established military bases across South Korea
to deter future aggression from the North. These bases have since
become critical for projecting American power in the Asia-Pacific
region, serving as staging points for U.S. operations, from the
Vietnam War to more recent military engagements in the Middle
East. The presence of approximately 28,000 U.S. troops in South
Korea today stands as a constant reminder of the unresolved
tensions on the Korean Peninsula and underscores the enduring
strategic importance of the region to U.S. foreign policy. This
military presence is not only aimed at North Korea but also
serves as a check on the growing influence of China in the
region, making South Korea a key ally in the broader U.S.
strategy of maintaining a balance of power in East Asia.

The war reshaped U.S.-China relations, as the two nations
became key adversaries during the conflict. China's entry into the
war in October 1950, sending hundreds of thousands of troops
to aid North Korea, marked its emergence as a significant military power on the global stage. For the United States, the war
highlighted the threat posed by communist China, leading to
decades of mistrust, tension, and a U.S. policy of diplomatic

isolation toward Beijing. This adversarial relationship would continue through much of the Cold War, with the U.S. and China supporting opposing sides in various conflicts around the world, including Vietnam. However, the war also set the stage for eventual rapprochement, as both nations realized the importance of managing their competition to avoid direct conflict, a balancing act that culminated in President Nixon's historic visit to China in 1972.

For North and South Korea, the war deepened the division of the peninsula and created a lasting rift that persists to this day. The conflict solidified the ideological divide between the communist North and the capitalist South, with each side developing along vastly different political, economic, and military lines. In North Korea, Kim Il-sung established a totalitarian regime centered around the ideology of self-reliance (Juche), with an emphasis on militarization and isolation. In contrast, South Korea, under U.S. protection, evolved into a thriving democracy and an economic powerhouse. The unresolved nature of the conflict—ending in an armistice rather than a peace treaty—has left both countries in a perpetual state of tension, with sporadic skirmishes and provocations, such as the sinking of the South Korean naval vessel Cheonan in 2010 and North Korea's continued nuclear tests. The Demilitarized Zone, one of the most fortified borders in the world, remains a visible reminder of the ongoing conflict.

The war also reinforced the need for flexible military strategies that integrated air, sea, and ground forces. The mountainous terrain of Korea, which made large-scale ground offensives difficult and costly, forced U.N. commanders to adopt a more adaptable approach, relying on a combination of air strikes, naval bombardments, and smaller, mobile ground units. This focus on integrated operations helped shape the U.S. Military's approach in later conflicts, where flexibility and coordination between different branches of the military became essential to success.

In addition, the Korean War provided critical lessons in the challenges of coalition warfare, as the U.S. led a U.N. force composed of troops from twenty-one nations. The logistical and operational difficulties of managing such a diverse coalition highlighted the importance of coordination, communication, and diplomacy in modern warfare. These experiences directly influenced how the U.S. approached future alliances, such as NATO, where joint operations and collective defense became foundational principles.

The Korean War's impact on global politics and military strategies was far-reaching and enduring. It shaped the U.S. policy of containment, influenced U.S.-China relations, entrenched the division of the Korean Peninsula, and transformed military doctrine by advancing the use of airpower, helicopters, and integrated operations. The war's unresolved outcome continues to affect global diplomacy and security efforts, making the Korean Peninsula a flashpoint of tension in East Asia and a reminder of the enduring complexities of Cold War geopolitics.

A WAR REMEMBERED BUT UNRESOLVED

The Korean War holds a paradoxical place in modern history. It is overshadowed by the monumental scale of World War II and the bitter divisiveness of the Vietnam War, yet its impact was both profound and far-reaching, shaping not only the immediate geopolitical landscape of the Cold War but also the military and diplomatic strategies that persist to this day. Despite the relative obscurity it suffers in popular memory, the Korean War left an indelible mark on the nations involved, the global order, and the millions of lives it touched. It was a war not of conquest or dominance, but of containment, fought to hold a line against the perceived monolithic threat of communism, a conflict emblematic of the broader ideological struggle that defined much of the twentieth century.

At its core, the Korean War was a conflict about boundaries—political, geographic, and ideological. The fighting on the Korean Peninsula was not just about territory but about which worldview would prevail: communism, as represented by North Korea, China, and the Soviet Union, or the capitalist, democratic ideals championed by the United States and its allies. For the U.S., the war became a test of its newly articulated policy of containment, an effort to prevent the spread of communism without igniting a broader, possibly nuclear, conflict. This was not a war for victory in the traditional sense but a battle to preserve the status quo and prevent a collapse that might trigger larger, more catastrophic consequences. The outcome—an armistice that merely froze the conflict in place—reflected the complexities and limitations of such a strategy.

One of the enduring legacies of the Korean War is the recognition of the costs of intervention, both in human terms and in strategic outcomes. The war claimed an estimated 5 million lives, with millions more displaced and entire cities reduced to rubble.

For the U.S., the human toll included over 36,000 soldiers killed and more than 100,000 wounded. South Korea, in particular, bore the brunt of civilian casualties and infrastructural destruction, yet it also emerged as one of the key beneficiaries of U.S. post-war aid and security guarantees. The war served as a painful reminder of the difficulties of intervening in conflicts that are geographically distant but ideologically significant. It exposed the limits of military power, where even overwhelming force could not bring about a decisive resolution, and underscored the fact that wars fought with constrained objectives often leave behind unresolved tensions.

These unresolved tensions are most evident in the ongoing division of the Korean Peninsula. The DMZ, a sad strip of land that has separated North and South Korea since the armistice in

1953, remains one of the most heavily militarized borders in the world. It is a living testament to the unresolved nature of the war, a visible reminder that the conflict was never truly settled, only paused. The division of Korea has created two vastly different states—one an isolated, totalitarian regime that has developed nuclear weapons as a means of survival, and the other a thriving, democratic, and economically powerful nation. The legacy of this division has not only shaped the lives of millions of Koreans but also continues to influence regional security dynamics, U.S. foreign policy, and global diplomacy.

The Korean War also taught invaluable lessons about the importance of alliances. The U.N.-led coalition, which included forces from twenty-one countries, was a precursor to the kind of multinational military cooperation that would become more common in the latter half of the twentieth century. For the U.S., the war reinforced the necessity of building and maintaining alliances, not only in terms of military partnerships but also in terms of political and economic support. The war also solidified the U.S. commitment to South Korea, resulting in a permanent military presence on the peninsula that continues to this day. The U.S.-South Korea alliance has been a cornerstone of American strategy in Asia, and the lessons learned about coalition warfare and the complexities of multinational command structures were carried forward into future conflicts, most notably in Vietnam, the Gulf War, and various peacekeeping operations.

Moreover, the Korean War illuminated the limits of military power in conflicts defined by broader ideological struggles. The war showcased how conventional military operations—no matter how advanced or well-coordinated—could not alone resolve conflicts deeply rooted in political, economic, and ideological divides. The inability to achieve a clear military victory despite massive firepower and technological superiority forced military and political leaders to reassess their approach to such conflicts. This realization would deeply influence U.S. strategy during the

Cold War, where the focus shifted from outright military victory to containment, deterrence, PSYOP, and maintaining balance in regions deemed geopolitically significant.

The Korean War also demonstrated the critical role of diplomacy and negotiation in conflict resolution. The armistice talks, which dragged on for over two years, were an example of the complexities involved in ending wars that have spiraled into stalemates. The debates over prisoners of war, the placement of the final border, and the future of the peninsula were fraught with political sensitivities that complicated the negotiations. These challenges highlighted the fact that wars of containment often end not with a clear victory but with fragile, negotiated settlements. The lessons from Panmunjom are echoed in many conflicts that have followed, where diplomacy, however difficult and protracted, has become the key to halting violence.

The sacrifices made during the Korean War, by soldiers and civilians alike, remain etched in the history of the nations involved. The war's intensity, fought across a landscape of mountains, rivers, and devastated cities, created heroes and tragedies on both sides. Battles like the Inchon Landing, the Chosin Reservoir, and Heartbreak Ridge have become symbols of resilience, endurance, and tactical brilliance. Yet, the human cost of these victories was enormous, with millions of lives lost, families separated by the DMZ, and generations shaped by the war's aftermath. The suffering endured in Korea serves as a sobering reminder that even wars fought with the best intentions—such as the defense of democracy and the containment of totalitarianism—carry heavy and enduring costs.

The Korean War remains a conflict remembered but unresolved, a symbol of the Cold War's complexities and the limitations of military power in achieving political stability. Its legacy continues to shape the geopolitics of East Asia, the strategies of the U.S. Military, and the lives of millions of Koreans living on either side of the DMZ. As the world grapples with new challenges of global security, the lessons of the Korean War remain as relevant today as they were over seventy years ago. It is a war that should not be forgotten, for its history offers insights into the costs of war, the limits of intervention, and the enduring quest for peace in a divided world.

Check out my podcast exploring the "what ifs" of military history, where alternative scenarios and fresh perspectives dive into the pivotal moments that shaped our world.

Go to danielwrinn.com to listen.

BIBLIOGRAPHY

Appleman, Roy E. *South to the Naktong, North to the Yalu*. Washington, D.C.: U.S. Army Center of Military History, 1961.
A detailed official history of the first year of the Korean War, compiled by the U.S. Army.

Armstrong, Charles K. *Tyranny of the Weak: North Korea and the World, 1950–1992*. Ithaca, NY: Cornell University Press, 2013.
Explores the role of intelligence, propaganda, and psychological warfare during the Korean conflict and beyond.

Bowers, Alex. "A Canadian Gamble at Kapyong." *Legion Magazine*, April 24, 2024. https://legionmagazine.com/a-canadian-gamble-at-kapyong/.

Bradley, Omar N. *A General's Life: An Autobiography*. New York: Simon & Schuster, 1983.
Provides insights into high-level strategic decision-making during the Korean War.

Clayton, James. *The Inchon Landing: A Turning Point in the Korean War*. Annapolis, MD: Naval Institute Press, 1995.
An in-depth analysis of the planning and execution of the Inchon Landing.

Cohen, Eliot A., and John Gooch. *Military Misfortunes: The Anatomy of Failure in War*. New York: Free Press, 1990.
Provides insight into strategic failures during the war and how they shaped future military doctrine.

Cumings, Bruce. *The Origins of the Korean War: Liberation and the Emergence of Separate Regimes, 1945–1947*. Princeton, NJ: Princeton University Press, 1981.
Focuses on the pre-war political landscape and intelligence failures that contributed to the conflict.

Dean, William F. *General Dean's Story: A Personal Account of Korea*. New York: Viking Press, 1954.
The story of General Dean's leadership and eventual capture by North Korean forces.

Fehrenbach, T.R. *This Kind of War: A Study in Unpreparedness*. New York: Macmillan, 1963.

One of the most influential histories of the Korean War, focusing on the human and tactical dimensions of the conflict.

Field, James A. *History of United States Naval Operations: Korea*. Washington, D.C.: U.S. Navy Department, 1962.
A comprehensive overview of naval operations during the conflict, including blockades and amphibious assaults.

"First Helicopter Rescue." *HistoricWings.Com: A Magazine for Aviators, Pilots and Adventurers*, September 4, 2012. https://fly.historicwings.com/2012/09/first-helicopter-rescue/.

Gaddis, John Lewis. *The Cold War: A New History*. New York: Penguin Press, 2005.
Provides context on how the Korean War fit into the broader Cold War framework.

Gough, Terrence J. *U.S. Army Mobilization and Logistics in the Korean War: A Research Approach*. Washington, D.C.: Center of Military History, 1987.
A valuable resource on logistics, supply chains, and troop movements during the war.

Hastings, Max. *The Korean War*. New York: Simon & Schuster, 1987.
A detailed, balanced account of the war, with focus on both military strategy and political context.

Hermes, Walter G. *Truce Tent and Fighting Front*. Washington, D.C.: U.S. Army Center of Military History, 1966.
Covers the war's stalemate phase and the negotiations leading to the armistice.

Jones, Matthew. *After Hiroshima: The United States, Race, and Nuclear Weapons in Asia, 1945–1965*. Cambridge: Cambridge University Press, 2010.
Analyzes the geopolitical context of the Korean War and its influence on U.S. intelligence strategy.

MacArthur, Douglas. *Reminiscences*. New York: McGraw-Hill, 1964.
MacArthur's memoir, reflecting on his time as commander during the early stages of the Korean War.

Ridgway, Matthew B. *The Korean War: How We Met the Challenge*. New York: Doubleday, 1967.
A memoir by General Ridgway, commander of U.N. forces, offering personal insights into the conflict.

Smith, Oliver P. *The March to the Yalu: A Marine's Memoir of Chosin Reservoir*. New York: Random House, 1964.
A first-hand account from the general who led the 1st Marine Division at Chosin.

Stueck, William. *The Korean War: An International History*. Princeton, NJ: Princeton University Press, 1995.
Examines the conflict within the broader framework of global Cold War dynamics.

United Nations Command. *Military Armistice Agreement between North Korea and the United Nations Command*, July 27, 1953.
The official document establishing the armistice and the DMZ.

U.S. Air Force Historical Research Agency. *The Air War in Korea, 1950–1953*. Montgomery, AL, 1954.
An official account of the U.S. Air Force's role in the Korean War.

Westad, Odd Arne. *The Global Cold War: Third World Interventions and the Making of Our Times*. Cambridge: Cambridge University Press, 2007.
Analyzes the global impact of U.S. and Soviet interventions, including the Korean conflict.

Werrell, Kenneth P. *Sabres over MiG Alley: The F-86 and the Battle for Air Superiority in Korea*. Annapolis, MD: Naval Institute Press, 2005.
Focuses on the air war over Korea, particularly jet warfare and dogfights in MiG Alley.

Air Force Historical Support Division. (n.d.-a). "Sebille – Maj. Louis J Sebille." *Air Force Historical Support Division*. https://www.afhistory.af.mil/FAQs/Fact-Sheets/Article/639634/sebille-maj-louis-j-sebille/.

Mongoose Bravo: Vietnam: A Time of Reflection Over Events
So Long Ago

"A frank, real, memoir" – Reviewer

Uncover the gritty, real-life story of a Vietnam combat veteran.

With an engaging and authentic retelling of his experiences as an infantry soldier of the B Co., 1/5th 1st Cavalry Division in the Vietnam War, this gripping account details the life and struggles of war in a strange and foreign country.

What started as a way of bringing closure to a grieving mother morphed into a memoir, covering the author's deployment, duty, and eventual return to the United States after the end of the war. Imbued with the emotion that he felt during this conflicted time, along with letters and journal entries from decades ago, this memoir is a testament to the sacrifice that these brave men and women made fighting on foreign soil.

Recounting the tragedies of war and the chaos of combat as an infantry soldier, in the words of the author: "We lived, and fought as a unit, covering each other's backs. Most came home to tell their own stories, many didn't."

If you like gripping, authentic accounts of life and combat during the Vietnam War, then you won't want to miss Mongoose Bravo: Vietnam: A Time of Reflection Over Events So Long Ago.

WORLD WAR II PACIFIC: BATTLES AND CAMPAIGNS FROM GUADALCANAL TO OKINAWA 1942-1945

"A brisk and compelling game changer for the historiography of the Pacific Theater in World War II." – Reviewer

An enlightening glimpse into nine battles and campaigns during the Pacific War Allied offensive.

Each of these momentous operations were fascinating feats of strategy, planning, and bravery, handing the Allies what would eventually become a victory over the Pacific Theater and an end to Imperialist Japanese expansion.

Operation Watchtower, a riveting exploration of the spark that set off the Allied offensive in the Pacific islands, detailing the grueling struggle for the island of Guadalcanal and its vital strategic position.

Operation Galvanic, an incredible account of the battle for the Tarawa Atoll and base that would give them a steppingstone into the heart of Japanese-controlled waters.

Operation Backhander, a gripping retelling of the war for Cape Gloucester, New Guinea, and the Bismarck Sea.

Battle for Saipan, Marines stormed the beaches with a goal of gaining a crucial air base from which the US could launch its new long-range B-29 bombers directly at Japan's home islands.

Invasion of Tinian, is the incredible account of the assault on Tinian. Located just under six miles southwest of Saipan. This was the first use of napalm and the "shore to shore" concept.

Recapture of Guam, a gripping narrative about the liberation of the Japanese-held island of Guam, captured by the Japanese in 1941 during one of the first Pacific campaigns of the War.

Operation Stalemate, Marines landed on the island of Peleliu, one of the Palau Islands in the Pacific, as part of a larger operation to provide support for General MacArthur, who was preparing to invade the Philippines.

Operation Detachment, the battle of Iwo Jima was a major offensive in World War II. The Marine invasion was tasked with the mission of capturing airfields on the island for use by P-51 fighters.

Operation Iceberg, the invasion and ultimate victory on Okinawa was the largest amphibious assault in the Pacific Theater. It was also one of the bloodiest battles in the Pacific, lasting ninety-eight days.

This gripping narrative sheds light on these often-overlooked facets of WWII, providing students, history fans, and World War II buffs alike with a captivating breakdown of the history and combat that defined the ultimate victory of US forces in the Pacific.

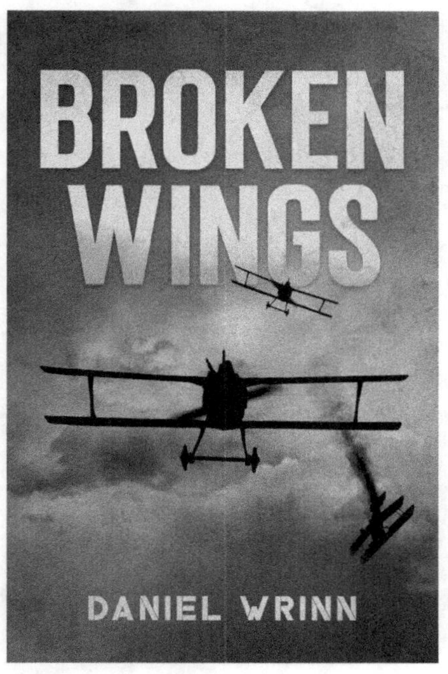

Broken Wings: WWI Fighter Ace's Story of Escape and Survival

"A masterfully told story of triumph and redemption in a powerfully drawn survival epic." – Reviewer

Hero WWI Fighter Pilot Shot Down and Captured.

With an engaging and authentic retelling of his experiences as an escaped prisoner of war, this gripping account details the life and struggles of a captured pilot in 1917 war-torn Europe.

Lieutenant John Ryan couldn't wait to see action in WWI. He joined up with the British colors out of Canada. As one of several American pilots in the Royal Flying Corps before the US joined the war, he earned his wings and became an Ace through fierce air battles over the skies of Germany.

www.ingramcontent.com/pod-product-compliance
Lightning Source LLC
Chambersburg PA
CBHW070851160726
48004CB00003B/1015